Communication and the Mass Media

Reference Sources in the Humanities Series
James Rettig, Series Editor

Communication and the Mass Media: A Guide to the Reference Literature. By Eleanor S. Block and James K. Bracken.

Journalism: A Guide to the Reference Literature. By Jo A. Cates.

Judaism and Christianity: A Guide to the Reference Literature. By Edward D. Starkey.

Linguistics: A Guide to the Reference Literature. By Anna L. DeMiller.

Music: A Guide to the Reference Literature. By William S. Brockman.

On the Screen: A Film, Television, and Video Research Guide. By Kim N. Fisher.

Philosophy: A Guide to the Reference Literature. By Hans E. Bynagle.

Reference Works in British and American Literature: Volume I, English and American Literature. By James K. Bracken.

COMMUNICATION AND THE MASS MEDIA

A GUIDE TO THE REFERENCE LITERATURE

ELEANOR S. BLOCK
The Ohio State University

JAMES K. BRACKEN
The Ohio State University

LIBRARIES UNLIMITED, INC.
Englewood, Colorado
1991

LIBRARIES UNLIMITED, INC.
P.O. Box 3988
Englewood, CO 80155-3988

Library of Congress Cataloging-in-Publication Data

Block, Eleanor S.
    Communication and the mass media : a guide to the reference
literature / Eleanor S. Block and James K. Bracken.
xii, 198p. 17x25cm. -- (Reference sources in the humanities series)
    Includes indexes.
    ISBN 0-87287-810-4
    1. Reference books--Communication--Bibliography. 2. Reference
books--Mass media--Bibliography. 3. Communication--Bibliography.
4. Mass media--Bibliography. I. Bracken, James K., 1952-   .
II. Title. III. Series.
Z5630.B54 1991
[P90]
016.3022--dc20   91-19866
                                                          CIP

Contents

Preface

Every discipline continuously renews its reference literature to record new theories, revised theses, discoveries, deaths, and developments in the application of theory. New editions of standard works and new titles appear from time to time, while serials bibliographies index each year's outpouring of journal articles, monographs, and festschriften. This series, Reference Sources in the Humanities, takes as its purpose the identification, description, and organization of the reference literature of the humanities disciplines. The volumes in this series, emphasizing the Anglo-American reference literature of recent decades, are intended to serve the needs of undergraduates, graduate students, professors exploring adjunct disciplines, librarians building and using reference collections, and intellectually curious adults interested in systematic, self-guided study of the humanities.

Like bibliographic guides to the literature of any discipline, guides in this series are intended to serve various users in various ways. Students being initiated into the ways of a discipline can use these guides to learn the structure of the discipline's secondary literature, to find sources which will enable them to find definitions of specialized terms, to identify significant historical figures, to gain an overview of a topic, etc. Specialists may use them to refresh their memories about once familiar sources and to advise their students on approaches to problems. Librarians will use them to build and evaluate reference collections and to answer patron questions.

The volumes in the Reference Sources in the Humanities Series are designed to serve all of these users and purposes. Each volume in the series is organized principally by reference genre, including types specific to each discipline. This will facilitate their efficient use by reference librarians, a group trained to think in terms of reference genre (e.g., encyclopedias, dictionaries, indexes and abstracts, biographical directories, bibliographies, etc.) within subject categories, when they seek a particular type of reference work in one of the humanities disciplines. Because no discipline's reference literature can completely convey its most recent discoveries, each volume also includes information on key journals and associations and research centers, the sources from which much of any discipline's new knowledge emanates and by means of which that knowledge is disseminated. While each of these guides describes the reference literature of its discipline as that literature presently exists, each also contributes to that literature's renewal and growth.

James Rettig
Series Editor

Acknowledgments

Few academic institutions maintain libraries of the dimensions needed to support the completion of a bibliographic work with the scope of the present one. Work on this volume, in fact, was completed almost exclusively with the resources of The Ohio State University Libraries. We are most grateful that its resources and facilities were available to us.

In addition, we thank several individuals and groups whose expertise and support were especially valuable in completing this guide. Professor Marjorie Murfin, Information Services Department, The Ohio State University Libraries, provided substantial bibliographic assistance. The Advisory Committee on Research of The Ohio State University Libraries provided monetary support for basic spadework. James Rettig, editor of the series of which this work is a part, helped us define *communication* to a scale that could be contained within the space of a few hundred pages. His sound comments and suggestions have improved this volume.

And, of course, our families offered sustaining support and encouragement. To Bernie and Nicole and to Cory, Andy, Sara, Laura, and Patrick—thanks.

Introduction

Communication and the Mass Media: A Guide to the Reference Literature is an annotated guide to basic English-language sources in communication, most published since 1970, as well as selected classic earlier works. Emphasis is on works published in the United States, although selected foreign imprints are also described. Coverage includes sources relevant to the various areas that constitute the curricula offered by departments of communication in colleges and universities throughout the United States. These most commonly include courses in communication theory, interpersonal and small group communication, organizational communication, mass communication (radio, television, and film), rhetoric, speech, applied linguistics, international and intercultural communication, telecommunication, and new communication technologies. Public relations, advertising, technical writing and business communication, and journalism are also naturally or, at least, in many programs, closely affiliated with the communication curricula.

Communication and the Mass Media aims to complement several presently available general and specialized guides, most notably Jean Ward and Kathleen Hansen's *Search Strategies in Mass Communication* (entry 17) and Rebecca Rubin, Alan Rubin, and Linda Piele's *Communication Research: Strategies and Sources* (entry 11), as well as Kim N. Fisher's *On the Screen: A Film, Television, and Video Research Guide* (entry 5); Jo Cates's *Journalism: A Guide to the Reference Literature* (entry 3); and Anne B. Passarelli's *Public Relations in Business, Government, and Society: A Bibliographic Guide* (entry 9). Useful general guides such as Ward and Hansen's and Rubin, Rubin, and Piele's focus on research strategies and skills but provide substantial detail for only a limited selection of major bibliographic sources. Specialized guides such as those by Fisher, Cates, and Passarelli, among others, provide comprehensive coverage within the particular limitations of specific fields — in these cases, the entertainment media, journalism, and public relations. Although they consciously link sources in their specialized areas to those of the general field of communication, these guides exclude sources in parallel areas.

Both the general and specific approaches to communication's increasingly broad literature are valid, and this guide does not attempt to supersede guides such as these. Rather, *Communication and the Mass Media* attempts to fill the spaces between these general and specialized guides by giving comprehensive and detailed information on a broad variety of both general and specialized resources, including research guides, bibliographies and bibliographic series, and annual reviews; dictionaries, encyclopedias, and handbooks; indexes, abstracts, and serial bibliographies; biographical sources; library catalogs; directories and yearbooks; electronic files; core periodicals; research centers and archives; and societies and associations. Aimed at the upper division undergraduate or beginning graduate communication student, *Communication and the Mass Media* might accurately be described as a guide to a selection of the full range of general and specialized resources useful in academic and professional research and practice in each of the many areas of communication. Certainly, this guide gives the more sophisticated undergraduate communication students advice on reliable alternatives to *Communication Abstracts* (entry 163) and *Journal of Communication* (entry 374). It also provides a depth of specialized coverage that a graduate student with interests in several areas, such as organizational communication and public relations or telecommunication and intercultural communication, will find helpful.

1
Bibliographies

Research Guides

1. Bowers, John Waite, and John A. Courtright. **Communication Research Methods.** Glenview, IL: Scott, Foresman, 1984. 367p. LC 83-11682. ISBN 0-673-15468-8.

Research guides that include discussions of bibliographic research methods and resources are typically quite rare in the broad field of communication or in any of its component areas. The majority simply ignore both the library and bibliographic resources. Often research guides are concealed as parts of textbooks. Such guides usually include brief notices of bibliographic information sources in addition to more detailed discussions of research methodologies that range from telephone surveys and polls to computerized statistical analyses. This is the case in Bowers and Courtright's *Communication Research Methods*, as well as several other works cited in this entry. Bowers and Courtright offer limited advice on bibliographic research and resources in chapter 7, "Finding a Researchable Idea and 'Searching the Literature'." Descriptions are provided for selected ICA (entry 468) and SCA (entry 482) journals, Matlon (entry 177), and general and specialized bibliographies. Despite Bowers and Courtright's stated interest in identifying "sources of ideas that are available to any reader of this book" (p. 215), *Communication Abstracts* (entry 163) is curiously overlooked. Guides like those by Rubin, Rubin, and Piele (entry 11); Ward and Hansen (entry 17); and (obviously) the guide in hand, among others, are superior to Bowers and Courtright's.

Another general guide (or, perhaps more accurately, introductory textbook) that addresses library research and bibliographic resources in communication is William J. Seiler's *Introduction to Speech Communication* (Glenview, IL: Scott, Foresman, 1988). Seiler includes a list of useful periodical indexes in an appendix to a chapter titled "Gathering and Using Information" (pp. 149-81). Likewise, Raymond K. Tucker, Richard L. Weaver II, and Cynthia Berryman-Fink's *Research in Speech Communication* (Englewood Cliffs, NJ: Prentice-Hall, 1981) includes a general discussion of library research and the use of specific major indexes and other reference works (pp. 43-65). Similar guides to research in more specialized areas of communication are also available. Alan D. Fletcher and Thomas A. Bower's *Fundamentals of Advertising Research*, 2d ed. (Columbus, OH: Grid Publishing, 1983) describes basic indexes, journals, directories, and dictionaries in a chapter titled "Secondary Research" (pp. 47-57). Likewise, Joseph R. Dominick and James E. Fletcher's *Broadcasting Research Methods* (Boston, MA: Allyn and Bacon, 1985) includes a chapter titled "Searching for Television's History" (pp. 16-25). By Fay C. Schreibman, the chapter includes descriptions of about 30 bibliographic resources and 24 archives and special libraries, such as ATAS-UCLA Television Archives (entry 448) and Broadcast Pioneers Library (entry 426).

2. Cassata, Mary, and Thomas Skill. **Television: A Guide to the Literature.** Phoenix, AZ: Oryx Press, 1985. 148p. LC 83-43236. ISBN 0-89774-140-4.

Cassata and Skill assemble a collection of bibliographic essays on selected topics related to television (television history, children and television, the television industry) and research strategies and resources. The guide is of general interest to researchers in mass communication theory and effects. It is most valuable for identifying and critically evaluating key scholarly works on the aesthetic, social, and technological significance of television. The first part covers broad issues in communication, communication theory, and mass communication theory. Seminal works like Jacques Ellul's *The Technological Society* (New York: Knopf, 1964) and Wilbur Schramm's *Men, Messages, and Media* (New York: Harper & Row, 1973) are reviewed. Chapters conclude with bibliographies of the works described. Chapter 3 covers basic reference sources, including research guides, indexes, and general and specialized bibliographies. Among these are some 40 works that should be regarded as important for research in the electronic media, like George Comstock's *Television and Human Behavior* (Santa Monica, CA: Rand, 1975) and Blake and Haroldsen's *A Taxonomy of Concepts in Communication* (entry 109). Chapters 4 and 5 focus on television's uses and effects, particularly as these are related to children. Specific topics surveyed include television and learning, advertising, and violence. Television news and politics are also discussed. Other parts and sections cover the television industry, regulation, new technologies, public broadcasting, programming, and television criticism. Collections and anthologies of criticism are evaluated. Access to extensive bibliographies of references is enhanced by separate author, title, and subject indexes. The reviews and surveys included in this guide are supplemented by articles included in the *International Encyclopedia of Communications* (entry 127).

3. Cates, Jo A. **Journalism: A Guide to the Reference Literature**. Englewood, CO: Libraries Unlimited, 1990. 214p. (Reference Sources in the Humanities Series). LC 89-78335. ISBN 0-87287-716-7.

Cates's guide includes descriptive and evaluative annotated entries for about 700 bibliographies and bibliographic guides; dictionaries and encyclopedias; indexes, abstracts, and databases; handbooks and manuals; directories and yearbooks; stylebooks and usage handbooks; filmographies, videographies, and library catalogs; core periodicals; professional associations and societies; and research centers in journalism. Coverage extends from the late 1960s through 1989. Separately published books, parts of works, and articles are included. Works related to book publishing, advertising, telecommunication, public relations, film, and television are cited only when journalism is addressed. Over 100 bibliographies are described. Most of the approximately 50 core journals described are highly specialized, such as *The Coaches' Corner* (1986-) and *The Masthead* (1948-). The most extensive coverage is provided for indexes, abstracts, and databases. In addition to traditional sources in communication, Cates includes entries for such sources as *ABC News Index* (Woodbridge, CT: Research Publications, 1969-) and *Graphic Arts Literature Abstracts* (Rochester, NY: Rochester Institute of Technology, 1954-). Some 40 professional organizations are described in detail, with additional notes for about 50 others. Cates's guide is impressive in coverage and detail. For specific resources for journalism history, researchers should consult Lucy Shelton Caswell's *Guide to Sources in American Journalism History* (Westport, CT: Greenwood Press, 1989).

4. Dziki, Sylwester. **World Directory of Mass Communication Periodicals**. Cracow, Poland: Press Research Center, 1980. 218p. (Library of Knowledge of the Press, vol. 14). OCLC 13606731.

Although significantly dated, Dziki's guide offers the most comprehensive annotated description of mass communication periodicals, particularly those published in other countries. Arranged alphabetically, English-language entries for 530 newsletters, popular magazines, scholarly journals, and broadcasting guides from 55 countries provide basic data (publisher, editor, frequency, target audience, and the like) as well as describe the character of each journal and its publication history. Non-roman alphabet titles have been transliterated, but not translated. Indexes for countries, languages, frequencies, and first years of publication increase accessibility.

5. Fisher, Kim N. **On the Screen: A Film, Television, and Video Research Guide.** Littleton, CO: Libraries Unlimited, 1986. 209p. (Reference Sources in the Humanities Series). LC 86-20965. ISBN 0-87287-448-6.

Fisher's guide is a good place to start to discover the reference and research resources on film, television, and video. Coverage also includes such topics as radio, television news, and broadcast journalism. Briefly annotated entries describe a judicious selection of 731 bibliographic, serial, and institutional resources, including bibliographical guides; dictionaries and encyclopedias; indexes, abstracts, and databases; biographies; compilations of film, television, and video credits; sources for film reviews and television programming; library catalogs; directories and yearbooks; filmographies and videographies; bibliographies; handbooks; core periodicals; research centers and archives; and societies and associations. An appendix lists database service suppliers. The separate author/title and subject indexes are helpful. Entries for sources related to advertising, commercials, and marketing, for example, are cross-referenced under "Television — Advertising."

Some of the listings in Fisher's guide can be effectively used to supplement the present guide. The sections for indexes and abstracts, databases, library catalogs, and filmographies identify specialized resources not included here. Examples of these resources are *Alternative Press Index*; *Hollywood Hotline* database; script catalogs; and listings of films and videos about women, youth, and western American topics. On the other hand, Fisher's guidance for core journals is weak. Of the 42 titles briefly described, only 11 deal directly with television and video. Similarly, descriptions of the many complicated indexes that are useful in media research are necessarily superficial. Little specific guidance or direction is offered for use of such resources as the *Social Sciences Citation Index* (entry 185) or *Topicator* (entry 189), for example. Complementary coverage of American popular film is offered in George Rehrauer's *The Macmillan Film Bibliography: A Critical Guide to the Literature of Motion Pictures* (New York: Macmillan, 1982) and in Robert A. Armour's *Film: A Reference Guide* (Westport, CT: Greenwood Press, 1980).

6. Garner, Ana C., and Carolyn Stewart Dyer. **The Iowa Guide: Scholarly Journals in Mass Communication and Related Fields.** 3d ed. Iowa City, IA: University of Iowa, Iowa Center for Communication Study, School of Journalism and Mass Communication, 1989. 70p. OCLC 20135484.

Garner and Dyer offer brief descriptions of nearly 100 selected journals in journalism, mass communications, and speech. The "biggies," like *Communication Quarterly* (entry 347) and *Journal of Communication* (entry 374), are covered. In addition, Garner and Dyer cover selected journals in other disciplines (*American Historical Review* and *American Economic Review*, for example) that have published articles on journalism or mass communication. Brief information is provided about each journal's topical focus and interests, institutional affiliation, readership, editorial offices, and publication frequency. Guidance for manuscript submission is also provided.

7. Gitter, A. George, and Robert Grunin. **Communication: A Guide to Information Sources.** Detroit, MI: Gale, 1980. 157p. (Psychology Information Guide Series, vol. 3). LC 79-26529. ISBN 0-8103-1443-6.

Ten years old and becoming more dated by the moment, even at its conception this slim volume was more a general bibliography than a research guide. The guide is a good example of where the bibliography of communication was only a decade ago. Gitter and Grunin describe 723 primary and secondary books, continuations, and articles in a seven-section arrangement for general communication research, interpersonal communication, international communication, political communication, attitude change, mass communication, and reference works. Subsections are provided for specific areas such as nonverbal communication and speech. Works relevant to mass communication are interspersed through all of the sections. Both the guide's bibliographic coverage as well as the annotations of specific works reveal wide inconsistency. The final section, reference materials, covers 44 different tools, such as the first edition of Blum's *Basic Books in the Mass Media* (entry 22) and the antecedent of the *Television and Cable Factbook* (entry 254). This work is no longer recommended as a guide to research.

8. Knapp, Mark L., and John A. Daly. **A Guide to Publishing in Scholarly Communication Journals.** Austin, TX: International Communication Association, 1986. 52p. OCLC 15207727.

This is not a guide to research, but rather a compilation of lots of good and practical advice for novice scholars about submitting research for publication in professional journals. Knapp and Daly speak as experienced editors of major journals and incorporate suggestions offered by other editors as well. Much of the advice is obvious (for example, the admonition to mail manuscripts first class). Such advice is nonetheless useful for reducing anxiety in new professionals.

9. Passarelli, Anne B. **Public Relations in Business, Government, and Society: A Bibliographic Guide.** Englewood, CO: Libraries Unlimited, 1989. 129p. (Reference Sources in the Social Sciences Series). LC 89-12211. ISBN 0-87287-741-8.

Passarelli provides briefly annotated entries for 633 reference works; periodicals; practical guides and textbooks; scholarly studies; and professional, educational, and special interest organizations in public relations. Emphasis is both current and historical; the guide covers descriptive works on present and past practices as well as theoretical discussions. Arrangement is by bibliographic format and by topic, including sections for public relations in government (with emphasis on American politics); nonprofit organizations (charities, churches, libraries, and social-welfare organizations); and corporate public relations (advocacy advertising, lobbying, and international public relations). These listings are most valuable. Seventy-two scholarly, professional, business, and educational journals are reviewed.

10. Rivers, William L., Wallace Thompson, and Michael J. Nyhan. **Aspen Handbook on the Mass Media 1977-79 Edition: A Selective Guide to Research, Organizations, and Publications in Communications.** New York: Aspen Institute for Humanistic Studies, 1977. 438p. (Praeger Special Studies in U.S. Economic, Social, and Political Issues). LC 77-14556. ISBN 0-03-023141-8.

Rivers's guide, familiarly referred to as the *Aspen Handbook*, is a classic bibliographic guide and sourcebook (as classic as a guide can get in a fairly newborn field) that deserves thorough revision and updating as well as wider emulation. First published in 1973 as a pamphlet of 97 pages, *Aspen Handbook*'s third edition provides information about academic and nonacademic research programs in mass communication, media action groups, and U.S. and Canadian government offices related to the media. Names of officials, addresses, and other data are hopelessly out of date, to be sure, but the interlined notes on bibliographic resources published by the various offices and agencies remain useful. Likewise, although the lists of key books, periodicals, and films are dated and incomplete, they retain some historical value.

11. Rubin, Rebecca B., Alan M. Rubin, and Linda J. Piele. **Communication Research: Strategies and Sources.** 2d ed. Belmont, CA: Wadsworth, 1990. 270p. LC 89-22651. ISBN 0-534-12144-6.

Although largely intended for undergraduates, this is among the best comprehensive guides now available to the bibliographic methods and resources for research in all fields of communication. Emphasis in the first edition (1986) on explaining the nature of communication as a research field has shifted in this revision toward bibliography and the research process. Initial chapters include "Searching the Communication Literature" (pp. 17-36) and "Using Computerized Data Bases" (pp. 37-64). A step-by-step explanation of an online search, with illustrations from DIALOG's version of *ABI/Inform* (entry 260), is retained. Selected online files relevant to communication research are listed and briefly described (pp. 60-61). As with the first edition, the guide's value for graduate students and above rests on its strong bibliography. Fully half of the volume is given to descriptions of research resources. "General Sources" includes comprehensive and selected subject-specific handbooks, textbooks, encyclopedias, dictionaries, and annual reviews and series. "Finding Tools" includes comprehensive and selected bibliographies, research guides, indexes (specialized, citation, microfilm, and media), and abstracts. "Communication Periodicals" lists general and selected scholarly and professional and trade journals. "Information Compilations" identifies general and specific collections (speeches, print media, electronic media, legal, and "attitude measurement"); statistical sources; U.S. government publications; yearbooks; directories; and manuals. The most significant resources, such as *Communication Yearbook* (entry 95), *Communication Abstracts* (entry 163), and *Human Communication Research* (entry 358), are described in detail. Other useful works are discussed in the narrative. "Designing the Communication Research Project" provides overviews of communication as a field and profession and of the mechanics of conducting literature reviews and writing papers and offers useful descriptions of typical research methodologies, including historical, critical, survey, observational, and experimental. Brief review questions conclude each chapter. A useful appendix outlines APA style. A glossary of terms used in communication and social science research, such as *internal validity* and *control*, as well as terms associated with libraries and research tools and resources is also provided. The volume is thoughtfully indexed by source and by subject. This is a good guide for undergraduate communication students.

12. Schreibman, Fay C., and Peter J. Bukalski. **Broadcast Television: A Research Guide**. Los Angeles, CA: American Film Institute, Education Services, 1983. 62p. (Factfile, no. 15). OCLC 10379233.

This is a no-nonsense, no-frills mimeographed guide to the full range of primary and secondary resources for research on television, including bibliographies; research collection catalogs and finding aids; government documents; glossaries and dictionaries; histories and critical studies of programming, business, technology, and regulation; indexes and abstracts; and serials. Annotations are descriptive and evaluative. Several of the sources listed are not typically cited elsewhere (for example, *New Books in the Communications Library* of the University of Illinois at Urbana-Champaign, a quarterly checklist of recently cataloged items). Schreibman and Bukalski's directory and descriptions of national, regional, and local special collections and libraries exceeds similar coverage in Fisher's guide (entry 5).

13. Schwarzlose, Richard A. **Newspapers: A Reference Guide**. New York: Greenwood Press, 1987. 417p. (American Popular Culture). LC 87-246. ISBN 0-313-23613-5.

This is more a major specialized sourcebook or bibliography of primary and secondary materials about newspapers than it is a research guide. The volume identifies and reviews the literature about all aspects of the newspaper, including history, personnel, operations, social and political relations, law, and technology. Schwarzlose surveys primary and secondary literature on topics such as news reporting and writing, press-government relationships, freedom of the press, and newspaper distribution. Emphasis is on the "core" of the literature — that is, what is recognized as significant as well as what is widely available. About 1,700 titles are covered, the majority being monographs of historical value. Indeed, approximately half of the guide is devoted to historical materials. The specific discussion of materials for systematic research on newspapers is limited to a chapter on bibliographies, reference works, indexes, annuals, and journals. An appendix details major newspaper research collections in libraries and other repositories. These specific research resources receive more detailed attention in Rubin, Rubin, and Piele's *Communication Research* (entry 11), among other guides.

14. Slide, Anthony. **International Film, Radio, and Television Journals**. Westport, CT: Greenwood Press, 1985. 428p. (Historical Guides to the World's Periodicals and Newspapers). LC 84-8929. ISBN 0-313-23759-x.

The title of Slide's volume might cause the researcher to expect to find a directory not unlike those by Garner and Dyer (entry 6) and by Knapp and Daly (entry 8). This, however, is not the case. Slide provides descriptions of some 300 selected international professional, popular, and scholarly journals that are sources of primary and secondary information for research in radio, television, and especially film. The interest here, however, is more in the histories and significant contributions of the specific journals than in the media. Among the journals described in the volume's main section are *Broadcasting* (entry 338) and *TV Guide* (entry 417). *Communication Booknotes* (entry 344) is here, too, but many of the other major scholarly journals that have featured research on the electronic mass media are missing. Uniform entries offer narrative surveys of each journal's important contributions to the literature of the media (such as discussions of technical innovations or significant programs, films, or personalities); references to bibliographic or other secondary studies about the journal, locations of complete or significant holdings, and availability in microform; and information about its "publication history" that largely consists of notes about the journal's ownership and editors. Appendixes record brief data for fan club journals, fan magazines, in-house journals, and national film journals (arranged by country). Another appendix arranges all of the journals by type and subject interest. Researchers needing practical advice about the coverage of journals in the mass media should consult any of the other guides identified in this chapter before turning to this volume. Slide's guide is largely useful for guidance about journals that might be used in historical research in the media as popular entertainment.

15. Startt, James D., and William David Sloan. **Historical Methods in Mass Communication**. Hillsdale, NJ: Lawrence Erlbaum, 1989. 210p. (Communication Textbook Series). LC 88-26033. ISBN 0-8058-0433-1.

Startt and Sloan offer a thorough discussion of theories and practices of historical research both in general and in the context of communication. Chapters on evaluating historical sources and writing history for publication, as well as "The Fundamentals of 'Good' History," deserve close attention. Similarly, the chapter "Quantification in History" is particularly relevant to communication research. The guide's bibliography, however, is not completely satisfactory or sufficient. "Searching for Historical Materials" (pp. 81-112) explains the uses of the card catalog (with little mention of online catalogs) and identifies and lists basic reference works, including bibliographies of bibliographies; bibliographies of U.S. history; indexes and abstracts; and finding aids for audiovisual materials, statistics, and government documents, and manuscripts and archival materials, among others. Descriptions of reference works are very limited; annotations are largely general comments. Online searching is briefly described. Nonetheless, in light of the otherwise limited and marginal discussions of historical research methods in communication offered in guides like that by Rubin, Rubin, and Piele (entry 11), Startt and Sloan's guide is the most important starting point for historical research in the field. All mass communication scholars should know this work.

16. Stempel, Guido H., III, and Bruce H. Westley. **Research Methods in Mass Communication.** 2d ed. Englewood Cliffs, NJ: Prentice-Hall, 1989. 418p. LC 88-20005. ISBN 0-13-773987-7.

This is the most important and authoritative general guide for mass communication research now available. Stempel and Westley identify and explain the key concepts and theories of various research methodologies, such as data processing, content analysis, surveys, and secondary analysis. Unfortunately, scarce attention is given to the role of the library and bibliographic information sources in supporting these methods. Important chapters detail historical and legal research in mass communication. Chapters 15 and 16, "The Nature of Historical Research" and "The Method of History," discuss historical research theories and strategies. Despite copious documentation, there is no direct reference to resources. On the other hand, chapter 17, "Legal Research in Mass Communication," is perhaps the best discussion of legal research strategies and resources in mass communication. Difficult-to-use resources, like *Pike & Fischer Radio Regulation* (mentioned in entry 398), are described in detail. Major legal indexes and journals as well as important government publications are also identified and discussed.

17. Ward, Jean, and Kathleen Hansen. **Search Strategies in Mass Communication.** New York: Longman, 1987. 274p. LC 86-18527. ISBN 0-582-99851-4.

Ward and Hansen's guide is unique in its emphasis on the wide range of possible methods in the "process" (p. xii) of research in communication. Here bibliographic research is viewed simply as a single alternative among a variety of research methodologies. Discussions of methods that employ bibliographic resources are limited, suggesting that these methods are not necessarily always of great importance in mass communication research. The bulk of the guide contains sections that discuss the viability of such information-gathering strategies as observation and consultation, interviewing, and polling and surveying. Appropriate supporting discussions of the concept of information as well as advice on information selection and synthesis are provided. Chapter 5 focuses on the use of libraries and bibliographic sources. "Approaching Libraries: Tactics and Tools" includes sections that explain the varieties of resources as well as the typical organizational and classification systems in public, academic, and special libraries; archives; and "media-organization libraries." Limited attention is given to specific bibliographic resources, although some discussion is integrated throughout the narrative. Chapter 6 discusses online information technologies. "Data-Base Searching in Mass Communication" explains Boolean logic and identifies selected databases relevant to mass communication research. Discussions here are more detailed than those for bibliographic sources. A useful "Topic Tool Index" cross-references resources cited in the guide. Ward and Hansen's guide offers a useful supplement to other guides that focus on bibliographic research methods and resources.

18. Williams, Emelda L., and Donald W. Hendon. **American Advertising: A Reference Guide.** New York: Garland, 1988. 208p. (Garland Reference Library of Social Science, vol. 398). LC 87-32148. ISBN 0-8240-8490-X.

In more of a subject bibliography than a guide to reference and research resources, Williams and Hendon arrange 648 books, journals, and articles in four chapters. The first part covers general, historical, and reference literature. Topical listings include advertising history; advertising management; ethical, economic, and social issues; motivation and psychological issues; and reference guides, professional journals, and advertising texts. The guidance provided for the reference literature of advertising is very limited. "Reference

Guides" includes briefly annotated entries for 14 resources ranging from *Business Periodicals Index* (entry 160) and *Readers' Guide* (entry 184) to *Standard Rate and Data Service* publications (entry 251). Among the 33 professional and scholarly journals described are *Advertising Age* (entry 330) and *Journal of Advertising* (entry 367) in addition to several others not included here, such as *Communication Arts, Direct Marketing*, and *Journal of Retailing*. Part 2, "Institution of Advertising," identifies works about agencies, suppliers, and the media, including media planning and selection, print and electronic media, direct marketing, and sales promotion. Works about the artistic and technical aspects of advertising, such as production, layout, copywriting, and graphics, are described in the third section. Part 4, "Special Types of Advertising," covers works on local advertising, corporate advertising and public relations, noncommercial and political advertising, international advertising, and professional and services advertising. A list of "advertising classics," largely consisting of early accounts and texts by American ad men, concludes the bibliography. An author index is provided. Lack of subject indexing greatly limits accessibility. For more comprehensive coverage of the primary and secondary literature on the history of advertising, researchers should consult Pollay's *Information Sources in Advertising History* (entry 71).

Bibliographies and Bibliographic Series

19. Belanger, Sandra E. **Better Said and Clearly Written: An Annotated Guide to Business Communication Sources, Skills, and Samples**. New York: Greenwood Press, 1989. 196p. (Bibliographies and Indexes in Mass Media and Communications, no. 3). LC 89-17227. ISBN 0-313-26641-7.

Belanger briefly describes reference sources (such as research guides, indexes, abstracts, handbooks, and directories); databases; local and national information sources (ranging from professionals and publishers through grammar hotlines); and basic practical guides and textbooks as well as scholarly studies of written and oral communication in business settings. Arrangement is by bibliographic format with topical subsections including "Editing and Revising," "Annual Reports," "Feasibility Studies," "Media Relations," and "Television Interviewing." Most useful is the solid list of bibliographies for such topics as résumé writing, questioning, and employee evaluation. Coverage is largely limited to publications from 1980 through 1989.

20. Bennett, James R. **Control of Information in the United States: An Annotated Bibliography**. Westport, CT: Meckler, 1987. 587p. (Meckler Corporation's Bibliographies on Communications and First Amendment Law, no. 1). LC 87-16475. ISBN 0-88736-082-3.

The bibliography includes annotated entries for nearly 3,000 items that deal with the varieties and impacts of censorship on governmental, community, and other social actions intended to create and sustain "a national consensus in the United States." Particular attention focuses on censorship sanctioned or condoned by government agencies or by other groups and forces. Separately introduced chapters include entries related to anticommunism and anti-Sovietism, the Pentagon, and intelligence agencies.

Treating similar topics, Jonathan Green's *The Encyclopedia of Censorship* (New York: Facts on File, 1990) offers comprehensive discussions of terms, governmental acts, titles, and individuals that are in some way related to official and unofficial censorship in literature, the press, speech, religion, book publishing, film, and society. Emphasis is on censorship in the United States and Great Britain.

21. Bishop, Robert L., and A. G. Leigh-James. **Public Relations: A Comprehensive Bibliography: Articles and Books on Public Relations, Communication Theory, Public Opinion and Propaganda, 1964-1972**. Ann Arbor, MI: University of Michigan Press, 1974. 212p. LC 74-20093.

Although approaching 20 years of age and somewhat dated, Bishop and Leigh-James's bibliography provides approximately 4,000 briefly annotated entries for books and articles published in the United States on the broadly defined field of public relations. Alphabetically arranged under nearly 200 topical headings (such as agriculture, food industry, libraries, women in public relations, disasters/emergencies, travel/tourism, and social unrest), the works included vary in specificity and timeliness. In addition, Bishop and Leigh-James list other bibliographies, periodical and book indexes, core periodicals, and domestic and international organizations in public relations and related fields. A cumulative personal and corporate names index provides access; additional subject indexing is lacking. Unfortunately, this is the most recent of the one-volume bibliographies on public relations and its related fields. It is preceded in the field by two editions of Scott Cutlip's *A Public Relations Bibliography* (Madison, WI: University of Wisconsin Press, 1957; 2d ed., 1965). Other widely cited but equally dated public relations bibliographies are Alice Norton's *Public Relations: Information Sources* (Detroit, MI: Gale, 1970) and William Ahler Nielander's *A Selected and Annotated Bibliography of Public Relations* (Austin, TX: Bureau of Business Research, University of Texas, 1967).

22. Blum, Eleanor, and Frances Goins Wilhoit. **Mass Media Bibliography: An Annotated Guide to Books and Journals for Research and Reference**. 3d ed. Urbana, IL: University of Illinois Press, 1990. 344p. LC 89-39705. ISBN 0-250-1706-4.

Eleanor Blum, author of the first (1972) and second (1980) editions of *Basic Books in the Mass Media* (Urbana, IL: University of Illinois Press), has been joined by Frances Wilhoit for the much-needed new edition of this standard bibliography. The first edition cited 665 titles and the second, 1,179. The third edition includes 1,947 titles, reflecting the recent growth of the field's literature. Coverage largely includes works published from 1980 through 1988. All of the selected materials focus in general terms on aspects of mass communication. Biographies and individual newspaper histories are excluded. Monograph entries are arranged in topical sections for general communication (treating two or more media), broadcasting, print, film, and advertising and public relations, with separate sections for bibliographies, directories, and handbooks. Coverage is limited to English-language books from the widest range of sources, including trade and university presses, professional associations, government agencies, the United Nations, and Unesco. Varying in length, annotations are descriptive as well as evaluative, with references to earlier editions or related works. New to this edition is a section describing selected current journals in mass communication. A concluding section describes relevant indexes and abstracts. Researchers need to consult all three editions of this important bibliography to locate significant works in mass communication published from 1970 through the present. Though it cannot replace more specialized or limited subject bibliographies, Blum and Wilhoit's *Mass Media Bibliography* is an excellent base for all mass communication literature searches.

23. **Bridging the Gap III: A Guide to Telecommunications and Development**. Washington, DC: Intelsat, 1987. 118p. OCLC 16464829.

The third volume in a bibliographic series published by Intelsat, a global satellite system that serves 170 countries and provides a worldwide range of programs to assist in communications development, *Bridging the Gap III* arranges studies on telecommunications in seven sections: socioeconomic development, rural and agricultural development, health, tele-education, training and assistance, communication technology, and global applications (subarranged by geographic regions). Substantial annotations describe (for the most part) English-language papers, government documents, dissertations, articles, symposia papers, and proceedings appearing after 1976. Most of the sources are highly technical, making the bibliography most applicable to advanced scholars.

24. Brightbill, George D. **Communications and the United States Congress: A Selectively Annotated Bibliography of Committee Hearings, 1870-1976**. Washington, DC: Broadcast Education Association, 1978. 178p. LC 78-108111.

This helpful and time-saving resource cumulates references to all congressional hearings held between 1870 and 1976 involving any topic related to communication. (References to committee prints and related documents are not included.) Major emphasis is on such topics as television and radio broadcasting, cable television, telecommunications, telephones, telegraphs, and censorship. As might be expected, the more recent years yield the most entries. To some extent this work duplicates coverage of the *Monthly Catalog* (entry 179), *CIS Index* (entry 162), and *PAIS* (entry 181). Chronologically arranged entries include brief annotations when titles are not sufficiently explanatory. The cumulation is most useful to researchers with ready access to holdings of congressional documents.

25. Christians, Clifford, and Vernon Jensen. **Two Bibliographies on Ethics**. 2d ed. Minneapolis, MN: Silha Center for the Study of Media Ethics and Law, School of Journalism and Mass Communication, University of Minnesota, 1988. 49 leaves. OCLC 18655218.

Each author contributes a different bibliography to this slender paperback. Christians, a noted writer on media ethics, provides "Books in Media Ethics," which contains chronologically arranged annotated entries for a selection of 37 important works. Most are English-language works published within the last decade; the earliest dates from 1924. Jensen contributes "Ethics in Speech Communication," an unannotated listing of about 400 English-language sources on such topics as ethics in interpersonal communication, freedom of speech, rhetorical criticism, journalistic ethics, and ethics in public speaking. Separate sections include books and dissertations, chapters and parts of books, articles, and bibliographic aids. Neither Christians's nor Jensen's bibliography is indexed, however; researchers are focused to read the entries and lists to locate particular citations.

26. **The Classical World Bibliography of Philosophy, Religion, and Rhetoric**. New York: Garland, 1978. 396p. (Classical World Bibliographies: Garland Reference Library of the Humanities, vol. 95). LC 76-52512. ISBN 0-8240-9878-1.

Researchers and scholars in classical rhetoric will most benefit from this source's 19 separate bibliographic essays and supporting annotated bibliographies. Seven essays focus exclusively on rhetoric in ancient Greece and Rome, with three on Cicero and two on Seneca. These essays, which originally appeared in the journal *Classical World*, largely review research on classical rhetoric published after 1940.

27. Cooper, Thomas W., Robert Sullivan, Christopher Weir, and Peter Medaglia. **Television & Ethics: A Bibliography**. Boston, MA: G. K. Hall, 1988. 203p. LC 88-7206. ISBN 0-8161-8966-8.

A total of 1,171 books, dissertations, journal articles, texts of speeches, conference papers, and ERIC documents (largely English-language works appearing after 1970) on the relationship between television broadcasting and ethical behavior are identified in a two-part arrangement. "Ethical Contexts" lists materials on classical ethics, professional ethics, communication and mass media ethics, journalistic ethics, and education (focusing on the teaching of media ethics). The second part lists materials on a variety of topics in television ethics, including advertising and television, public and educational television, children and television, and history. Annotations (limited to about one-third of the entries) range in length from a sentence to a paragraph.

28.   Courtney, Alice E., and Thomas W. Whipple. **Sex Stereotyping in Advertising: An Annotated Bibliography.** Lexington, MA: Lexington Books, 1983. 239p. LC 80-8115. ISBN 0-669-03955-1.
      Courtney and Whipple offer annotated entries for 253 (primarily scholarly) books, journal articles, proceedings, and conference papers related to how the sexes are or should be portrayed in advertising. Most of the sources are American, British, or Canadian in origin and were published in the 1970s. Listings in eight major subject areas with topical subdivisions cover the existence of sex stereotyping, attitudes toward stereotyping, effectiveness of sexual stimuli, changes in sex roles, improving the portrayal of the sexes, and the future of sex stereotyping research. A key indicates the methodological orientation or research process of each source. Leslie Friedman's *Sex Role Stereotyping in the Mass Media: An Annotated Bibliography* (New York: Garland, 1977) provides somewhat similar coverage, although its annotations are mainly aimed at undergraduates and advertising is only one of several media addressed.

29.   Crano, William D., Suellen Ludwig, and Gary W. Selnow. **Annotated Archive of Communication References: Empirical and Theoretical Works.** East Lansing, MI: Center for Evaluation and Assessment, Michigan State University, 1981. 275p. OCLC 7826588.
      Only the most dedicated — or desperate — researcher will profit from the sources listed in this bibliography owing to its nearly incomprehensible and challenging coding scheme, which was intended to categorize each source by type of publication, type of laboratory situation, research subject, and other variables. A two-part arrangement offers (in part I) a list of numbered, alphabetically arranged sources with descriptive codes and (in part II) the same sources rearranged by codes. Selectively and briefly annotated entries identify 4,215 books, journal articles, dissertations, conference proceedings, and technical reports, including non-English-language publications, on all areas and aspects of communication, including organizational communication, propaganda, persuasion, uses of the mass media, rhetoric, and public broadcasting. The listings are good even if access by subject is virtually impossible. The bibliography will be most useful to researchers who require studies employing specific types of methodologies. Other researchers interested in subject access, however, should probably skip this source.

30.   Dannelley, Paul. **Fund Raising and Public Relations: A Critical Guide to Literature and Resources.** Norman, OK: University of Oklahoma Press, 1986. 145p. LC 85-40951. ISBN 0-8061-1990-x.
      This is an effective resource tool, despite the fact that more than half of the entries cite publications of organizations, foundations, and other service groups that effectively bury items representing critical scholarship from commercial and academic presses. Dannelley evaluates about 170 books and 100 magazine and journal articles published from 1975 through 1985. Annotations range from one sentence to several paragraphs. A unique and interesting feature, a geographically arranged list of fund-raising directories, enhances access to the literature.

31.   Davis, Martha, and Janet Skupien. **Body Movement and Nonverbal Communication: An Annotated Bibliography, 1971-1981.** Bloomington, IN: Indiana University Press, 1982. 294p. (Advances in Semiotics). LC 81-7881. ISBN 0-253-34101-9.

Sponsored by the Institute for Nonverbal Communication, this bibliography includes annotated entries for 1,411 works in all languages that explore the psychological, anthropological, and communication aspects of body movement. An appendixed descriptive listing of journals that feature research in this area is particularly valuable. This work supersedes Davis's earlier *Understanding Body Movement: An Annotated Bibliography* (New York: Arno Press, 1972).

32. Dorn, Nicholas, and Nigel South. **Message in a Bottle: Theoretical Overview and Annotated Bibliography of the Mass Media and Alcohol**. Aldershot, Hants, England: Gower, 1983. 178p. LC 83-201044. ISBN 0-566-0621-9.

The principal focus of this British work is literature concerned with the mass media and its ability (and inability) to communicate information on the health risks of alcohol abuse to the general public. British, Canadian, and American books, journal and magazine articles, reports on research, and working papers are emphasized. Two introductory essays explore theoretical models of the mass media and alternatives to "effects" models. Annotations are generally quite extensive. Unfortunately, no indexes are provided. Dorn and South prepared this work at the Institute for the Study of Drug Dependence in London. Because of its highly technical nature, *Message in a Bottle* is recommended to advanced communication scholars.

33. Du Charme, Rita. **Bibliography of Media Management and Economics**. 2d ed. Minneapolis, MN: Media Management and Economics Resource Center, University of Minnesota, 1988. 131p. ISBN 0-944866-01-8.

Du Charme arranged unannotated entries for over 400 books (mostly current American imprints) in 35 subject categories, including advertising, book publishing, broadcasting, cable, mass media, media management, minorities, telecommunications, video, public relations, and organizations, that focus on economic and management issues. Journal articles are excluded. Surprisingly, Du Charme's coverage only slightly overlaps that provided by Middleton and Jussawalla in *The Economics of Communication* (entry 63), despite the similar titles. Undergraduates will find Du Charme's bibliography useful. The omission of scholarly and popular articles, however, greatly reduces the volume's research value.

34. **Ethics and Candor in Public Relations and Organizational Communication: A Literature Review**. San Francisco, CA: IABC Foundation, 1984. 89p. OCLC 11547112.

The International Association of Business Communicators (entry 467) commissioned this and two similar works that summarize the recent literature on public relations and organizational communication. This particular volume focuses specifically on the issues of ethics and professionalism. Extensively annotated entries for approximately 200 books, journal and newspaper articles, conference papers, dissertations, theses, speeches, research reports, and correspondence are arranged in topical sections for advertising ethics, business ethics, codes of conduct, communication ethics, mass media ethics, organizational standards, personal ethics, philosophy of ethics, and training of ethics. Most of the materials date from 1970 through 1984. Companion volumes in this series include Carolyn Garrett's *Evaluation and Measurement in Public Relations and Organizational Communication: A Literature Review* (San Francisco, CA: IABC Foundation, 1984) and William Roach's *Planning in Public Relations and Organizational Communication: A Literature Review* (San Francisco, CA: IABC Foundation, 1984).

35. Fejes, Fred. **Gays, Lesbians and the Media: A Selected Bibliography**. Boca Raton, FL: Florida Atlantic University, 1987. 23p. OCLC 16881402.

Fejes gleaned the standard periodical indexes, including *Communication Abstracts* (entry 163), as well as several bibliographic resources and gay publications, such as *The Advocate*, for materials focusing on topics related to homosexuality and the media, such as the gay image, the gay media, advertising directed toward gays, and the treatment of gays in the mainstream press. Only English-language books and journal and newspaper articles are cited. With the exception of *The Advocate* (cited very extensively) and other gay-oriented publications, most sources (such as *Ms.,* the *New York Times*, and the like) are readily available.

36. Flannery, Gerald V. **Mass Media: Marconi to MTV: A Select Bibliography of New York Times Sunday Magazine Articles on Communication, 1900-1988**. Lanham, MD: University Press of America, 1989. 342p. LC 89-5592. ISBN 0-8191-7421-1.

The *New York Times* and its Sunday magazine section are undoubtedly the most widely available newspaper archives in the United States. The magazine is thoroughly indexed by both *The New York Times Index* (entry 180) and *Readers' Guide* (entry 184). Flannery has ferreted out articles on communication appearing in the magazine beginning from 1900 and arranged their references chronologically with subdivisions for such topics as the telephone, the wireless, telegraphy, public relations, advertising, radio, newspaper, theater, communication, and other media. The compilation's chief fault is the absence of an index. This is an updated version of Flannery's *Marconi to McLuhan: A Select Bibliography of N.Y. Times Sunday Magazine Articles on Communication, 1900-1980* (Lafayette, LA: 1984).

37. Garay, Ronald. **Cable Television: A Reference Guide to Information**. New York: Greenwood Press, 1988. 177p. LC 87-24955. ISBN 0-313-24751-x.

Nearly all current broadcasting bibliographies include materials on cablecasting. Identifying over 400 books, journal articles, and government documents published from 1980 through 1987, Garay's is the most comprehensive bibliography presently available on cable television in the United States. The volume consists of five bibliographic essays, with supporting bibliographies, that survey general sources; business and industry/economics; program services, contents, uses and effects, viewing habits, and criticism; cable law and regulation; and videotext. The chapters include detailed overviews of each topic. The bibliographies also identify special information sources, such as trade and professional journals, newsletters, and bulletins. Earlier bibliographies of cable television literature include Felix Chin's *Cable Television: A Comprehensive Bibliography* (New York: IFI/Plenum, 1978). A serial publication, *BCTV: Bibliography on Cable Television* (San Francisco, CA: Communications Library, 1975-), provides complementary coverage.

38. Gazdar, Gerald, Ewan Klein, and Geoffrey K. Pullum. **A Bibliography of Contemporary Linguistics**. New York: Garland, 1978. 425p. (Garland Reference Library of the Humanities, vol. 119). LC 77-83358. ISBN 0-8240-9852-8.

No separate linguistics bibliography of note has been published in several years. Four useful works, however, appeared in the United States and Japan through the early 1980s. This bibliography includes unannotated entries for 500 English-language journal articles, conference proceedings, working papers, and dissertations (mostly appearing after 1970) relevant to linguistic research and the teaching of linguistics. Books are specifically excluded. A topical index provides access to entries on such subjects as artificial intelligence, semantics, conversational analysis, and grammar. Other works that should be consulted include Minoru Yasui's *Current Bibliography on Linguistics and English Linguistics, 1960-1978* (Tokyo: Kaitakusha, 1979) and *Current Bibliography on Linguistics and English Linguistics, 1979-1982* (Tokyo: Kaitakusha, 1983); and Harold B. Allen's *Linguistics and English Linguistics*, 2d ed. (Arlington Heights, IL: AHM Publishing, 1977).

39.   Georgi, Charlotte, and Terry Fate. **Fund-raising, Grants, and Foundations: A Comprehensive Bibliography**. Littleton, CO: Libraries Unlimited, 1985. 194p. LC 84-21821. ISBN 0-87287-441-9.

Georgi and Fate identify about 1,500 English-language books, primarily published in the United States, that deal with the topics of fund-raising, grants, and foundations. Section I, "Reference Information Sources," and section II, "Subject Information Sources" (arranged in 10 categories), consist of unannotated listings. Section III, the briefest section, lists the "best" literature on these topics, with extensive annotations, arranged by publisher. The bibliography complements Dannelley's more comprehensive *Fund Raising and Public Relations* (entry 30).

40.   Gillmor, Donald M., Theodore L. Glasser, and Victoria Smith. **Mass Media Law: A Selected Bibliography**. Minneapolis, MN: Silha Center for the Study of Media Ethics and Law, School of Journalism and Mass Communication, University of Minnesota, 1987. 31 leaves. OCLC 16885982.

This slim paperback provides unannotated entries for books and articles (mainly from law and communication law journals and predominately from the 1970s and 1980s) on such subjects as the First Amendment, privacy, obscenity, propaganda, reporting and the courts, broadcast and cable regulation, commercial speech, libel, and the student press. The list's selectivity reflects both considered judgment and appropriateness. No subject index is provided. Researchers who expect comprehensiveness or evaluative guidance will be disappointed.

41.   Gottsegen, Gloria Behar. **Group Behavior: A Guide to Information Sources**. Detroit, MI: Gale, 1979. 219p. (Psychology Information Guide Series, vol. 2). LC 79-63744. ISBN 0-8103-1439-8.

Group influence, power in groups, group therapy, and group problem solving are among the 13 subjects treated in this selective annotated guide to sources on small and social group behavior, training, and communication. Other subjects include organization, education, social, and general applied settings. The guide is highly selective. Only major English-language books, most published in the late 1960s through 1977, are included. Although somewhat dated, this is the most recent bibliography on group behavior and, therefore, remains useful for identifying major monographic works on the subject. Researchers must update it by consulting indexes and abstracts in the field.

42.   Greenfield, Thomas Allen. **Radio: A Reference Guide**. New York: Greenwood Press, 1989. 172p. (American Popular Culture). LC 88-24647. ISBN 0-313-22276-2.

Each of the seven chapters in this volume is an extended bibliographic essay on a particular aspect of American radio broadcasting. Lists of cited sources support the essays. Emphasis throughout is on historical and current scholarly research materials, including privately published reports, regional publications, archival sources, books, journal articles, and dissertations. Sources are on such topics as radio networks and station history, radio news, radio music, radio comedy and variety programs, and sports. The last chapter, "Shortwaves," identifies sources for research on women in radio, radio advertising, Armed Forces Radio, and religious radio programming. A list of radio archives and research centers, organizations, and journals is also included. Greenfield's guide greatly facilitates locating sources on radio broadcasting in the United States. It is presently the best reference guide for American radio studies.

43. Grisko-Kelley, Hannelore. **Annotated Bibliography of Rural-Urban Communications**. Urbana-Champaign, IL: Office of Agricultural Communications and Extension Education, College of Agriculture, University of Illinois at Urbana-Champaign, 1987. 40p. (Agricultural Communications Research Reports, vol. 30). OCLC 16724276.

Stunning economic losses, farm foreclosures, disastrous weather, and other natural and unnatural forces have made the American farm and agriculture a staple topic in the media. This bibliography pulls together 142 sources (books, journal articles, dissertations, proceedings, industry reports, speeches, and other publications) that focus on the communication aspects of these issues. Many sources (with extensive descriptive annotations) are agricultural extension or agri-business publications appearing after 1973. Grisko-Kelley also cites a few works dating from 1928 for their historical interest. Separate listings cover such topics as media coverage of agriculture, organization of rural-urban communication, public and farmer opinions, and programs for rural-urban communication. Many of the sources are not indexed by other general or agricultural sources. Although Grisko-Kelley's list is not comprehensive, it is a good starting point for research on this topic.

44. Higgens, Gavin. **British Broadcasting, 1922-1982: A Selected and Annotated Bibliography**. London: BBC Data Publications, 1983. 279p. LC 85-169267. ISBN 1-563-12137-0.

Briefly annotated (most, but not all) entries for 1,200 books, journal articles, government reports, and other materials on a broad range of subjects in British broadcasting are included in this bibliography. Coverage includes materials on the relationship of broadcasting and society, cable and satellite broadcasting, engineering, pirate broadcasting, broadcasting and government, and broadcasting personalities, among other topics. A detailed list of programs arranged by topic and by genre is also featured. Separate appendixes list titles of British broadcasting periodicals and of volumes in the *BBC Engineering Division Monographs* and *BBC Lunchtime Lectures* series. Coverage is less than comprehensive; only materials of British origin are included. In that many of the sources are not commonly available, the bibliography's usefulness is limited mainly to advanced researchers.

45. Hill, George H. **Black Media in America: A Resource Guide**. Boston, MA: G. K. Hall, 1984. 333p. (Reference Publication in Black Studies). LC 84-15672. ISBN 0-8161-8610-3.

Including 4,069 sources, this bibliography provides comprehensive coverage of African-Americans and newspapers, radio and television broadcasting, magazine and book publishing, public relations, and advertising. Part I consists primarily of annotated entries for books and dissertations (theses are generally unannotated) largely published from 1960 through 1983. Hill also cites a few seminal works from the late nineteenth and early twentieth centuries. Other parts include (mostly) unannotated entries for journal, magazine, and newspaper articles arranged in subsections for the various media. Of particular interest is coverage of sources on specific black radio and television stations. Hill, with Sylvia Saverson Hill, also compiled *Blacks on Television: A Selectively Annotated Bibliography* (Metuchen, NJ: Scarecrow Press, 1985).

46. Hill, George H., and Lenwood Davis. **Religious Broadcasting, 1920-1983: A Selectively Annotated Bibliography**. New York: Garland, 1984. 243p. (Garland Reference Library of Social Sciences, vol. 216). LC 83-20813. ISBN 0-8240-9015-2.

Hill and Davis provide entries for some 1,100 English-language works, arranged in separate lists for books, dissertations and theses, articles, and indexes, on topics related to religious broadcasting in the United States and published from 1920 through 1983. The section for articles is the most extensive, with the bulk consisting of references to articles in general, broadcasting, and religious magazines. Subdivisions within this section list materials on media topics and religious denominations (networks, personalities, controversies, Protestant, Catholic, and the like). Entries for articles are not annotated. An addendum cites 147 articles published after 1983 or otherwise overlooked. In addition to author and title indexes, a religious program index enhances access. It is noteworthy that coverage is largely limited to Christian broadcasting; very few materials for other religions are cited. Comprehensive within the scope of the Christian faiths, this bibliography can be used for research on all levels.

47.   Hill, Susan M. **Broadcasting Bibliography: A Guide to the Literature of Radio & Television**. 3d ed. Washington, DC: National Association of Broadcasters, 1989. 74p. ISBN 0-89324-076-1.

Compiled by the staff of the National Association of Broadcasters Library and Information Center, this compact bibliography lists 520 books on the broadcasting industry, including sections for basic reference works, business, regulation, technology and production techniques, societal concerns, comparisons with other systems, and telecommunications technologies. No annotations are provided. A list of 110 scholarly and trade periodicals in mass communication with brief descriptions completes the volume. The listings for books and journals are solid bases for research in broadcasting.

48.   Hoffman, Frank W. **Intellectual Freedom and Censorship: An Annotated Bibliography**. Metuchen, NJ: Scarecrow Press, 1989. 244p. LC 88-18811. ISBN 0-8108-2145-1.

Like Bennett's *Control of Information in the United States* (entry 20), Hoffman's bibliography addresses the limits that are placed on communication. Hoffman describes 900 books, periodical articles, and legal and governmental materials. Entries are arranged in five sections, covering the theoretical foundations of censorship and intellectual freedom; professions concerned with intellectual freedom; pro- and anti-censorship; and cases of censorship in the mass media. Interspersed throughout are various tables illustrating milestones in the history of censorship in the United States, legal abbreviations, the First Amendment, and mass media titles of all types (books, films, magazines, newspapers, music, television, videotapes, and the like) that have been censored at some point in American history. This coverage updates Ralph E. McCoy's classic bibliography on press freedom (and control of intellectual freedom), *Freedom of the Press: An Annotated Bibliography* (Carbondale, IL: Southern Illinois University Press, 1968), and his *Freedom of the Press: A Biblioencyclopedia: Ten-Year Supplement (1967-1977)* (Carbondale, IL: Southern Illinois University Press, 1979).

49.   Horner, Winifred Bryan. **Historical Rhetoric: An Annotated Bibliography of Selected Sources in English**. Boston, MA: G. K. Hall, 1980. 294p. LC 80-21947. ISBN 0-8161-8191-8.

Horner arranges entries in five sections covering the classical period, the Middle Ages, the Renaissance, the eighteenth century, and the nineteenth century. Each section separately lists entries (all annotated, many very extensively) for primary works (arranged chronologically) and secondary studies appearing as books and journal articles (arranged alphabetically). Additional historical resources and works on current rhetoric are listed in Horner's *The Present State of Scholarship in Historical and Contemporary Rhetoric* (entry 50).

50.   Horner, Winifred Bryan, ed. **The Present State of Scholarship in Historical and Contemporary Rhetoric**. Columbia, MO: University of Missouri Press, 1983. 230p. LC 82-20002. ISBN 0-8262-0398-1.

Horner's collection of literature reviews cites a wide variety of works on rhetoric in all historical periods. Different subject specialists provide essays and supporting bibliographies that identify the primary and secondary works on rhetoric during the classical period, the Middle Ages, the Renaissance, the eighteenth century, the nineteenth century, and the twentieth century.

51. Hudson, Heather E. **A Bibliography of Telecommunications and Socio-Economic Development.** Norwood, MA: Artech House, 1988. 241p. LC 87-35089. ISBN 0-89006-288-9.

Hudson identifies 1,124 sources published through 1985 that address the role of telecommunications in economic and social development. Emphasis is on point-to-point interactive means of communication, such as the telephone, telex, new technologies, videotext, electronic mail, satellites, two-way radio, and rural telecommunication. Entries are unannotated. Instead, keyword codes for geographical regions, types of technology, contents, applications, or organizations (such as Intelsat, ITU [International Telecommunications Union], Unesco, and others) describe the sources to some degree. Coverage is limited to English-language books, journal articles, dissertations, conference reports, ERIC documents, texts of speeches, technical reports, domestic and foreign government documents, and Unesco documents. Godwin C. Chu and Brent Cassan's *Modern Communication Technology in a Changing Society: A Bibliography* (Honolulu, HI: East-West Communication Institute, East-West Center, 1977) should be consulted for older but still important sources on this topic.

52. Kaid, Lynda Lee, and Anne Johnston Wadsworth. **Political Campaign Communication: A Bibliography and Guide to the Literature, 1973-1982.** Metuchen, NJ: Scarecrow Press, 1985. 217p. LC 84-23508. ISBN 0-8108-1764-0.

Kaid and Wadsworth identify 2,461 books, pamphlets, scholarly articles, and dissertations on subjects in communication related to political campaigns in the United States from 1973 to 1982. Among the topics covered are campaign debates, the mass media and elections, political advertising, political rhetoric, television news, interpersonal aspects of campaigns, and the agenda-setting functions of campaigns. No annotations are provided. Despite the exclusion of articles in popular journals and newspapers, government documents, and unpublished papers, this bibliography doubles the number of entries in Kaid's earlier *Political Campaign Communication: A Bibliography and Guide to the Literature* (Metuchen, NJ: Scarecrow Press, 1974).

53. Key, Mary Ritchie. **Nonverbal Communication: A Research Guide & Bibliography.** Metuchen, NJ: Scarecrow Press, 1977. 439p. LC 76-53024. ISBN 0-8108-1014-x.

About one-half of this volume is a collection of essays on different aspects of nonverbal communication and a review of the literature on kinesic communication, speech, body movement, notation systems, and related topics. The remaining half lists (without annotations) books, journal and newspaper articles, research papers, dissertations, and other materials on topics in nonverbal communication that are of historical and current interest, including works in English, German, Italian, and French. Although the essays and bibliography were originally intended to support Key's *Paralanguage and Kinesics: Nonverbal Communication with a Bibliography* (Metuchen, NJ: Scarecrow Press, 1975), the bibliography capably stands alone. Despite its age and lack of annotations, the bibliography remains an effective tool for the study of gestures, body and hand movements, baby talk, and similar topics. Additional coverage of materials on these topics is available in Obudho's *Human Nonverbal Behavior* (entry 67).

54. Kruger, Arthur N. **Argumentation and Debate: A Classified Bibliography**. 2d ed. Metuchen, NJ: Scarecrow Press, 1975. 520p. LC 74-17198. ISBN 0-8108-0749-1.

First published as *A Classified Bibliography of Argumentation and Debate* (New York: Scarecrow Press, 1964), the second edition includes 5,972 books, articles, dissertations, and theses that constitute the secondary literature on debate. Topical sections identify entries on general principles of debate, writings before 1900, history, the debate, the case, teaching and coaching, research and evidence, logic, forms of debate, ethics, organization, and judging. Works published in the United States in the twentieth century predominate. Although greatly outdated, Kruger's work remains valuable for research on the study and teaching of debate.

55. Langham, Josephine, and Janine Chrichley. **Radio Research: An Annotated Bibliography, 1975-1988**. 2d ed. Aldershot, England: Averbury, 1989. 357p. ISBN 0-566-07130-4.

This Radio Academy survey, sponsored by Britain's Independent Broadcasting Authority, intends to provide a current comprehensive list of information sources for radio research and analyses of data on audiences and the ways listeners use and perceive radio broadcasts. Annotated entries for the exclusively English-language sources are organized in four parts. Parts I and II, "BBC Research" and "IBA Research," identify highly specialized and not commonly available agency reports, arranged chronologically under the issuing agencies. A section titled "Other British Research" includes separate listings for such topics as advertising and industry-related research, local radio, community radio, and academic and scholarly research. The last section, "Foreign Research," presents a brief and highly selective list of books, journal articles, BBC publications, and Unesco documents in a geographical arrangement. This specialized bibliography is recommended for serious researchers who need information on broadcasting from a British perspective. This edition largely updates Langham's *Radio Research: A Comprehensive Guide, 1975-1985: An Annotated Bibliography of Radio Research Resources* (London: BBC Data, 1986).

56. Larson, Keith A. **Public Relations, the Edward L. Bernayses, and the American Scene: A Bibliography**. Westwood, MA: F. W. Faxon, 1978. 774p. (Useful Reference Series, no. 114). LC 77-79472. ISBN 0-87305-118-1.

If one had to select a truly comprehensive bibliography (regardless of the narrowness of its topic), this title would be an excellent choice. Larson has identified 4,079 books, chapters and parts of books, articles, published talks, printed letters, and the like either by or about Edward L. Bernays and/or Doris E. Fleischman (Mrs. Bernays). Because both are seminal figures in the historical development of public relations in the United States, this bibliography of works related to them additionally offers a first-rate source for studies about public relations in general through the late 1970s. All entries are annotated, many quite extensively. Five separate indexes are provided. This is a revision and enlargement of Larson's *Public Relations, Edward L. Bernays, and the American Scene* (Westwood, MA: F. W. Faxon, 1951).

57. Lent, John A. **Caribbean Mass Communication: A Comprehensive Bibliography**. Los Angeles, CA: Crossroads Press, 1981. 152p. (Archival and Bibliographic Series). LC 82-126147. ISBN 0-9184-5639-8.

Lent describes 2,250 secondary sources on all aspects of mass communication (including the press, book and magazine publishing, advertising, radio, television, and films) related to the island nations of the Caribbean. Coverage dates from the eighteenth century to 1979. Books, articles, U.S. government documents, local publications, and reports of the International Organization of Journalists are included. Although English-language items predominate, works in Spanish, French, and Russian (titles are transliterated for these) are also cited. It is noteworthy that about one-fourth of the entries deal with Cuban media. Lent's *Global Guide to Media & Communications* (entry 60) supplements this bibliography. Jim Richstad and Michael McMillan's *Mass Communication and Journalism in the Pacific Islands* (Honolulu, HI: University of Hawaii Press, 1978) is a similar bibliography covering mass communication in the Pacific Islands.

58.   Lent, John A. **The New World and International Information Order: A Resource Guide and Bibliography**. Republic of Singapore: Asian Mass Communication Research and Information Centre, 1982. 103p. LC 83-672538. ISBN 9971-905-01-9.

Lent selected the sources in this guide to illustrate the concepts and policies of the development of technology and the control of news flow, particularly in the Third World. This concept, usually referred to as the "new world information order" or "new world order," has caused significant controversy in Western nations. Lent devotes substantial attention to the issues of this controversy in his introductory essay. He also analyzes the development of the new world order as expressed in worldwide conferences. The bibliography is a comprehensive list of books, theses, documents, and articles from 250 international journals, the majority of which are English-language sources. Most are briefly annotated. For additional sources on the new world order from a different perspective, researchers should consult *The New World Information and Communication Order: A Selective Bibliography* (New York: United Nations, Dag Hammarskjold Library, 1984).

59.   Lent, John A. **Women and the Mass Media in Asia: An Annotated Bibliography**. Republic of Singapore: Asian Mass Communication Research and Information Centre, 1985. 54p. ISBN 9971-905-18-3.

The 150 items in this bibliography address such topics as women in the media, women as audience, and women's media in Asia. All of the alphabetically arranged items are in English. Lent reports that locating these required searching 1,000 periodicals as well as books, conference proceedings, bibliographies, dissertations, and theses. The depth of this obviously restricted coverage varies for each country. Forty-three items relate to women in India; only one is cited for women in Vietnam. Most citations date from the early 1960s through the early 1980s. Items are selectively annotated, although some annotations are extensive. Unfortunately, neither subject nor country indexes are included. This slim paperback is a valuable resource for research on women and the media in Asia in that most of the items cited are not readily identified in other sources.

60.   Lent, John A., ed. **Global Guide to Media & Communications**. Munich: K. G. Saur, 1987. 145p. ISBN 3-598-10746-3.

It seems a bit mystifying that a "global" guide would purposefully eliminate coverage of the United States, but that is exactly what Lent has done. This bibliographic guide covers communication in all other areas of the world through 1984. Lent arranges geographically both general and specialized studies on all aspects of the mass media and mass communications, including newspapers, magazines, radio, television, advertising, new technologies, telecommunication, and public relations. Lent contributed the section on Asia and co-edited the sections on Eastern Europe and Latin America. Six other highly respected scholars were responsible for the other sections. The depth of coverage varies for different regions. The most extensive bibliographies cover mass communication in France, Great Britain, and West Germany. Although coverage is selective, the guide cites a wide variety of materials, including books, articles, government documents, dissertations, and theses. English-language materials predominate. Most annotations are in English. The volume's inconsistent (and occasionally absent) pagination as well as its lack of an index, however, will frustrate some researchers. Nonetheless, the guide offers a useful starting point for research on communication in nations other than the United States.

61. **Marxism and the Mass Media: Towards a Basic Bibliography.** Paris: International Center, 1972- . Irregular. LC 75-64245. ISSN 0098-9509.

Volumes in this series include studies of Marxist and leftist communication methods, networks, and theories in the French, German, Spanish, Italian, and English languages. All items included are held by the International Mass Media Research Center (entry 434) in Paris. Coverage extends to books, pamphlets, reviews, articles, dissertations, and unpublished manuscripts related to all mass media, including television, radio, public opinion, advertising, journalism and the press, film, and mass culture. About 500 annotated entries (all in English) appear in each issue. Indexing by country, author, and subject facilitates access. This interesting and valuable resource focuses on material not easily found elsewhere.

62. McKerns, Joseph P. **News Media and Public Policy: An Annotated Bibliography.** New York: Garland, 1985. 171p. (Public Affairs and Administration Series; Garland Reference Library of Social Science, vol. 219). LC 83-49290. ISBN 0-8240-9004-7.

McKerns provides annotated entries for 713 books, periodical and magazine articles, dissertations, and theses on the relationship between governmental public policy and the mass media in the United States. Most items date from the late 1960s to the present, although earlier seminal works are also included. McKerns arranges the entries in 10 topical sections, including mass communication theory, government and the press, and the news media and the bureaucracy (such as the executive, legislative, and judicial branches of American government). Of particular interest is the coverage of the historical framework of the relationship of government and the press in the second chapter.

63. Middleton, Karen P., and Meheroo Jussawalla. **The Economics of Communication: A Selected Bibliography with Abstracts.** New York: Published in cooperation with the East-West Center, Hawaii, by Pergamon Press, 1981. 249p. (Pergamon Policy Studies on International Development). LC 80-20505. ISBN 0-08-026325-9.

Middleton and Jussawalla concentrate on sources that address both communication and economics, providing extensively annotated entries for nearly 400 books, journal articles, Unesco reports, and documents of the East-West Center of Hawaii on the economic analysis of communication media (print, braodcast, and telecommunications) as well as satellites, cables, computers, libraries, and other communication exchange systems. Such multidisciplinary coverage makes this bibliography equally useful to researchers in economics and political science as to those in communication. A complementary bibliography is Snow and Jussawalla's *Telecommunication Economics and International Regulatory Policy* (entry 80).

64. Muller, Werner, and Manfred Meyer. **Children and Families Watching Television: A Bibliography of Research on Viewing Processes.** Munich: K. G. Saur, 1985. 159p. (Communication Research and Broadcasting, no. 7). ISBN 3-598-20206-7.

This bibliography, originally published in German, identifies research materials on the television viewing processes of children between 2 and 12 years of age. Some 454 unannotated references to books, journal articles, reports, and other documents in English, French, and German are included, most appearing from 1975 through 1985. Selected earlier works are also cited. Arrangement is in sections for bibliographies and studies of reception processes, viewing situations, and media education. English-language keywords or topic headings describe each source. Meyer and Ursula Nissen have also compiled

Effects and Functions of Television, Children and Adolescents: A Bibliography of Selected Research Literature, 1970-1978 (Munich: K. G. Saur, 1979), which lists research studies of television's effects on children and youths.

65. Murphy, James Jerome. **Medieval Rhetoric: A Select Bibliography**. 2d ed. Toronto, Canada: University of Toronto Press, 1989. 198p. (Toronto Medieval Bibliographies, vol. 3). LC 89-93504. ISBN 0-8020-5750-0.

This edition identifies 971 items on rhetoric from the year 400 through the early fifteenth century. Murphy arranges the selectively annotated entries in nine topical and chronological sections, including background studies, early Middle Ages, high Middle Ages, letter-writing, poetics and grammar, sermon theory, and university disputation and scholastic method, with subarrangements for different types of rhetoric and authors. Both primary and secondary works in Latin, Italian, French, German, Spanish, and English from all historical periods are included. In that this edition omits sources cited in Murphy's first edition (Toronto, Canada: University of Toronto Press, 1971), scholars requiring comprehensive coverage of the topic will need to consult both editions.

66. Murray, John P. **Television & Youth: 25 Years of Research & Controversy**. Boys Town, NE: Boys Town Center for the Study of Youth Development, 1980. 278p. LC 80-27601. ISBN 0-938510-00-2.

This bibliography is a classic, identifying 2,886 sources dating from 1955 through 1980 that evaluate television's impact on children and adolescents. More than half of the sources appeared between 1975 and 1980. The volume's arrangement provides sections for surveys of the general research literature on television and youth as well as for specific topics and various supporting bibliographies. Separate bibliographies focus on types of violence and their effects, television advertising, audience patterns, public policy, and other topics. The comprehensive coverage encompasses books, journal articles, dissertations, reports, government documents, unpublished manuscripts, and proceedings. The majority are English-language sources published in the United States, Australia, and Western Europe. About 15 percent are non-English-language sources.

67. Obudho, Constance E. **Human Nonverbal Behavior: An Annotated Bibliography**. Westport, CT: Greenwood Press, 1979. 196p. LC 79-7586. ISBN 0-313-21094-2.

Obudho includes non-evaluative annotations for 536 books, papers, articles, proceedings, speeches, and dissertations on human nonverbal behavior appearing from 1940 through 1978. Studies of normal individuals are distinguished from those about individuals with psychiatric problems and encompass body posture, distance, eye behavior, facial expression, and personal space, as well as nonverbal behavior within different racial groups. This bibliography supplements listings in Mary Ritchie Key's *Nonverbal Communication* (entry 53).

68. **Organizational Communication: Abstracts, Analysis, and Overview**. Newbury Park, CA: Sage, 1976-1983. 8 vols. LC 78-645212.

This source proves that an index that ceases annual publication remains valuable as a bibliography. The literature of organizational communication encompasses the areas of interpersonal, intragroup, and intergroup communication; communication factors and organizational goals; skill improvement and training; communication media; and communication system analysis and research methodology. These eight areas, as well as a ninth titled "Texts, Anthologies, Reviews, and General Bibliographies," comprise the major classifications of literature in *Organizational Communication*. It is the primary resource for an analysis of the literature in this specialized and interdisciplinary aspect of communication. Under the sponsorship of the International Communication Association (entry 468) and the American Business Communication Association, the series was first published as *Organizational Communication Abstracts* (1974-1975). In 1976 it acquired a new publisher and its subsequent title. The annual provides a general review of published and unpublished literature for both practitioners and scholars in the field. Each volume features a summary overview of organizational communication and additional summaries of communication in the nine areas previously cited. These are further subdivided into two categories: books and dissertations and articles, papers, and government documents. The main body of the volume consists of literature abstracts. Appendixes list the resources used in compiling the year's literature and a review of the contributors' research method. Separate indexes by author, type of organization, and data collection instrument complete each annual volume.

69. Paine, Fred L., and Nancy E. Paine. **Magazines: A Bibliography for Their Analysis with Annotations and Study Guide**. Metuchen, NJ: Scarecrow Press, 1987. 690p. LC 86-29825. ISBN 0-8108-1975-9.

Anyone researching the history, audience, literary or journalistic content, production, design, advertising, law, ethics, censorship, or other aspects of periodical publishing will find this bibliography immensely valuable. The Paines list and briefly annotate more than 2,000 books, articles, and dissertations about magazines. Items generally date from 1979 to the present, although selected historical or other early important works are also cited. The volume's bulk consists of the selected bibliography. Part I lists journals, magazines, and newspapers that regularly feature articles about magazines, in addition to bibliographies, directories, handbooks, statistical sources, and indexes. Researchers should consult John Hammond Schacht's *A Bibliography for the Study of Magazines* (Urbana, IL: College of Communications, University of Illinois, 1972) and its earlier editions (1966, 1968) for older works on magazine publishing.

70. Palzer, Michaela. **Neue Medien und Technologien in Asien und im Sudpazifik: Auswahlbibliographie. (New Media and Technologies in Asia and the South Pacific: A Selected Bibliography)**. Hamburg: Deutsches "Übersee-Institut," Übersee-Dokumentation, Referat Asien und Südpazifik, 1988. 181p. (Dokumentationsdienst Asien, Series A, no. 23). ISBN 3-922852-25-4.

Palzer profiles 500 books, United Nations documents, journal articles, industrial reports, and research papers published between 1985 and 1988 that focus on the development and proliferation of electronics in Asia and the South Pacific, including such topics as mass media, telecommunications, information systems, computers, and technological development, as well as new technology and media economics, trade, policy, and effects. Entries, arranged in broad topical sections, include keywords (in German) and abstracts in German or English. Despite international coverage, German- and English-language materials predominate. Indexes by author and by journal title provide access. Currency makes this bibliography most valuable to advanced researchers.

71. Pollay, Richard W. **Information Sources in Advertising History**. Westport, CT: Greenwood Press, 1979. 330p. LC 78-75259. ISBN 0-313-21422-0.

This guide features bibliographic essays by different contributing specialists on the history of advertising and marketing; an introductory survey of the literature of advertising history; and lists of specialized statistical sources, reference resources for advertising research, and advertising industry publications. The bulk of the volume contains annotated entries for 1,600 sources arranged alphabetically in topical listings for reference works; histories; biographies and memoirs; organizations; institutions, associations, and agency operations; psychology and sociology; advertising and copy research; criticism; ethics and polemics; textbooks and "how-to" works; copywriting texts; case histories; and fictional literature about advertising, among others. Additionally, separate directories list archives, special collections, manuscript repositories, and professional advertising associations. Coverage is limited to English-language books, dissertations, reports, journal articles, and textbooks. Pollay indicates that the bibliography is most valuable for identifying pre-1960 publications. This is an excellent guide to resources on American advertising history.

72. Pringle, Peter K., and Helen H. Clinton. **Radio and Television: A Selected, Annotated Bibliography: Supplement Two, 1982-1986.** Metuchen, NJ: Scarecrow Press, 1989. 237p. LC 88-23968. ISBN 0-8108-2158-3.

Nearly 1,000 English-language books, pamphlets, and reports on broadcasting and related technologies published from 1982 through 1986 are cited. Articles in periodicals are specifically excluded. Pringle and Clinton provide topical sections for broadcasting, radio, television, cable, new technologies, and home video. Pringle's supplement continues William E. McCavitt's *Radio and Television: A Selected, Annotated Bibliography* (Metuchen, NJ: Scarecrow Press, 1978), which covered materials published from 1920 through 1976, and McCavitt's *Radio and Television: A Selected, Annotated Bibliography: Supplement One, 1977-1981* (Metuchen, NJ: Scarecrow Press, 1982), which covered 1977 through 1981. Pringle retains the format of previous volumes and adds a title index. Researchers should consult all three volumes for comprehensive coverage of books on radio and television. Selective coverage of similar topics is provided by Susan Hill's *Broadcasting Bibliography* (entry 47).

73. Shearer, Benjamin F., and Marilyn Huxford. **Communications and Society: A Bibliography on Communications Technologies and Their Social Impact.** Westport, CT: Greenwood Press, 1983. 242p. LC 83-12659. ISBN 0-313-23713-1.

Shearer and Huxford include a selection of 2,732 books, scholarly articles, dissertations, and Rand reports that "explore the diversity of communication technologies from a humanistic perspective." Unannotated entries represent scholarship of about the past 40 years on media theory, the history of technological development, the shaping of mass media content, the social effects of the new media, mass media as creators and reflectors of public opinion, politics and the mass media, advertising, the future of mass communications, and fine art and literature in the technological society. Emphasis is on publications after the late 1970s. Both English- and non-English-language materials are included. Although researchers will find this bibliography useful, they should consult Zureik and Hartling's *The Social Context of the New Information and Communication Technologies* (entry 89) for more up-to-date coverage.

74. Signorielli, Nancy. **Role Portrayal and Stereotyping on Television: An Annotated Bibliography of Studies Relating to Women, Minorities, Aging, Sexual Behavior, Health & Handicaps.** Westport, CT: Greenwood Press, 1985. 214p. (Bibliographies and Indexes in Sociology, no. 5). LC 85-9823. ISBN 0-313-24855-9.

Sponsored by the Corporation for Public Broadcasting, this bibliography focuses on five different topics related to audiences: women and sex roles, racial and ethnic minorities, age roles, sexual behavior and orientation, and health and handicaps. Coverage includes books, scholarly and popular journal articles, and government documents appearing through 1984. The most useful sources cited here deal with television's handling of specific audiences. Entries include extensive descriptions of audiences/subjects used in specific studies.

75. Signorielli, Nancy, and George Gerbner. **Violence and Terror in the Mass Media: An Annotated Bibliography**. Westport, CT: Greenwood Press, 1988. 233p. (Bibliographies and Indexes in Sociology, no. 13). LC 87-29556. ISBN 0-313-26120-2.

In this bibliography, originally commissioned by Unesco in 1984 and supported by The Annenberg School of Communication, Signorielli and Gerbner offer a significant new scholarly contribution to the literature on the portrayal of violence in the mass media. Briefly annotated entries are provided for 784 international books, dissertations, scholarly and popular journal articles, government documents, and conference reports that examine such topics as violence in relation to mass media content and effects, terrorism an the mass media, and pornography. Most of the sources appeared from the early 1970s through 1987. This bibliography substantially supplements the bibliography on violence and the mass media included in volume 2 of the Canadian government's exhaustive seven-volume *Report of the Royal Commission on Violence in the Communications Industry* (Toronto, Canada: Royal Commission on Violence in the Communications Industry, 1977).

76. Slide, Anthony, ed. **Selected Radio and Television Criticism**. Metuchen, NJ: Scarecrow Press, 1987. 203p. LC 86-27891. ISBN 0-8108-1942-2.

Slide is a prolific author in the area of critical analysis of the cinema and theater. Over 100 entries present critical comments on individual programs, series, and personalities. The texts of one to three critical reviews or articles are reprinted from magazines, newspapers, and John Crosby's *With Love and Loathing* (New York: McGraw-Hill, 1933). These original sources date from the late 1920s through the 1950s and are arranged alphabetically by personal name or program title. Separate indexes, one of personalities and programs and one of critics, are provided. As with any volume of selective materials, not all will agree with the group of radio and television shows, series, and personalities that Slide has chosen for this collection. Among the programs and individuals included in the section dealing with radio criticism, for example, are *Lassie, The Lone Ranger, One Man's Family*, Don Wilson, and Father Charles E. Coughlin. Not covered are the memorable *Baby Snooks, Mr. District Attorney*, and *Breakfast with Dorothy and Dick*. Nevertheless, despite such omissions, Slide's volume must be regarded as the best handbook of analyses of radio criticism that is now available.

77. Sloan, W. David. **American Journalism History: An Annotated Bibliography**. New York: Greenwood Press, 1989. 344p. (Bibliographies and Indexes in Mass Media and Communications). LC 88-35800. ISBN 0-313-26350-7.

Journalism historians will find this bibliography of resources on American journalism from 1690 through 1987 most valuable. Annotated entries for 2,657 books and journal articles are arranged in sections for general history, historical periods (the colonial press, the antebellum and Civil War press), and historical topics (freedom of the press, the penny press, frontier and regional journalism). Coverage of the scholarly journal literature is particularly comprehensive: Articles appearing in over 200 mass communication, journalism, history, business, and legal journals are identified. A separate section serves as a research guide, including a list of reference works. Sloan's volume complements coverage provided by Caswell's *Guide to Sources in American Journalism History* (mentioned in entry 3).

78. Smith, Myron J., Jr. **U.S. Television Network News: A Guide to Sources in English**. Jefferson, NC: McFarland, 1984. 233p. LC 82-42885. ISBN 0-89950-080-3.

The American public has displayed a fascination with the happenings on network news programs and with the individuals associated with these shows. Recent magazines and newspapers have produced an extraordinary number of articles that reflect this preoccupation. Smith offers an excellent introducton to the older literature dealing with the growth and development of television network news in the United States, including selectively annotated entries for some 3,215 books, journal and magazine articles, dissertations, theses, and government documents published in English from the late 1940s through 1982. An addendum includes selected items from 1983. Newspaper articles are excluded. The volume includes separate sections, each preceded by a brief introductory overview, for reference works, general works on history and audiences, news reporting and writing, news in controversy, news and domestic affairs, news and U.S. presidents, presidential elections, foreign affairs, and biography. Smith's bibliography is particularly useful for identifying works on network news coverage of particular historical events and about network news personalities. In that the majority of the references are to readily available sources, Smith's work is especially useful to undergraduates.

79. Snorgrass, J. William, and Gloria T. Woody. **Blacks and Media: A Selected, Annotated Bibliography, 1962-1982**. Tallahassee, FL: Florida A&M University Press, 1985. 150p. LC 84-15296. ISBN 0-8130-0810-7.

This bibliography contains brief, non-evaluative annotations of about 700 books, chapters and parts of books, scholarly and popular journal articles, and other sources on African-Americans in the print and broadcast media, advertising and public relations, and film and theater. Many of the references have been culled from such black-oriented publications as *Jet, Black Collegian*, and *Sepia*. Researchers should consult Hill's *Black Media in America* (entry 45) for additional sources.

80. Snow, Marcellus S., and Meheroo Jussawalla. **Telecommunication Economics and International Regulatory Policy: An Annotated Bibliography**. New York: Greenwood Press, 1986. 216p. (Bibliographies and Indexes in Economics and Economic History, no. 4). LC 86-12130. ISBN 0-313-25370-6.

Snow and Jussawalla provide comprehensive coverage of the scholarly literature dealing with both the regulatory policies in general and the regulatory economics of telecommunication. Many of the sources specifically focus on the international aspects of regulation. Although some of the sources date from the 1960s and early 1970s, the majority date from the late 1970s through 1985. Arrangement is in three parts. Part 1 covers telecommunication's concepts and theoretical backgrounds while part 2 deals with technical, institutional, and legal frameworks. Part 3 includes empirical studies, research resources, and research desiderata. Among the main topics of this bibliography are trade issues, pricing theory, distribution, and worldwide regulatory issues, with the most substantial emphasis on the United States, West Germany, Japan, the United Kingdom, and Canada. Coverage is largely limited to English-language books, journal articles, International Telecommunications Union reports, proceedings, and government reports. Fairly extensive annotations are provided. Although many of the sources included in this bibliography are very technical, the work's thoroughness makes it an excellent basic research resource. It should be used in conjunction with Middleton and Jussawalla's *The Economics of Communication* (entry 63).

81. Soukup, Paul A. **Christian Communication: A Bibliographical Survey**. New York: Greenwood Press, 1989. 400p. (Bibliographies and Indexes in Religious Studies). LC 89-12076. ISBN 0-313-25673-x.

Soukup identifies over 1,300 works (books, journal and newspaper articles, and dissertations) that deal with the broad theme of Christian communication. Popular articles and works on homiletics (the art of preaching) are specifically excluded. Topical sections include annotated entries in the areas of rhetoric, interpersonal communication, intercultural communication, and other media as related to art, music, drama, video, videotext, and the like. The most extensive listings are for mass communication. Introductory chapters offer a history of Christian communication and an analysis of related issues as well as descriptions of relevant reference resources. English-language works dating from the 1950s through the late 1980s predominate, although selected older works are also cited.

82. Sterling, Christopher H. **Foreign and International Communications Systems: A Survey Bibliography: An Annotated Listing of Selected Books and Documents on Foreign Communication Systems and International Communication**. 4th ed. Columbus, OH: Center for Advanced Study in Telecommunications, 1989. 13p. (Basic Bibliography, no. 3). OCLC 22403634.

First published in 1982 by the Center for Telecommunications Studies in Washington, D.C., Sterling's guide includes briefly annotated entries for a representative selection of about 150 English-language books and government and agency (such as the International Telecommunications Union [ITU] and Unesco) documents on transborder and foreign communication systems. Journal articles are excluded. Separate topical listings are included for reference works, surveys of international and foreign systems, history, regulations and policy, world satellite communications, transborder communication, telecommunications trade, propaganda, and the role of the United States in international telecommunications, as well as telecommunications in OECD (Organization for Economic Cooperation and Development), communist, and Third World nations. Emphasis in this edition is on recent publications. For older sources on similar topics the three previous editions should be consulted. Sterling, editor of *Communication Booknotes* (entry 344), has produced several other volumes in this series, including *Telecommunications Policy*, 5th ed. (Washington, DC: George Washington University, Telecommunications Policy Program, 1986), and *Mass Communication and Electronic Media*, 11th ed. (Washington, DC: George Washington University, Telecommunications Policy Program, 1986).

83. Sutton, Roberta Briggs. **Speech Index: An Index to 259 Collections of World Famous Orations and Speeches for Various Occasions**. 4th ed., revised and enlarged. New York: Scarecrow Press, 1966. 947p. LC 66-13749.

This is supplemented by:

83.1. Mitchell, Charity. **Speech Index: An Index to Collections of World Famous Orations and Speeches for Various Occasions: Fourth Edition: Supplement, 1966-1980**. Metuchen: NJ: Scarecrow Press, 1982. 466p. LC 81-23282. ISBN 0-8108-1518-4.

Despite the field's current interest in mass communication, telecommunications, and other hi-tech things, public speaking remains a fundamental part of communication. Students and scholars alike need to identify texts of speeches, whether the speech is Abraham Lincoln's *Gettysburg Address*, Pericles's *Funeral Orations*, or former FCC chairman Newton Minow's speech before the National Association of Broadcasters in which he called television "a vast wasteland." The *Speech Index* provides author/speaker and subject access to historical and current speeches published in English-language anthologies since 1900. Mitchell's supplement analyzes an additional 115 collections, including a large number of standard public speaking textbooks.

84. Unesco. **List of Documents and Publications in the Field of Mass Communication**. Paris: Unesco, 1976- . Annual. LC 80-649024.

Unesco annually publishes this paperbound checklist of its own publications and other materials on mass communication published internationally during the preceding year. Coverage includes United Nations documents, conference reports, working papers, proceedings, and books from trade and academic presses in all languages, as well as articles published in the *Unesco Courier*. The main listing alphabetically interfiles main entries, acronyms, titles (both in the language of the original as well as translated into English), and subjects. Subject (keyword) and personal-name indexes are provided. This bibliography is most valuable for identifying materials on communication in Third World and other developing nations.

85.   Walsh, Ruth M., and Stanley J. Birkin. **Business Communications: An Annotated Bibliography**. Westport, CT: Greenwood Press, 1980. 686p. LC 79-8296. ISBN 0-313-20923-5.

Walsh and Birkin identify and briefly abstract more than 1,000 English-language books, articles, and dissertations published from 1960 through 1978 that deal with such topics in interpersonal and organizational communication in business as employee-employer interaction, data and word processing, telecommunication, and written communication. A rather confusing three-part arrangement of author-title and keyword-in-context indexes and an abstracts section is intended to permit cross-referencing by item numbers. Scholars should use the volume selectively. The listings on interpersonal communication in business are of the most value. Others on telecommunication and management information systems are already dated.

86.   **Webster's Comprehensive Marketing Bibliography**. Kawkawlin, MI: Data Publishers Corporation, 1986. 13 vols. in 46 vols. OCLC 15000096.

This extremely impressive set offers comprehensive coverage on marketing. Specific volumes deal exclusively or partially with various aspects of advertising and, to a lesser degree, public relations. The great depth of coverage of the subject of advertising is most evident in volume VII-2, *Advertising Types, Strategies, and Audiences*, which includes annotated entries (many very extensive) for 3,500 sources. Topical chapters list sources on advertising and children, advertising in the professions, corrective advertising, deceptive and false advertising, and public relations publicity and strategies. Coverage is limited to English-language books, journal and newspaper articles, conference papers, dissertations, and government reports, most dating from the 1960s through the present. Usefulness of this otherwise excellent series is severely hindered by lack of subject indexing of any kind in combination with the broad subject classifications employed in the general organization of the volumes and chapters. Thus, despite excellent coverage and description of the literature, this bibliography is not recommended as a primary reference resource for materials on advertising and public relations except in the context of the broader field of marketing.

87.   Wedell, George, George-Michael Luyken, and Rosemary Leonard, eds. **Mass Communication in Western Europe: An Annotated Bibliography**. Manchester, England: European Institute for the Media, 1985. 327p. (Media Monograph, no. 6). ISBN 0-948195-04-5.

The editors, all of whom are or have been affiliated with the European Institute for the Media, have selected 757 items published from 1980 through 1985 that deal with topics in mass communication (such as radio, television, telecommunication, teledistribution, the press, informatics, and information technology) in 20 Western European countries. The geographically arranged sources include scholarly critical studies, policy-oriented texts, and legislative and official documents. Other sections include listings for intergovernmental organizations, such as Unesco, Council of Europe, the European Community, the

Commission of the European Community, and the European Parliament. A significant number of items are in languages other than English. Although English translations of titles are frequently provided, annotations are in the language of the original publication. Indexing is by a complicated coding system. Many of the cited sources are relatively obscure. Because of these limitations, this useful bibliography is only recommended to advanced students and researchers.

88. Woll, Allen L., and Randall M. Miller. **Ethnic and Racial Images in American Film and Television: Historical Essays and Bibliography**. New York: Garland, 1987. 408p. (Garland Reference Library of Social Science, vol. 308). LC 84-48883. ISBN 0-8240-8733-4.

This work's most interesting features are the introductory essays for each chapter. These provide histories of the television and film images of such varied ethnic and racial groups as Hispanics, Arabs, Asians, Jews, Irish, Italians, Eastern Europeans and Russians, Germans, Africans, and Native Americans. The collective history of media images of other groups (Greeks, Armenians, and others) is provided in another chapter. Unannotated checklists of books, articles in scholarly and popular journals and newspapers, dissertations, theses, and government documents accompany each essay. Coverage extends beyond English-language sources. This guide is particularly valuable for its coverage of scholarship on the images of smaller ethnic groups in the media.

89. Zureik, Elia, and Dianne Hartling. **The Social Context of the New Information and Communication Technologies: A Bibliography**. New York: Peter Lang, 1987. 310p. (American University Studies, Series XV: Communications, vol. 2). LC 87-3450. ISBN 0-8204-0413-6.

This bibliography is of use to a broad range of communication students. Zureik and Hartling, both faculty of Queen's University, Ontario, identify more than 6,000 books, journal articles, dissertations, and proceedings that illustrate the role of new information technologies in present and future societies. Entries are arranged in about 80 widely varied topical groups, including cable and pay television, organizational planning, electronic publishing, satellites and space communication, information theory, and transnational data flow. Coverage is limited to English-language sources published for the most part since 1975. Emphasis is on American and Canadian sources, with selected British and Australian publications also included. For complementary coverage researchers should consult Shearer and Huxford's *Communications and Society* (entry 73). Additional coverage of earlier sources is provided by Thomas F. Gordon and Mary Ellen Verna's *Mass Communication Effects and Processes: A Comprehensive Bibliography, 1950-1975* (Beverly Hills, CA: Sage, 1978) and their *Mass Media and Socialization: A Selected Bibliography* (Philadelphia, PA: Radio-Television-Film Department, Temple University, 1973).

Annual Reviews

90. **Advances in Experimental Social Psychology**. New York: Academic Press, 1964- . LC 64-23452. ISSN 0065-2601.

Each annual volume in this well-established series is typically divided into 10 chapters concerned with the development, status, and literature of experimental social psychology study and research. Essays in recent volumes have focused on such topics as the relationship between media violence and aggressive behavior as well as international trends in the study of television's impact on children and adults. Both *Applied Social Psychology Annual* (entry 94) and *Annual Review of Psychology* (entry 92) should be consulted for more thorough and detailed analyses of current research trends in communication psychology and sociology. Review essays featured in *Advances in Experimental Social Psychology* are indexed in *SSCI* (entry 185).

91. **Annual Review of Applied Linguistics**. Rowley, MA: Newbury House, 1980- . LC 84-649237. ISSN 8756-5625.

The field of applied linguistics is the exclusive theme of *Annual Review of Applied Linguistics (ARAL)*. *ARAL* surveys the research literature on such topics as languages and politics, language teaching, computer-assisted language instruction, linguistics and written discourse, bilingualism, and language in the areas of business, law, education, political science, science, and the media (including the role of language in journalism and advertising). Research on the language of pedagogy, psycholinguistics, and sociolinguistics is also surveyed. Each volume begins with an introductory essay and an overview of research in a particular aspect of applied linguistics, with an unannotated bibliography of cited literature. Chapters include brief "state of the art" statements, annotated bibliographies of the year's most significant scholarship, and unannotated bibliographies of less important works. Coverage is comprehensive; non-English-language scholarship is cited. For reviews of scholarship in theoretical linguistics, communication researchers should consult *YWES* (entry 103) and *YWMLS* (entry 104). Essays in *ARAL* are selectively indexed in *MLA* (entry 178).

92. **Annual Review of Psychology**. Palo Alto, CA: Annual Reviews, Inc., 1950- . LC 50-13143. ISSN 0066-4308.

The principal annual review in the field of psychology, *Annual Review of Psychology* is particularly valuable for reviewing current research in interpersonal, intrapersonal, small group, and organizational communication and psychology. Major critical essays reflect the categories in the annual volume's master list of topics. These typically include attention, clinical and community psychology, cognitive processes, developmental psychology, learning and memory, psychology and the law, personnel-organizational psychology, psycholinguistics, social psychology, and sex roles. The master list is modified annually to reflect research trends. Each review begins with a table of contents and concludes with an annotated bibliography of cited literature. Essays focus on such pertinent topics as the effects of political behavior on agenda-setting in the mass media, the relationship of the mass media and political psychology, media technology, the psychological uses of television, and the processing of stimuli in advertising. Coverage of research is international. Volumes feature separate author and subject indexes and cumulative five-year indexes to contributors and chapter titles. Although substantial, *Annual Review of Psychology*'s coverage of the literature of organizational communication is not as comprehensive as that provided by *Organizational Communication* (entry 68). *Applied Social Psychology Annual* (entry 94) and *Advances in Experimental Social Psychology* (entry 90) offer complementary literature reviews in psychology. Annual Reviews, Inc., also publishes *Annual Review of Sociology* (entry 93). Review essays featured in *Annual Review of Psychology* are indexed in *CC* (entry 164), *PA* (entry 183), *SSCI* (entry 185), and *SSI* (entry 186).

93. **Annual Review of Sociology**. Palo Alto, CA: Annual Reviews, Inc., 1975- . LC 75-648500. ISSN 0360-0572.

"The primary purpose of the *Annual Review of Sociology* continues to be to provide authoritative surveys of recent important sociological theory and research in specialized fields [that are] ... important for the development of specialties with sociology." It also surveys recent literature from the related disciplines of anthropology, psychology, law, political science, psycholinguistics, and history. Its reviews provide critical assessments of current topics of research, summarize past contributions, and identify future research trends. The essays are arranged in 12 broad categories: theory and methods, social processes, institutions and culture, formal organizations, political and economic sociology, differentiation and stratification, individuals and society, demography, urban and rural sociology, policy, historical sociology, and sociology of world regions. Each essay is abstracted and includes an unannotated bibliography of cited literature. Essays by distinguished scholars in the field of sociology preface recent volumes. *Annual Review of Sociology* provides strong bibliographic coverage of the literature on the sociology of organizations, complementing that offered by *Annual Review of Psychology* (entry 92) and *Organizational Communication* (entry 68). It also offers occasional surveys of literature on the sociology of mass media and mass communications. As neither of these subjects nor communication in general is specifically indicated, researchers must use either the subject index or the cumulative chapter title index at the end of each volume to identify appropriate entries. Review essays included in *Annual Review of Sociology* are indexed in *PA* (entry 183) and *SSCI* (entry 185).

94. **Applied Social Psychology Annual**. Newbury Park, CA: Sage, 1980-1988. 8 vols. LC 80-645341. ISSN 0196-4151.

This annual, sponsored by the Society for the Psychological Study of Social Issues, a division of the American Psychological Association, provides a more narrowly focused review of the social aspects of psychological research than the reviews found in either *Annual Review of Psychology* (entry 92) or *Annual Review of Sociology* (entry 93). *Applied Social Psychology Annual* includes a review of the research literature of social psychology. A recent issue, for example, featured a detailed report of research on the role of the media in terrorism as well as a chapter entitled "The Media and Nuclear War: Fall Out from TV's *The Day After*." Another psychological-sociological annual that should be consulted is *Advances in Experimental Social Psychology* (entry 90). Review essays featured in *Applied Social Psychology Annual* are indexed in *PA* (entry 183).

95. **Communication Yearbook**. Newbury Park, CA: Sage, 1977- . LC 76-45943. ISSN 0147-4642.

Sponsored by the International Communication Association (ICA) (entry 468), *Communication Yearbook* offers essay reviews of research and other articles that reflect the broad range and variety of interests in the field of communication, including information systems, interpersonal communication, mass communication, organizational communication, intercultural and development communication, health communication, philosophy of communication, and human communication technology. Through volume 10 (1987), *Communication Yearbook* featured "commissioned overviews" and selected papers from ICA conventions. Beginning with volume 11 (1988), commissioned papers continue to form a volume's contents while convention papers are published separately as proceedings. In addition, in principle, contributed reviews and articles are now written for the larger field rather than for divisional interests and typically reflect or connect to particular central themes. Volume 11, for example, addressed "themes in media, conversational analyses, criticism, phenomenology, persuasion, methodology, and opinion formation" (pp. 11-12). Other volumes will cover focal "themes in power, friendship, technology, the self and others, life stages, intercultural relations, media and politics, confrontation, and contextualism." In volume 11, general themes are arranged in individual sections consisting of two to three features. These sections are concluded by signed commentaries and critical analyses. A chapter on agenda-setting, for example, includes an overview essay, "Agenda-Setting Research: Where Has It Been, Where Is It Going?" and several critical responses, including "New Directions in Agenda-Setting Research" and "Feeling the Elephant: Some Observations on Agenda-Setting Research." Other articles in the volume address such topics as rural health communication, male-female communication on the job, and children's perceptions of moral themes in television. In general, this change in *Communication Yearbook*'s composition provides researchers with a more substantial body of research on a more intradisciplinary (read: narrower) range of topics. *Communication Yearbook* remains a convenient source for bibliographies on topics of current interest in the field. Most contributions include extensive lists of cited works. Name and subject indexes make access relatively straightforward.

96. **Communications Law.** New York: Practising Law Institute, 1982- . LC 79-643817. ISSN 0898-2457.

The Practising Law Institute annually publishes two volumes containing detailed legal discussions of communications issues as well as a detailed topical analysis of the law of communications and its literature. Volumes present major articles and legal interpretations of such issues as the regulation of cable television, antitrust and the media, and advertising law. Typical contributions in a single volume included "Battle Intensifying over Explicit Sex on Cable TV," "FCC Due to Rule on Radio Station's Future," and "The Media and Communications Revolution: An Overview of the Regulations Framework and Developing Trends." *Communications Law* is complemented by *LDRC 50-State Survey* (entry 98), which presents a state-by-state analysis of media law in the United States and its territories.

97. **Current Issues and Research in Advertising.** Ann Arbor, MI: Division of Research, Graduate School of Business Administration, University of Michigan, 1978- . LC 78-646623. ISSN 0163-3392.

According to editor James H. Leigh, "a definite need for the advertising community is the timely review of developments in the functional areas of the discipline." *Current Issues and Research in Advertising* (*CIRA*) fills that need. *CIRA* offers the most fundamental and comprehensive review of advertising research and literature. It should be consulted first among other reviews that cover this area. *CIRA* summarizes and analyzes research and discussion of advertising concepts, theories, and issues and identifies areas in need of research. Review areas include ad stimulus effects, consumer information, processing of advertisements, copy testing and measurement, creative function and assessment, legal and regulatory aspects of public policy, advertising education, advertisement management (such as agency-client relations), economic impact of advertising, international advertising, and societal and social aspects of public policy. Research in most of these topics is surveyed and updated at least once every two years; updates for advertising education and international advertising are provided every four years. *CIRA* was formerly issued in one volume divided into two sections, "Theory, Practice and Current Developments" and "Research." Since 1983 *CIRA* has been published in two volumes. Volume I, *Original Research and Theoretical Contributions*, features previously unpublished original research. "A Comparison of Advertising Self-Regulation in the U.K. and the U.S.A.," "Senior Citizens and Television Advertisements: A Research Note," and "Responses to Physician Advertising in the Yellow Pages" are typical articles. Volume II, *Reviews of Selected Areas*, typically contains four or five substantive review essays that analyze the literature in particular areas and topics in advertising. These reviews cite research largely published in mainstream advertising and communication periodical literature, such as *Journal of Marketing* (entry 380), *Journal of Advertising Research* (entry 368), *Journal of Advertising* (entry 367), and *Journal of Communication* (entry 374).

98. **LDRC 50-State Survey: Current Developments in Media Libel and Invasion of Privacy Law**. New York: Libel Defense Resource Center, 1982- . LC 84-10646.

Television, radio, newspapers, and magazines are all constantly facing challenges in the courts concerning libel and privacy rights. Attorneys in all 50 states and United States overseas territories annually contribute individual updates and evaluations of the current media laws in the United States, Guam, Puerto Rico, and the Virgin Islands. Each geographically arranged section includes a summation of current laws, definitions of terms, and an analysis of fault, privileges, damages, burden of proof, retraction, insurance, and so on. All entries identify the preparer by name and firm and indicate the date of preparation. Some entries include bibliographies of citations of pertinent local media laws. The 1987 edition featured a comparative review of extant media laws in England, Australia, New Zealand, Singapore, Hong Kong, Israel, West Germany, and France. *LDRC 50-State Survey*'s review of the current status of media laws and regulations should be used in conjunction with *Communications Law* (entry 96).

99. **Mass Communication Review Yearbook**. Beverly Hills, CA: Sage, 1980-1987. 6 vols. LC 80-159. ISSN 0196-8017.

Published in cooperation with the Center for Research in Public Communication of the University of Maryland, *Mass Communication Review Yearbook* included original review essays as well as previously published research articles. The contents of each annual volume (biennial in 1987) were chosen "to alert mass communication scholars to the shifting contours of the field." Among the areas of research reviewed were media effects, media conflict, media and culture, mass communication, feminism and the media, media and society, mass media and the individual, the role of the state in media performance, new technologies, telecommunication policy, and political communication. While featuring some original commissioned essays, volumes largely consisted of essays that had appeared in previously published books or core periodicals, such as *Critical Studies in Mass Communication* (entry 351), *Public Opinion Quarterly* (entry 404), *Journal of Broadcasting and Electronic Media* (entry 370), *Journal of Communication* (entry 374), and *Communication Research* (entry 348). Contributors represent a cross-section of noted communication scholars, including Elihu Katz, Kaarle Nordenstreng, Denis McQuail, and Wilbur Schramm, to name only a few. Although international in scope, most features concentrated on topics in mass communication in the United States and Europe. *Mass Communication Review Yearbook* ceased publication in 1987.

100. **Progress in Communication Sciences**. Norwood, NJ: Ablex, 1979- . LC 79-643016. ISSN 0163-5689.

Review essays in volumes in this series detail research in the areas of information, information transfer, information systems, the effects of communication, and the control and regulation of communication and information. Much of the cited research deals with major conference papers and recently published articles. Due to the interdisciplinary nature of communication, the series approaches topics from the perspectives of sociology, psychology, linguistics, political science, economics, and information science. The topics cover a wide range of areas in the broad field of communication, including interpersonal, organizational, mass, and international communication. Essays have addressed such topics as information technology, speech, verbal and nonverbal communication, communication codes, and crosscultural communication. Recent issues have included features on communication and ethnicity, communication and the unconscious, the communication of deviance, satellite communication, television viewer behavior, the impact of new communication technologies, and theory of discourse. Volumes typically feature eight or nine essays. Most essays are thoroughly documented and contain extensive bibliographies.

All conclude with summary discussions. Cumulative chapter title lists now appear in all volumes; however, no cumulative subject or author indexes are provided. While *Progress in Communication Sciences* does not offer the broad coverage of communication that is provided by other serial publications, such as *Communication Yearbook* (entry 95), it does give complementary coverage of a variety of topics in more limited but fundamental areas of communication research.

101. **Public Relations Research Annual**. Hillsdale, NJ: Lawrence Erlbaum, 1989- . LC 88-3470. ISSN 1042-1408.

A project of the Public Relations Division of the Association for Education in Journalism and Mass Communication (entry 460), this annual continues *Public Relations Research and Education* (1984-1985), a journal whose run ceased after only three issues. Edited by James E. Grunig and Larissa Grunig, the annual is a first attempt to consolidate examples of academic research on public relations in a single volume. The contents reflect historical and critical scholarly research in public relations and thus cannot be compared to the majority of publications in this field, which deal primarily with practical public relations applications and methods. It offers a broad review of scholarship in a relatively new area of academic publication and research. Volume I of the series is divided in two sections. Part I, "Research Reviews," includes two chapters that provide an overview of recent progress and development of public relations research. The editors promise that subsequent volumes of the annual will include at least two reviews of this kind. The remaining chapters constitute Part II, "Reports of Original Research." This section describes the results of original research previously presented as papers at the annual meetings of major academic public relations associations, including Public Relations Society of America (entry 479), International Association of Business Communicators (entry 467), and International Communication Association (entry 468), as well as other groups with interests in the field, such as Speech Communication Association (entry 482). Studies in the inaugural volume focused on conflict management, organizational structure, models for public relations, public services activities, design of organizations, ethics of public relations, and dialogue. Also among the subjects covered are some of perennial concern to the field, such as ethics and credibility, public relations as a profession, and public relations theory. James E. Grunig is a well-established author in the public relations field. His previous publications include *Organizations and Public Relations* (1976) and *Managing Public Relations* (1984).

102. **Sage Annual Reviews of Communication Research**. Beverly Hills, CA: Sage, 1972- . LC 80-50. ISSN 0099-1414.

Each volume in the *Sage Annual Reviews of Communication Research* series (this is a series title; each volume is separately titled) is a major monograph that surveys the scholarly and professional research literature on a particular area or topic in communication. To date, 16 volumes in this review series have been published. Among the titles in this series are *Organizational Communication: Traditional Themes and New Directions* (1985), *Advances in Content Analysis* (1981), *Strategies for Communication Research* (1977), *Explorations in Interpersonal Communication* (1976), *New Models for Communication Research* (1973), and *Current Perspectives in Mass Communication* (1972). Other volumes have explored research in nonverbal interaction, the communication of children, intrapersonal communication, the theory of persuasion, and political communication. Other relevant monographic series include *Advances in the Study of Communication and Effect* (New York: Plenum, 1974-); *Sage Series in Interpersonal Communication* (London: Sage, 1975-); *People and Communication* (Beverly Hills, CA: Sage, 1977-); and *Contributions to the Study of Mass Media and Communications* (Westport, CT: Greenwood Press, 1983-).

103. **Year's Work in English Studies**. New York: Humanities Press, 1921- . LC 22-10024. ISSN 0084-4144.

Sponsored by the English Association, *Year's Work in English Studies* (*YWES*) is the most important and prestigious review of scholarship on literature in English and the English language. In *YWES* interest in literature and literary scholarship prodominates. Chapters are provided for reference works, literary history and bibliography, literary theory, Old English literature, Milton, American literature to 1900, and the like. Discussion of topics relevant to research in rhetoric, speech, communication theory, and other areas of communication is concentrated in a specific chapter on the English language. In addition, the "Subjects Treated List" references research on the language of advertising, linguistics, discourse, mass media, rhetoric, television, and radio included elsewhere in each volume. Separate indexes of critics/authors and subjects are included. Essays in *YWES* are indexed in *MLA* (entry 178).

104. **Year's Work in Modern Language Studies**. London: Modern Humanities Research Association, 1931- . ISSN 0084-4152.

Complementing *Year's Work in English Studies* (entry 103) in style, format, and coverage, *Year's Work in Modern Language Studies* (*YWMLS*) provides critical reviews of the literature in the areas of medieval and modern Romance, Germanic, and Slavic languages and literatures. Each volume includes sections for general linguistics, Latin, Romance languages, Celtic languages, Germanic languages, and Slavic studies, with further specific subdivisions. Romance languages, for example, includes subdivisions for French, Occitan, Spanish, Catalan, Portuguese, Latin American languages, Italian, Romansh, and other Western European languages. *YWMLS* is most valuable in communication research for comprehensive coverage of both linguistics and rhetoric. Subdivisions in linguistics include bilingualism, organizational linguistics, contrastive linguistics, textual linguistics, and linguistic theory. Similarly extensive coverage is offered for rhetoric. "Abbreviations Lists" include periodical titles, acta, festschriften, and other collective and general works as well as the names of publishers, institutions, and places. Both subjects and names are indexed. Emphasis in *YWMLS* is on theoretical aspects of linguistics and rhetoric. More comprehensive coverage of applied linguistics is provided by *Annual Review of Applied Linguistics* (entry 91). Essays in *YWMLS* are indexed in *MLA* (entry 178).

2
Dictionaries, Encyclopedias, and Handbooks

105. Arnold, Carroll C., and John Waite Bowers, eds. **Handbook of Rhetorical and Communication Theory**. Boston, MA: Allyn and Bacon, 1984. 916p. LC 83-11806. ISBN 0-205-08057-x.

Covering the most theoretical and fundamental aspects of communication, the handbook includes contributed essays that present the "state of the theoretical art." Emphasis is on "the pragmatics of human communication—how people practically use and, in a sense, are used by symbolic behavior" (p. vii). The essays are arranged in three sections. The first focuses on the underlying bases of the theories of communication and rhetoric. The second includes discussions of communication as "facilitator or inhibitor" in human activities. Articles address formation of self-image, attitude formation, pleasing behavior, interpersonal relations, organizational communication, persuasion and propaganda, and communication in social movements. The concluding section identifies topics for future research. All articles contain extensive notes and documentation. Contributors include prominent scholars like Phillip K. Thompkins, Gerald R. Miller, Michael Burgoon, and Judee K. Burgoon. A cumulative index of names and subjects concludes the handbook.

106. Asante, Molefi Kete, and William B. Gudykunst. **Handbook of International and Intercultural Communication**. Newbury Park, CA: Sage, 1989. 520p. LC 88-32672. ISBN 0-8039-3202-2.

Contributed articles in this handbook review the research literature on communication across the numerous and varied cultural boundaries in the global society. Communication across the boundaries of race, ethnicity, and social status or class are just a few of the topics discussed. Considerable emphasis is on communication between North-South, information rich-information poor societies and cultures. Articles are arranged in four sections. Introductory overviews survey the field in general and its underlying theories; its relationship to anthropology; "etic" and "emic" approaches to intercultural communication (that is, the study of the communication between different cultures and the study of communication within a specific culture); the role of communication in cultural development; and the issues involved in the New International Information Order debate. "Process and Effects" reviews research on the intercultural communication channels of language and nonverbal behavior from various cultural perspectives; the roles of social networks, social cognition, emotions, communication competence, and influence in interpersonal intercultural communication; and the role of electronic mass media in communication across cultures. Research on interpersonal bonding, intercultural communication in the workplace, diplomatic communication in international development, and intercultural communication training is also reviewed. The volume concludes with a review of problems in intercultural communication research methodologies. Bibliographic references accompany each essay. This handbook updates the review of research provided in Asante, Eileen Newmark, and Cecil A. Blake's *Handbook of Intercultural Communication* (Beverly Hills, CA: Sage, 1979). The earlier volume remains particularly valuable, however, for discussions of communication between genders, age groups, and races in the United States. Additional research on the role of intercultural communication in training is surveyed in Dan Landis and Richard W. Brislin's *Handbook of Intercultural Training* (New York: Pergamon Press, 1983).

107.   Barban, Arnold M., Donald W. Jugenheimer, and Peter B. Turk. **Advertising Media Sourcebook**. 3d ed. Lincolnwood, IL: NTC Business Books, 1989. 122p. LC 88-62120.

A textbook (complete with exercises), *Advertising Media Sourcebook* offers a fine overview of and introduction to the numerous marketing and advertising rate guides used in the U.S. by media and advertising planners. Over 30 titles are separately profiled. Entries provide publication information (address, frequency, and the like), reproduce typical pages, and explain and illustrate the efficient uses of the sources. Simmons's *Study of Media and Markets* (entry 145) and *Standard Rate & Data Service* publications (entry 251) are among the sources described. This useful handbook also features a list of media resource contacts, a glossary of advertising media terms, and valuable formulas for computing basic advertising media costs.

108.   Berger, Charles R., and Steven H. Chaffee, eds. **Handbook of Communication Science**. Beverly Hills, CA: Sage, 1987. 946p. LC 87-9783. ISBN 0-8039-2199-3.

This is the most important handbook for the study of communication in general. *Handbook of Communication Science* offers scholarly discussions of the specific orientations of nearly every specialized area in the field. It is modeled on Wilbur Schramm and D. F. Roberts's *Process and Effects of Mass Communications* (1954; rev. ed., Urbana, IL: University of Illinois Press, 1971); and Ithiel de Sola Pool's *Handbook of Communication* (entry 139). The handbook is arranged in four major sections, with an epilogue. The initial section presents an overview of the field. Here Jesse G. Delia provides an extensive history of communication research, with thorough documentation. The second part includes essays that describe analyses of communication at the individual, interpersonal, network/organizational, and "macrosocietal" levels. The third part features discussions of the role of language in reflecting and creating social power; the role of nonverbal communication in deception; socialization and communication; persuasion and compliance; and communication and conflict management. Articles in the last major section describe the particular "contexts" of communication, focusing on the family, marital relations, children (language acquisition and prosocial development), consumer behavior, health care (patient-physician communication), organizational assimilation, mass communication, public opinion, political communication (election campaigning), and cross-cultural communication (national differences). Although the subjects of telecommunication and new communication technologies, communication policy, and communication research methods are not specifically addressed, they are related throughout the discussions. All chapters are extensively documented. Contributors include prominent communication scholars like William B. Gudykunst, Frederic M. Jablin, Mark L. Knapp, and Denis McQuail. The intentional "disciplinary integration" of the discussions of the various areas of the field makes the handbook particularly useful as a general introduction.

109.   Blake, Reed H., and Edwin O. Haroldsen. **A Taxonomy of Concepts in Communication**. New York: Hastings House, 1975. 158p. (Humanistic Studies in the Communication Arts; Communication Arts Books). LC 74-34359. ISBN 0-8038-7154-6.

This is a classic dictionary/handbook of major terms in communication. Unlike similar works, however, this one can be read from start to finish. And while the coverage certainly shows the work's age, it is nonetheless useful, particularly for students researching the basic theories of communication. Blake and Haroldsen provide extended (one- to two-page) explanations of 60 broad terms that represent communication's basic elements, forms, contents, processes and effects, functions, social environments, and research approaches and methods. Entries are authoritative and critical. Most typically indicate each term's historical origins and note its uses by prominent critics and theorists. However, it is the taxonomic arrangement that makes this dictionary so uniquely useful. Terms are arranged from the most general to the specific. The initial entry is for *communication*; others follow for its components, *language, symbol, sender/receiver*, and *message*, with each part in turn figuratively sending "branches" toward related terms for specific types (*organizational communication*), uses (*advertising/publicity*) and other aspects (*canalization*). Running cross-references relate broader and narrower terms. *Gatekeeper*, for example, is cross-referenced to formal and informal channels of communication as well as censorship. An alphabetical list of terms, a bibliography of sources, and indexes of authors and subjects enhance access. Datedness most shows in the absence of discussions of topics that are presently in vogue, such as rhetoric, semiotics, and intercultural communication. This is not the place to find a quick definition of *media imperialism*, for example. For terms of this ilk, researchers should consult *The Communication Handbook* (entry 115) and *Key Concepts in Communication* (entry 137).

110.   Britt, Steuart Henderson, and Norman F. Guess, eds. **The Dartnell Marketing Manager's Handbook**. 2d ed. Chicago, IL: Dartnell, 1983. 1,293p. ISBN 0-85013-135-9.
      This is the most recent handbook that offers comprehensive reviews of the research literature of advertising and consumer behavior—included here as aspects of marketing—by academic and professional experts in the field. Richard H. Stansfield's *Dartnell Advertising Manager's Handbook*, 3d ed. (Chicago, IL: Dartnell, 1982) pre-dates this handbook and largely represents one professional's experiential perspectives on advertising. For research on advertising theory, practice, and research, Britt and Guess's handbook is preferable. Survey chapters by 132 expert contributors are arranged in 10 sections. Each contains information relevant to advertising, as well as to various aspects of organizational, political, and mass communication as applied in marketing. Part 2, about organizing and staffing a marketing organization, includes a chapter on advertising agencies. "Establishing Marketing Objectives" offers several chapters about research on consumer motivation and behavior and assessment of consumer needs. Part 4, "Marketing Research," includes a review of methods in "Advertising Research and Measurement," such as copy and commercial testing. Use of computers in marketing, the marketing campaign, marketing ethics, and government regulation of marketing are reviewed in part 5. Part 6, "Putting the Marketing Plan into Action for Consumer Products and Services," includes discussions of the marketing of services and "Brand Names and Branding Strategies." Part 8, "Promoting Products and Services," contains the bulk of the discussions relevant to advertising and communication. Chapters review the importance of communication in marketing; the use of imagery and symbolism to motivate consumers; interpersonal communication in personal selling and in promotion of products to sales personnel; advertisement creation, design, and production; development and production of advertising media, both printed and electronic; telephone marketing; and public relations. Theories, practices, and research in international advertising are described in part 9. All chapters include brief bibliographies. A subject and name index provides access. For research on marketing research, students should consult Robert Ferber's *Handbook of Marketing Research* (New York: McGraw-Hill, 1974).

111.   Brown, Les. **Les Brown's Encyclopedia of Television**. exp. ed. New York: New York Zoetrope, 1982. 496p. LC 82-7867. ISBN 0-918432-28-6.

All books on the mass media seem to be out of date at the moment of publication. This encyclopedia is certainly no exception. On the other hand, Brown has skillfully selected just enough information about the significant things related to television to make this collection more long-lived and valuable than numerous others. *Les Brown's Encyclopedia of Television* is truly an encyclopedia, including entries for a complete range of programs, personalities, institutions, terminology, topics, and issues. A representative sampling of entries includes synopses of the themes of such primetime and special programs as "Ding Dong School," "Charlie's Angels," "Miss America Pageant," and "Victory at Sea"; biographies of Dick Clark, Bob Hope, and Dan Rather; descriptions of the major and minor networks, such as NBC and HBO, and of other players in telecommunication, such as the European Broadcasting Union, the Federal Communications Commission, and the International Telecommunications Union; glossaries of television's management, advertising, and technical vocabularies; and longer discussions of topics like football on TV, pay television, and television in The Netherlands. Other entries explain influential legal cases and court decisions in television's history. There is even an entry for *Channels* (entry 340). That the entries lack bibliographic references somewhat weakens the encyclopedia's value in research. Similarly, for general research literature about the larger topics identified by Brown, students should start with *International Encyclopedia of Communications* (entry 127). For television's terminology, Diamant's dictionary (entry 116), among others is more comprehensive. Likewise, more comprehensive biographical sources are also available. And, of course, no compendium of programming is ever up-to-date. All of these considerations aside, no other single volume includes as much general information about so much of television as Brown's convenient encyclopedia. For similar descriptive coverage of both American and British programming, Leslie Halliwell and Philip Purser's *Halliwell's Television Companion*, 2d ed. (New York: Granada, 1982) can be consulted.

For more comprehensive information on television programming, researchers should consult the most recent editions of any one of a number of similar compilations, such as Larry James Gianakos's *Television Drama Series Programming: A Comprehensive Chronicle, 1982-1984* (Metuchen, NJ: Scarecrow Press, 1987), *Television Drama Series Programming: A Comprehensive Chronicle, 1980-1982* (Metuchen, NJ: Scarecrow Press, 1983), *Television Drama Series Programming: A Comprehensive Chronicle, 1975-1980* (Metuchen, NJ: Scarecrow Press, 1981), *Television Drama Series Programming: A Comprehensive Chronicle, 1959-1975* (Metuchen, NJ: Scarecrow Press, 1978), and *Television Drama Series Programming: A Comprehensive Chronicle, 1947-1959* (Metuchen, NJ: Scarecrow Press, 1980); Tim Brooks and Earle Marsh's *The Complete Dictionary to Prime Time Network TV Shows, 1946-Present*, 3d ed. (New York: Ballantine Books, 1985); Alex McNeil's *Total Television: A Comprehensive Guide to Programming from 1948 to the Present*, 2d ed. (New York: Viking Penguin, 1984); and Vincent Terrace's *The Complete Encyclopedia of Television Programs, 1947-1979*, 2d ed. revised (South Brunswick, NJ: A. S. Barnes, 1979), *Encyclopedia of Television: Series, Pilots and Specials, 1974-1984* (New York: New York Zoetrope, 1985), and *Encyclopedia of Television: Series, Pilots and Specials: The Index: Who's Who in Television, 1937-1984* (New York: New York Zoetrope, 1986).

112.   Bryant, Jennings, and Dolf Zillmann, eds. **Perspectives on Media Effects**. Hillsdale, NJ: Lawrence Erlbaum, 1986. 358p. (Communication). LC 85-13110. ISBN 0-89859-641-6.

A successor to Wilbur Schramm and D. F. Roberts's *The Process and Effects of Mass Communication* (1954; rev. ed., Urbana, IL: University of Illinois Press, 1971), this handbook of scholarly research also complements Gerbner and Siefert's *World Communications* (entry 120). Whereas *World Communications* examined the global influences of mass communication, the 16 contributed chapters in Bryant and Zillmann's handbook examine the effects of specific types of mass communication on specific groups. As in other handbooks, the interest here is the state-of-the-art interpretation and evaluation of research. The initial chapters review 25 years of research regarding the impacts on culture of the television news media and of television programming in general. Several of the chapters that follow address both the positive and negative influences of the media. Discussions of positive effects address the uses of television in education and in cognitive skill development as well as in development of prosocial behavior. Those on the negative effects focus on social learning of aggression and antisocial behavior from television violence, the effects of pornography, and television as an addiction. Other chapters review research on television portrayals of minorities in relation to attitudes and stereotypes; television's influences on political behavior, particularly in respect to election polling; the creation of pop culture personalities; television's effects on children; television's effects on attention; uses and gratifications; and television as entertainment. The final chapter indicates innovative uses of television in business and education and suggests future research areas. All chapters include extensive bibliographic references. Contributors include George Gerbner, Leonard Berkowitz, and Alan M. Rubin. Author and subject indexes provide access.

113. **Communications Industry Forecasts**. New York: Veronis, Suhler & Associates, 1987- . Annual. LC 89-29856.

Communications Industry Forecasts offers annual statistics, overviews, and forecasts for the financial market status of the communication industries, including radio and television broadcasting; magazine, newspaper, and book publishing; filmed entertainment; recorded music; cable television; and advertising and promotion. Filled with extensive charts, tables, and graphs that illustrate trends and project outlooks, the handbook is prepared by an in-house research team of Veronis, Suhler & Associates, a New York banking firm that specializes in communications banking. The 1989 subscription price was $500. Although few researchers will have ready access to this source, they should be aware of its existence.

114. Connors, Tracy Daniel, ed. **Longman Dictionary of Mass Media and Communication**. New York: Longman, 1982. 255p. (Longman Series in Public Communication). LC 82-92. ISBN 0-582-28337-x.

Communication researchers will find brief, current definitions of words, phrases, and abbreviations used by professionals in advertising, broadcasting, public relations, graphic arts, and publishing. Definitions are labeled to identify the specific areas of the field in which the terms are used. Included are such terms as *flack* and *market segmentation* (public relations) and *combination* (advertising). Illustrations would have been helpful in a number of cases. Terms dealing with the theoretical aspects of communication have been omitted. Diamant's *The Broadcast Communications Dictionary* (entry 116) is more up-to-date for terms associated with new communication technologies.

115. DeVito, Joseph A. **The Communication Handbook: A Dictionary**. New York: Harper & Row, 1986. 337p. LC 85-17547. ISBN 0-06-041638-6.

Of the numerous dictionaries described in this section, three merit the most attention simply because they are the most generally useful communication dictionaries available. These are Diamant's *The Broadcast Communications Dictionary* (entry 116), Weik's *Communications Standard Dictionary* (entry 149), and DeVito's work. *The Communication Handbook* offers the broadest coverage of the terminology associated with the social scientific and humanistic aspects of communication and communication research. Terminology is included from interpersonal, small group, organizational, and nonverbal communication; mass media; persuasion; public speaking; and language and verbal messages. Entry length is dependent upon the significance and complexity of the term. Specific rhetorical terms are defined in a few words. Other terms, such as *attraction, family communication patterns*, and *tactile communication*, are described in essays of several pages. Most entries include bibliographic references.

116. Diamant, Lincoln. **The Broadcast Communications Dictionary**. 3d ed. New York: Greenwood Press, 1989. 255p. LC 88-25093. ISBN 0-313-26502-x.
       Dictionaries of the specialized terminology of mass communication are abundant. Diamant's is perhaps the best and most up-to-date, all-purpose dictionary of general mass communication terminology. It is also the most precisely written. Indeed, the definitions might be called austere or spartan in detail. On the one hand, this is quite advantageous. Diamant includes about 6,000 technical, common, and slang words "that make up the language of broadcast communicators in English-speaking countries around the world" (p. ix). Terms are taken from "radio and television programming and production; network and station operations; broadcast equipment and engineering; audio and videotape recording; performing talent; agency and client advertising procedures; media usage; research; defense, government, trade, and allied groups." Particular attention is given to acronyms of media organizations and agencies as well as to terms associated with telecommunication and new communication technologies. The result is that Diamant defines many more terms in general and, particularly, many more current terms than either Connors (entry 114) or Graham (entry 123). On the other hand, Diamant's precision typically requires the user to look well beyond the term initially sought in order to interpret its definition. *Matrix*, for example, is defined as *"quadraphonic FM broadcast* and *recording/playback* system, encoding two extra *channels* atop two existing *stereo channels*. See: *SQ, QS*. Compare: *discrete*." Learning what *matrix* means requires obtaining the definitions of several other terms. Connors and Graham offer more palatable, nontechnical definitions.
       Other general dictionaries of mass communication terminology include William P. Brown and Kathryn Sederberg's *The Complete Dictionary of Media Terms* (Chicago, IL: Commerce Communications, 1986); Edmund Penney's *A Dictionary of Media Terms* (New York: Putnam, 1984); Lynne Naylor Ensign and Robin Eileen Knapton's *The Complete Dictionary of Television and Film* (Briarcliff Manor, NY: Stein and Day, 1985); Virginia Oakey's *Dictionary of Film and Television Terms* (New York: Barnes and Noble, 1982); and James Watson and Anne Hill's *A Dictionary of Communication and Media Studies*, 2d ed. (Maidenhead, England: Edward Arnold, 1989). The last work emphasizes the terminology of British mass communication. Diamant's compilation is generally more valuable than these. On the other hand, for the specialized terminologies of the specific mass communication media (video, cable, and the like), Diamant's dictionary must be supplemented by consulting more specialized dictionaries, such as James R. McDonald's *The Broadcaster's Dictionary: Dictionary of Terms ... Directory of Associations and Government Agencies ... Broadcasting Techniques, Solutions, and Circuits* (Denver, CO: Wind River Books, 1986); Larry Langman's *The Video Encyclopedia* (New York: Garland, 1983); and Glenn R. Jones's *Jones Dictionary of Cable Television Terminology: Including Related Computer & Satellite Definitions*, 3d ed. (Englewood, CO: Jones 21st Century, 1988). For the most technical terminology, Weik's *Communications Standard Dictionary* (entry 149) should be consulted. For terms associated with mass communication effects, see DeVito's *The Communication Handbook* (entry 115).

117. Dilenschneider, Robert L., and Dan J. Forrestal. **The Dartnell Public Relations Handbook**. 3d ed., revised. Chicago: IL: Dartnell, 1987. 875p. LC 87-71012. ISBN 0-85013-159-6.

Dilenschneider and Forrestal, two successful public relations professionals, review topics in public relations from a marketing perspective. The authors maintain that the object of public relations in all things—from crisis management to strategic planning to image enhancement—is to market ideas. Dilenschneider contributes chapters in parts 1 through 3 that provide an overview of the profession and its external functions; that is, public relations outside a particular organization. Introductory chapters address public relations' role in social change and work with the media. Other chapters describe public relations approaches and methods for specific types of clients and situations, such as financial institutions; businesses; corporate trade associations; industry and labor; professional services; environmental, occupational, and health care organizations; public agencies and government; and nonprofit organizations. Crisis communication is emphasized. In chapters 4 and 5, Forrestal focuses on internal public relations; that is, public relations methods and approaches within specific organizations. Topics include various devices of organizational communication, such as house organs, training movies and tapes, and bulletin boards, as well as the importance of leadership and written communication in creating a climate conducive to productivity. Case studies of successful internal public relations programs are provided. An additional chapter, "Public Relations for Health Care Facilities," by David B. Williams, reviews external and internal public relations strategies and programs in hospital marketing, public communication, and crisis management. A bibliography of general and specialized public relations studies, bibliographies, directories, and periodicals is included. The handbook is indexed by name and subject. More readable than *Lesly's Public Relations Handbook* (entry 133), *The Dartnell Public Relations Handbook* offers practical but also experiential and anecdotal advice for the public relations professional.

118. Dunning, John. **Tune in Yesterday: The Ultimate Encyclopedia of Old-Time Radio, 1925-1976**. Englewood Cliffs, NJ: Prentice-Hall, 1976. 703p. LC 76-28369. ISBN 0-13-932616-2.

Information on radio programming is much more difficult to locate than that for television. No single source currently provides a comprehensive record of radio programming. Dunning's work, however, is about the most thorough compilation available. Narrative entries detail the themes, characters, and credits for several thousand programs. The work is far more detailed than Harrison B. Summers's *A Thirty-Year History of Programs Carried on National Radio Networks in the United States, 1926-1956* (1958; reprint, New York: Ayer, 1971); Frank Buxton and Bill Owen's *The Big Broadcast, 1920-1950* (New York: Viking, 1972); and Vincent Terrace's *Radio's Golden Years: The Encyclopedia of Radio Programs, 1930-1960* (San Diego, CA: A. S. Barnes, 1981). Buxton and Owen offer brief facts about casts and credits while Terrace notes lengths of programs and sponsors. On the other hand, because each compilation identifies programs not included in the others, all are required. For additional coverage of radio programming, researchers should also consult Anthony Slide's *Selected Radio and Television Criticism* (entry 76). Tom Kneitel's *Radio Station Treasury, 1900-1946* (Commack, NY: CRB Research, 1986) is a collection of historically important documents or otherwise interesting information (call letters, slogans, reproductions of radio advertisements, and the like) from radio's early years.

119. Gehring, Wes D. **Handbook of American Film Genres**. New York: Greenwood Press, 1988. 405p. LC 87-31784. ISBN 0-313-24715-3.

Contributed essays survey the historical development of 18 genres in American film as well as the major critical bibliographical resources for the study of these genres. The genres discussed include action/adventure—the adventure film, the western, the gangster film, *film noir*, and the World War II combat film; comedy—"screwball" comedy, "populist" comedy, parody, black humor, and "clown" comedy; the fantastic—the horror film, the science fiction film, and the fantasy film; songs and soaps—the musical and the melodrama; and the nontraditional—the "social problem" film, the biographical film, and the art film. Researchers interested in discussions of the classic films will be disappointed here. Emphasis is always on the genre; that is, on films that represent the genre's development. *Citizen Kane* is cited only twice and Sam Peckinpah, only once. Accompanying filmographies of two to three pages are of limited use. Examples cited for the *film noir* include *The Maltese Falcon* (1941) and *Body Heat* (1981). Among examples for the horror film are *Dracula* (1931) and *The Texas Chain Saw Massacre* (1974). More valuable are the surveys of critical studies of the genres. This volume is an excellent starting point for researchers who need to identify sources for further research.

120. Gerbner, George, and Marsha Siefert. **World Communications: A Handbook**. New York: Longman, 1984. 527p. (Annenberg/Longman Communication Books). LC 82-24963. ISBN 0-582-28457-0.

This is a first attempt at a handbook that reflects the "globalness" of critical and cultural perspectives on mass communication. The issues and topics addressed in 54 essays by contributing experts representing 25 different nations are devisive, dynamic, and unresolved. This is evident in the 10 articles included in part 1, "Global Perspectives on Information." Differing national perspectives on the value of information to a nation and on the role of policies in maintaining and/or adjusting world order are identified. The perspectives of the United States, the First World, the North, and the West clash with those of developing nations, the Third World, the South, and the East. It is most appropriate that a version of Mustapha Masmoudi's controversial paper "The New World Information Order" is included here. Articles in part 2, "Transnational Communication: The Flow of News and Images," emphasize the role of the United States as both distributor and controller of information. "U.S. Television Coverage of the World's Press" and "U.S. Image of Other Cultures: The Need for Education" reflect the polemics. Other essays focus on transnational advertising and global television. "Telecommunications: Satellites and Computers" includes articles that examine the policy, financial, legal, and security implications resulting from the dissemination of communication technologies that do not recognize political boundaries. Ten articles emphasize international cooperation in data flow, the establishment of global data networks, and the need for access to this technology in the Third World. In contrast, articles in part 5 address the development of mass communication programs and systems and implications for social change within individual nations. Essays profile media development in Iran, China, Peru, Belgium, Egypt, India, and Austria. Additionally, significant emphasis is on intercultural media development; that is, the relations of rural and urban or national and local interests within a specific country. "Intergovernmental Systems: Toward International Policies" examines the roles of Intelsat, WARC (World Administrative Radio Conference), Unesco, and other organizations promoting media development. Appendixes include additional bibliographic references, a chronology (1944-1982) relevant to world communication development, a glossary of terms and acronyms, and a list of global satellite systems. Among the prominent contributors are Herbert S. Dordick, Elihu Katz, William H. Melody, Edwin B. Parker, Marcellus S. Snow, and Humphrey Tonkin. This is as much a collection of critical comments on global mass communication as it is a reference handbook of research.

121.   Goldhaber, Gerald M., and George A. Barnett, eds. **Handbook of Organizational Communication**. Norwood, NJ: Ablex, 1988. 502p. LC 87-19380. ISBN 0-89391-446-0.

Contributed chapters in this scholarly handbook emphasize the "theoretical and methodological directions" of research on organizational communication as well as the implications for future research. In contrast to Jablin, Putnam, Roberts, and Porter's *Handbook of Organizational Communication* (entry 128), greater attention is focused on the wide range of theoretical and critical perspectives and approaches to assessment and interpretation of communication in organizations. These variations, the editors suggest, reflect the different disciplinary origins and backgrounds that underlay the specific critical orientations. W. Charles Redding, regarded as the father of organizational communication, and Phillip K. Thompkins provide an introductory essay, "Organizational Communication — Past and Present Tenses." The bulk of the volume contains chapters in three sections. The most extensive section, including 10 essays, reviews and interprets current research on organizational culture, symbols and symbolic processes in organizations, assimilation and socialization, participative processes, leadership and power, and other organizational theories. "Methodological Approaches" includes three essays that review research on evaluation of organizational communication from 1950 through 1981, network analysis, the validity of communication gradients, and the use of computer technology in auditing communication. The final section, "Organizational Communication in the Information Age," contains three essays on the influence of information technology on communication in organizations. All chapters include extensive documentation. In general, however, essays are much shorter than those in the *Handbook of Organizational Communication*. Author and subject indexes identify specific references and topics within the discussions. Although this work is valuable for discussions of a wide range of approaches to organizational communication, the Jablin et al. handbook is preferable for identifying studies and research on specific topics in the field.

122.   Gordon, Michael, Alan Singleton, and Clarence Rickards. **Dictionary of New Information Technology Acronyms**. Detroit, MI: Gale, 1984. 217p. ISBN 0-8103-4309-6.

Brief identifications and definitions of acronyms used for technical expressions, such as DREAM for data retrieval entry and management, as well as those for more readily known organizations and products, such as ALA and JASIS, are included in this dictionary of about 10,000 acronyms. Additionally, the national origin of most terms (FDR, D.D.R., U.K., U.S., U.S.S.R.) is indicated. More up-to-date coverage of communication acronyms, abbreviations, and initialisms (in addition to those of other fields) is provided by *Acronyms, Initialisms & Abbreviations Dictionary* (Detroit, MI: Gale, 1976-). Julie E. Towell and Helen E. Sheppard's *Computer and Telecommunications Acronyms: A Selection of Approximately 25,000 Acronyms, Initialisms, Abbreviations, Contractions, Alphabetic Symbols, and Similar Condensed Appellations* (Detroit, MI: Gale, 1986) is largely a specialized extract from the comprehensive listing.

123.   Graham, John. **The Facts on File Dictionary of Telecommunications**. New York: Facts on File, 1983. 199p. LC 82-15675. ISBN 0-87196-120-2.

Graham's dictionary should be used as a source of brief, clearly written, nontechnical definitions of about 2,000 words and terms associated with telecommunication and new communication technologies. Like everything else that is one or more years old in this field, the dictionary is out of date. On the other hand, it remains particularly valuable for the intelligibility of the entries. Graham's style is intentionally "informative" rather than precise. The definition of *video signal* is an excellent example of the dictionary's accessibility: "When a television picture is created, the image of the scene is formed on a light-sensitive surface inside the television camera. This establishes an electrical charge pattern which is related to the light covering the object in the scene. This pattern is scanned by an *electronic beam* inside the camera to create a video signal" (p. 175). Entries also typically include useful examples of a particular term's usage. Users should compare Graham's entries with relevant and more up-to-date entries in Diamant's *The Broadcast Communications Dictionary* (entry 116) and Weik's *Communications Standard Dictionary* (entry 149).

124. Grinnell, J. D. **The National Register of Advertising Headlines & Slogans**. Westbury, NY: Asher-Gallant, 1987. 355p. LC 87-17577. ISBN 0-87280-159-4.

Advertising professionals searching for possible slogan ideas and others interested in the famous slogans of the past will find helpful information here. *The National Register of Headlines & Slogans* arranges thousands of slogans by product, company, and brand name in addition to broad subject classifications, such as money, strength, style, taste, ease, simplicity, cleanliness, and the like. A separate chapter identifies selected slogans by literary and rhetorical forms, including alliteration, double-talk, chiasmus, power, irony, and misleading statement. Only English-language slogans are covered. All are familiar to American audiences even though the products and brands are not necessarily domestic in origin. In addition to this source, Laurence Urdang and Ceila A. Robbins's *Slogans* (Detroit, MI: Gale, 1984) arranges by subject more than 6,000 advertising, political, and popular slogans.

125. Hudson, Robert V. **Mass Media: A Chronological Encyclopedia of Television, Radio, Motion Pictures, Magazines, Newspapers, and Books in the United States**. New York: Garland, 1987. 435p. (Garland Reference Library of Social Science, vol. 310). LC 85-45153. ISBN 0-8240-8695-3.

Hudson has assembled "one handy, comprehensive reference for historical facts about the mass media" in the United States from 1638 through 1985. Separate chapters, with subdivisions for printed and electronic media, are provided for 16 historical periods. A brief introductory essay, "Trends in Mass Media History," touches on the high points in American media history. "Selected Firsts in Mass Media" dates accomplishments like the first press in America in 1638 through the first public station to experiment with teletext in 1981, with numerous other firsts in between, such as the first newspaper in New Mexico, the first lawyer's magazine, and the first broadcast of orchestra music. An index of names, titles, and broad (obscenity and the First Amendment) and specific (the beginning of commercial television) subjects concludes the volume. This is a good source for quick historical facts about the media.

126. Inge, M. Thomas. **Handbook of American Popular Culture**. 2d ed. New York: Greenwood Press, 1989. 3 vols. LC 88-39092. ISBN 0-313-25406-0.

Inge assembles topical chapters, prepared by subject experts, that chronologically survey specific media and topics, provide critical reviews of the major bibliographic resources (histories, journals, and the like), and identify and evaluate significant research collections and other primary sources. Among the 46 areas covered are advertising, debate and public address, newspapers, pornography, propaganda, radio, and television.

127. **International Encyclopedia of Communications**. Erik Barnouw, ed. New York: Oxford University Press, 1989. 4 vols. LC 88-18132. ISBN 0-19-504994-2.

Previous to the publication of this encyclopedia, students requiring basic or introductory information to most topics in the field were typically either referred to such classic but limited volumes as Ithiel de Sola Pool's *Handbook of Communication* (entry 139) and Blake and Haroldsen's *A Taxonomy of Concepts in Communication* (entry 109) or, more frequently, advised to browse through several volumes of *Communication Yearbook* (entry 95). *International Encyclopedia of Communications*, the first attempt at an authoritative and comprehensive encyclopedia in the field, is now the best source for information of this kind.

Two qualities of the encyclopedia stand out above all others: its authority and its comprehensiveness. Everything about the *International Encyclopedia of Communications* is authoritative. The Oxford imprint goes a long way to legitimize a field that other, more established academic disciplines have frequently disdained as "soft." The encyclopedia was, in fact, jointly published with the Annenberg School of Communications of the University of Pennsylvania, a prestigious communication program. Its editor and contributing editorial staff include Erik Barnouw, George Gerbner, and Wilbur Schramm, three of the field's most recognized and influential scholars. Gerbner authored the article on the study of communication; Barnouw contributed articles on sponsors, syndication, Orson Welles, and early television history, among others; and Schramm wrote articles on George Gallup, Harold D. Lasswell, and the history and theory of development communication, among others. Other notable contributors and a selection of their articles include Hazard Adams ("Literary Criticism"), Michael Argyle ("Social Skills"), Carroll C. Arnold ("Rhetoric"), Albert Bandura ("Social Cognition Theory"), Asa Briggs ("History of Publishing"), George Comstock ("Violence"), Terry Eagleton ("Reading Theory"), Elihu Katz ("Mass Media Effects"), Denis McQuail ("Models of Communication"), John A. Lent ("Newspaper Trends in Asia"), Lawrence Lichty ("Radio"), W. Charles Redding ("Organizational Communication"), John Tebbel ("William R. Hearst," "Joseph Pulitzer," and "E. W. Scripps"), and Brian Vickers ("Classicism"). The contributors, in fact, include several hundred leading international authorities from all disciplines.

To call the encyclopedia's topical coverage comprehensive would be a misleading understatement. The coverage is nothing short of catholic. The lines that distinguish, for example, literature or theater from communication, are here rendered transparent: Everything is communication. The subjects listed in the handy "Topical Guide" included in volume 4 clearly reveal the wide intellectual scope of communication that various practitioners usually view from their own sides of arbitrarily erected fences. These broad topics include advertising and public relations, the ancient world, animal communication, area studies, the arts, communications research, the computer era, education, folklore, government regulation, institutions, international communication, journalism, language and linguistics, literature, media, the Middle Ages, motion pictures, music, nonverbal communication, photography, political communication, print media, radio, religion, speech, television, theater, and theories of communication. Among the important communication theorists identified are the likes of Aristotle, Cicero, John Milton, Max Weber, Claude Levi-Strauss, Karl Marx, Mikhail Bakhtin, Marshall McLuhan, Kenneth Burke, Harold D. Lasswell, and Paul F. Lazarsfeld. This abandoning of disciplinary partisanship makes the articles in the encyclopedia all the more useful to students.

Articles range from a few paragraphs to several pages. The brief article on gesture, for example, discusses types of gestures (such as pointing and characterizing gestures), the cultural variations of gesticulation, and children's learning of gestures. Cross-references to related articles on body movement, ritual, language, and animal signals and an up-to-date bibliography of studies of gesture are included in the article. By comparison, the article on advertising extends to 19 pages. The topic in general, its history, the role of agencies, and its economic aspects (including advertising theory, the influences of competition, economies of scale, and consumer behavior) are discussed in separate sections. Cross-references are included throughout and bibliographies accompany the sections of the discussion. The "Topical Guide," mentioned above, identifies major concepts, figures, institutions, and the like that are associated with specific broad subjects. Among the terms listed under "Communication Research," for example, are *agenda-setting, bandwagon effects, cognition, cultural indicators, performance*, and *selective reception*. Prominent theorists are also listed under appropriate subjects. Charles Darwin is cited under "Animal Communication"; Alfred Hitchcock, under "Motion Pictures"; and Philo Farnsworth, under "Television." The encyclopedia's biographical coverage is substantial. Individuals born before 31 December 1919 are included. The entry for Lazarsfeld is typical: The biography extends to one and one-half pages. Emphasis is on contributions to the field. The selected bibliography includes both primary and secondary writings. The encyclopedia's subject index provides access to topics, such as interpersonal communication and intercultural communication, that are discussed both in specific articles as well as in numerous other articles throughout the work.

The editors intended to "define, reflect, summarize, and explain the field in an accessible, comprehensive, and authoritative way." The *International Encyclopedia of Communications* succeeds magnificently. Scholars in the field who were trained before its publication are justly envious yet grateful that this resource exists for the present generation of students.

128. Jablin, Fredric M., Linda L. Putnam, Karlene H. Roberts, and Lyman W. Porter. **Handbook of Organizational Communication: An Interdisciplinary Perspective**. Newbury Park, CA: Sage, 1987. 781p. LC 87-23417. ISBN 0-8039-2387-2.

Other handbooks have addressed research on the subject of communication in organizational settings as an aspect of management. Among these are James G. March's *Handbook of Organizations* (Chicago, IL: Rand McNally, 1965) and Marvin D. Dunnette's *Handbook of Industrial and Organizational Psychology* (Chicago, IL: Rand McNally, 1976). This *Handbook of Organizational Communication* and Goldhaber and Barnett's *Handbook of Organizational Communication* (entry 121) are the first to discuss research in the area in its own right. Contributed chapters in the scholarly handbook offer comprehensive reviews and interpretations of the research literature of organizational communication. The first part presents a review of the "theoretical underpinnings of the field" and of communication and organizational theories. Part 2, "Contexts: Internal and External Environments," includes discussions of factors—such as corporate discourse, communication climate, organizational culture, and cross-cultural variables of gender and race—that "affect the nature, types, and outcomes of communication." "Structure: Patterns of Organizational Relationships" is the title of the third part of the volume. Networking; communication with superiors, peers, and subordinates; organizational structure; and the role of electronic media in reshaping organizational structure and communication are among the major topics addressed. A final section, "Process: Communication Behavior in Organizations," reviews the current understanding of message exchange; power and influence; conflict negotiating; message flow and decision making; feedback, motivation, and performance; and organizational entry, assimilation, and exit. All chapters include extensive bibliographic documentation. In addition to the editors, prominent contributors include Phillip K. Thompkins, W. Charles Redding, and Karl E. Weik. Separate indexes of authors and subjects are provided. For research information on a broad range of topics in organizational communication, this handbook is preferable to Goldhaber and Barnett's.

Two other handbooks, written from the perspectives of management, are worth noting. These are Robert L. Craig's *Training and Development Handbook: A Guide to Human Resource Development*, 3d ed. (New York: McGraw-Hill, 1987) and P. J. D. Drenth, H. Thierry, P. J. Williams, and C. J. de Wolff's *Handbook of Work and Organizational Psychology* (Chichester, England: John Wiley & Sons, 1989). Both review research on topics relevant to organizational communication, such as interviewing, feedback, and performance evaluation.

129.   Kahn, Frank J. **Documents of American Broadcasting**. 4th ed. Englewood Cliffs, NJ: Prentice-Hall, 1984. 501p. LC 83-11025. ISBN 0-13-217133-3.

This is a collection of selected seminal or otherwise important documents and other primary source materials—laws, commission materials, court decisions, commentaries, and the like—that are the bare structure of American electronic media history. The 43 excerpted texts range from the Constitution to Newton Minow's address to the National Association of Broadcasters in which he called television "a vast wasteland," to *Chandler v. Florida*, which allowed each state to determine if television cameras could enter the courtroom. Other documents, such as the "Code of Ethics" of the National Association of Broadcasters and *FCC v. Pacifica*, represent the professional and legal struggles to broadcast in the public's interest. Each text is accompanied by a historical introduction and a list of related readings. Most documents are extensively annotated and glossed. An index of legal decisions and a general index of names and topics conclude the volume. All communication students should know this important and useful collection.

130.   Knapp, Mark L., and Gerald R. Miller. **Handbook of Interpersonal Communication**. Beverly Hills, CA: Sage, 1985. 768p. LC 85-1869. ISBN 0-8039-2120-9.

Contributed chapters in *Handbook of Interpersonal Communication* review and interpret the research literature on the elemental variables relevant to all types of communication—the communicator, the message, the receiver, and the environment. Emphasis here is on verbal and nonverbal communication from basic cognitive and social behavioral perspectives. Research on these themes is reviewed in "Basic Positions and Issues." "Fundamental Units" focuses on the communicator, the communication environment, language, and nonverbal signals. "Basic Processes" discusses conversation, social power, emotion, and influence. Interpersonal communication in the workplace, social relationships, and the family are described in "Contexts." All chapters include extensive documentation. Prominent contributors include Judee K. Burgoon, Charles R. Berger, John Waite Bowers, and Fredric M. Jablin. Helpful indexing of names and broad and specific keywords (like *gaze, touch,* and *marriage*) is provided. Information in this handbook largely supersedes that related to interpersonal communication in A. Paul Hare's *Handbook of Small Group Research*, 2d ed. (New York: Free Press, 1976).

Covering a more specific kind of interpersonal communication, Charles V. Roberts, Kittie W. Watson, and Larry L. Barker's *Interpersonal Communication Processes: Original Essays* (New Orleans, LA: Spectra, 1989) assembles 26 surveys by different specialists on research in such fundamental areas of discourse and conversation as "self-talk" and inner speech, writing as intrapersonal communication, message processing, and listening.

131.   Kurian, George Thomas. **World Press Encyclopedia**. 2 vols. New York: Facts on File, 1982. LC 80-25120. ISBN 0-87196-621-2.

This is a good supplement and update of the data for national communication systems in *World Communications* (entry 152). Kurian provides descriptions and statistics for the history and current political and economic status of media in 180 countries. The surveys are arranged in four sections. The first part includes surveys relevant to the international press and its organizations, laws, press councils, and advertising, including statistics. Surveys and data for media in individual nations are segregated in parts 2 through 4 in the categories of developed, smaller and developing, and minimal and underdeveloped media systems. The most extensive coverage is provided for developed media systems, including those in the United States and the United Kingdom as well as those in Albania and Zimbabwe. The uniform entries for each country and national media system provide tabular demographic data and narrative descriptions of the economy, press laws, tradition of censorship, political status of the domestic and foreign media, news agencies, broadcast media, and professional education and training of journalists. Brief chronologies of media development and bibliographies conclude each entry. Descriptions of smaller and developing national media systems, such as those in Afghanistan, Iceland, Iran, Puerto Rico, and Zaire, are much less detailed and consist of just a few paragraphs. Data for the least developed national media systems, including those in the Bahamas, Monaco, the Vatican, and Yemen, are contained in tables. Appendixes list the world's 50 leading daily newspapers, international news agencies, press-related associations and organizations (by nation), and comparative data for ranking each nation's media (number of daily newspapers, daily newspaper circulation, advertising expenditures, radio transmitters and receivers, and television sets and transmitters). A cumulative index of names, titles, agencies, and organizations as well as broad and specific topics is very helpful. Subject headings for topics like censorship and computers and computerization aid national comparisons. Although significantly dated, information in Kurian's compilation is most valuable for supporting the comparative studies of national media. Data can be updated by consulting general statistical resources, like *Europa Year Book* (London: Europa Publications, 1926-) and the United Nations' *Statistical Yearbook* (New York: United Nations, 1949-), as well as national almanacs.

132.   Lass, Norman J., Leija V. McReynolds, Jerry L. Northern, and David E. Yoder, eds. **Handbook of Speech-Language Pathology and Audiology**. Toronto, Ontario, Canada: B. C. Decker, 1988. 1,399p. LC 87-72670. ISBN 1-55664-037-4.

This is a comprehensive sourcebook of research on the "processes and pathologies of speech, language, and hearing." Speech and hearing are the most basic devices of communication. This *is* verbal communication. Communication researchers who need basic information on the operation of the human body in communication should consult this work. The handbook includes 52 contributed articles by authorities arranged in 3 sections. "Normal Processes" includes chapters that describe the basic physiology and physics of speech, including the acoustics and aerodynamics of speech, speech production and perception, and the acquisition of speech and language in children. Part 2 reviews research on speech and language disorders. Assessment and intervention principles and methods are described in addition to the various disorders of articulation, fluency, language, and voice. Specific attention is given to disorders that affect "special populations," such as the aged, the handicapped, autistics, and the mentally retarded. Augmentative communication is also included here. The final section reviews research on hearing disorders. Methods of assessment, testing and evaluation, and diagnosis; corrective surgical and medical procedures and treatments; and rehabilitation and therapy, including implants and hearing aids, are identified. Bibliographic documentation in each chapter is extensive.

For information on research on more specialized aspects of the physiology of human communication, researchers should consult Sheldon Rosenberg's *Handbook of Applied Psycholinguistics: Major Thrusts of Research and Theory* (Hillsdale, NJ: Lawrence Erlbaum, 1982). Similarly, essays by contributing specialists in the annual volumes of Harris Winitz's *Human Communication and Its Disorders: A Review* (Norwood, NJ: Ablex, 1988-) review research on such topics as apraxia, cleft palate speech and language, and speech perception.

133.   Lesly, Philip. **Lesly's Public Relations Handbook**. 3d ed. Englewood Cliffs, NJ: Prentice-Hall, 1983. 718p. LC 83-8667. ISBN 0-13-530691-4.

A professional handbook (as contrasted to a handbook of research), this contains articles by prominent public relations professionals (nonacademics) that offer experiential and (more or less) anecdotal descriptions of typical problems in the field and advice about possible solutions. Emphasis is on the practical: what public relations is and what it does, with whom it works, how it works, when it works, and the like. Chapters address representing clients that need to work with federal and state government and consumers; public relations for specialized organizations, such as religious groups and broadcasters; and the techniques of public relations, including the use of publicity in newspapers, magazines, books, broadcast media, films, advertising, and "direct" media (telephones, mail, and so forth). Only a few of the articles contain bibliographies, and most of these reflect superficial knowledge of research and resources. Appendixes include a bibliography (consisting substantially of how-to books), a glossary of professional terms, the text of the "Code of Ethics of the Public Relations Society of America," and a useful directory of specialized public relations associations. This handbook should not be confused with others with a significant research orientation that are described in this section. *The Dartnell Public Relations Handbook* (entry 117) provides similar kinds of information on public relations theories and practices from a more scholarly perspective. For analyses of research on communication and mass communication that underlay public relations, students should consult relevant entries in *International Encyclopedia of Communications* (entry 127) and Berger and Chaffee's *Handbook of Communication Science* (entry 108), among other scholarly resources.

134. Lindzey, Gardner, and Elliot Aronson, eds. **The Handbook of Social Psychology**. 3d ed. New York: Random House, 1985. 2 vols. LC 84-18509. ISBN 0-394-35049-9 (vol. 1); 0-394-35050-2 (vol. 2).

This scholarly reference handbook, first edited in 1935 by Carl Murchison, is intended to serve as a text and a "portable companion" for the study of social psychology, defined here as a discipline that attempts to "understand and explain how the thoughts, feelings, and behavior of individuals are influenced by the actual, imagined, or implied presences of others" (p. 3). In this context, the 30 contributed essays included in volume 1, *Theory and Method*, and volume 2, *Special Fields and Applications*, describe the current state of scholarly understanding of communication's role in society. Several chapters deserve close examination. "Language Use and Language Users," by Herbert H. Clark, focuses on conversation and conversational analysis. In "Effects of Mass Communication," Donald F. Roberts and Nathan Maccoby identify trends in research on mass communication effects, describing findings on patterns of media use, uses and gratification studies, and influences on cognition, politics, and socialization. "Attitude and Attitude Change" is particularly relevant to research in interpersonal communication. Other essays in volume 1 include "Decision Making and Decision Theory," "Organizations and Organizational Theory," "Attitude and Opinion Measurement," and "Survey Methods." Volume 2 includes the chapters "Social Influence and Conformity," "Interpersonal Attraction," "Leadership and Power," "Intergroup Relations," and "Public Opinion and Political Action." Chapters conclude with strong bibliographies of cited references. Each volume is separately indexed by name and by subject. The subject indexes are essential for identifying discussions relevant to topics such as interviewing, the role of advertising in attitude change, and organizational communication. This handbook offers discussions of broad topics and issues in the field that supplement Berger and Chaffee's *Handbook of Communication Science* (entry 108).

135. Meyers, Robert A., ed. **Encyclopedia of Telecommunications**. San Diego, CA: Academic Press, 1989. 575p. LC 88-22343. ISBN 0-12-226691-9.

Meyers has compiled a collection of 28 authoritative essays by contributing scholars and professionals in the theoretical, policy, economic, and, most especially, the technical aspects of telecommunication and new communication technologies. According to Meyers, the three major components of telecommunications—transmitters, communications channels, and receivers—are discussed in an "interlocking manner." Novices should start with the broad discussion in the chapter on telecommunication and use its glossary of key terms. Prominent contributors include Herbert S. Dordick as well as representatives of AT&T, Bell Communications Research, RCA Laboratories, Motorola, and COMSAT. Articles cover antennas, computer networks, data transmission media, digital speech processing, fiber optics, microwave communication, satellite communication, television image sensors, and videotext and teletext, among other topics. Each article includes a thumbnail outline of the topic, a glossary of relevant terms, and a bibliography of relevant technical and critical literature. Articles are extensively illustrated with photographs, schematics, and tables. The subject index cross-references the numerous overlapping discussions of LANs, WANs, cable television, facsimile transmission, and PBXs.

136. Nimmo, Dan D., and Keith R. Sanders, eds. **Handbook of Political Communication.** Beverly Hills, CA: Sage, 1981. 732p. LC 81-9362. ISBN 0-8039-1714-7.

In this scholarly handbook for the analysis of political communication in public discourse and printed and electronic media, emphasis is on the results of empirical research. The historical literature of research on political communication receives limited treatment in an introductory assessment of the field, "The Emergence of Political Communication as a Field." The contributed essays that follow are arranged in four parts. The first part addresses current theoretical approaches to political communication. Major topics include process, uses and gratification, diffusion of information, agenda-setting, and critical theory. The methods of persuasive communication in politics are covered in part 2. Essays discuss the language of politics, political rhetoric, advertising, and political debates. Political socialization, election campaigns, mass communication and formation of public opinion, public policy, and the uses of rhetoric in political movements are discussed in part 3 as aspects of the setting of political communication. The final part, "Methods of Study," identifies research methodologies applicable to political communication. Essays discuss cultural criticism, experimental studies, content analysis, surveys, and intensive analysis. Lynda Lee Kaid provides a guide to the literature of political communication in an appendix. All chapters contain extensive bibliographic documentation. An index of names concludes the volume; no subject index is provided. Interesting and somewhat useful definitions and discussions of the terminology and language of international political communication (or the politics of international communication) are included in Timothy G. Brown's *International Communications Glossary* (Washington, DC: Media Institute, 1984) and Leonard R. Sussman's *Glossary for International Communications: Communications in a Changing World: Volume III* (Washington, DC: Media Institute, 1983).

137. O'Sullivan, Tim, John Hartley, Danny Saunders, and John Fiske. **Key Concepts in Communication.** London: Methuen, 1983. 270p. (Studies in Communication). LC 83-13180. ISBN 0-416-34250-7.

This dictionary of communication terminology combines the best features of the classic *A Taxonomy of Concepts in Communication* (entry 109) and *The Communication Handbook* (entry 115). It will be most useful to researchers on communication theory. Like Blake and Haroldsen's work, *Key Concepts in Communication* provides extended definitions for communication's major forms, uses, contents, and research approaches. Entries include extensive historical detail that notes uses by prominent communication scholars and theorists and cross-references to related terms. Coverage does not include terms associated with advertising, public relations, or even journalism. On the other hand, particular emphasis is on current communication theories and models as well as topics currently in vogue, such as intercultural communication, rhetoric, and semiotics. As in

DeVito's more recent compilation, here are terms like *dyad, mediation*, and *popular culture*, which are not found in Blake and Haroldsen's work. While DeVito's work covers more terms, *Key Concepts in Communication* offers more depth and discussion. An extensive bibliography complements that found in Blake and Haroldsen's work. Although an index of terms is provided, one for authors is unfortunately absent.

138.   Paneth, Donald. **The Encyclopedia of American Journalism**. New York: Facts on File, 1983. 548p. LC 81-12575. ISBN 0-87196-427-9.

This is regarded as the best comprehensive compilation of facts, definitions, descriptions, and the like for topics relevant to American journalism, largely because it is the only such work presently available. For broad topics such as advertising, freedom of the press, printing, and public relations, its significance recently has been somewhat diminished by the more comprehensive *International Encyclopedia of Communications* (entry 127). Similarly, biographical coverage of prominent personalities in American journalism, such as Joseph Pulitzer and Sheila Graham, is now better provided by McKerns's *Biographical Dictionary of American Journalism* (entry 203). Paneth's work remains very valuable for information about the numerous aspects of American journalism that are too minor (or commonplace) to receive attention elsewhere. Entries for "House of Fugger," *Graham's Magazine*, Ben Grauer and *The Search* are good examples of this coverage of less significant media organizations, particular media, personalities, and specific programs. Paneth's subject index consists of lists of the entries arranged under broad subject headings. "Awards and Prizes" identifies the Peabody Awards and Pulitzer Prizes. Likewise, "Satellite, Communications" lists dish and Domsat, among other related subjects. Although the entries themselves are as uneven in depth of detail as the various subjects that they cover, this encyclopedia remains most useful because it covers topics not included elsewhere.

139.   Pool, Ithiel de Sola. **Handbook of Communication**. Chicago, IL: Rand McNally, 1973. 1,011p. (Rand McNally Sociology Series). LC 72-7851.

This classic handbook in the field remains valuable today as a source of historical research on a wide range of topics that just recently have been more efficiently covered by articles in the *International Encyclopedia of Communications* (entry 127). Contributing authorities provide reviews of the research literature on (1) communication proces- ses — communication systems, language, sociolinguistics, nonverbal communication, audi- ences, communication and children, persuasion, resistance and attitude change, political persuasion, and mass media and interpersonal communication; (2) communication set- tings — communication and development, communication in totalitarian societies, the press as a communication system, film as communication, broadcasting, communication in small groups, communication between bureaucracy and the public, communication in poli- tical parties, advertising, scientific communication, public opinion, propaganda, and free- dom and control of information; and (3) communication research (methodologies) — content analysis, interviews, and experiments in effects. The handbook most shows its age in the section on research methods: References to computers are absent. The bibliographies that accompany the chapters are slim by 1990s standards. In addition to de Sola Pool, con- tributors include Wilbur Schramm, Nathan Maccoby, Elihu Katz, Edwin B. Parker, and William L. Rivers. Name and subject indexes provide access.

140.   Rose, Brian G., ed. **TV Genres: A Handbook and Reference Guide**. Westport, CT: Greenwood Press, 1985. 453p. LC 84-22460. ISBN 0-313-23724-7.

Contributors provide chapters that survey and review the historical developments, major distinguishing characteristics and features, and primary and secondary resources for

19 different types of television programming. These are identified as the police show, detective show, western, medical melodrama, science fiction and fantasy, situation comedy, soap opera, American made-for-television movie, docudrama, television news, documentary, sports telecast, game show, variety show, talk show, children's program, educational and cultural program, television church, and television commercial. The uniform narrative entries include overviews of the genres, descriptions of historical developments (with significant references to particular programs), discussions of major themes and issues, bibliographies of primary and secondary sources, and videographies of selected programs. As much attention is paid to research on programming and media effects and uses as to historical topics. The unevenness of the various chapters typically results from scholars' sustained attention to children's programming and other genres rather than reflecting the quality of the chapters themselves. This is a good source for both programming history and research.

141.   Rosen, Philip T., ed. **International Handbook of Broadcasting Systems**. New York: Greenwood Press, 1988. 309p. LC 87-29986. ISBN 0-313-24348-4.

According to Rosen, "at present no reference work exists where one can readily ascertain what the broadcasting structure is in a given nation and how it came to be" (p. xvii). Rosen and other contributing editors provide information on the history, regulations, economic structure, programming, broadcast reform, and new technologies of the broadcasting systems in separate chapters for 24 countries, including the United States, China, the U.S.S.R., Japan, Israel, and Great Britain. In addition, chapters conclude with forecasts for the future and selective bibliographies. Although the information on broadcasting provided by Rosen is more limited than that provided in *World Press Encyclopedia* (entry 131), statistical data and bibliographies are more current and descriptive.

142.   Schumacher, Rose, Gail K. Sevrens, Timothy S. O'Donnell, Lee Torrence, and Kate Carney. **World Communication and Transportation Data**. Santa Barbara, CA: ABC-Clio, 1989. 99p. ISBN 0-87436-548-1.

This handbook gives brief data in uniform entries on radio, television, newspapers, and telephones in 172 nations. Based largely on United Nations, Unesco, and Europa statistical compilations, information ranges in currency from 1982 through 1988. Although very conveniently packaged, the data generally lack the detail presented in other sources. On the other hand, data are reported as ratios to population—a presentation that students of comparative communication will find both interesting and revealing.

143.   Sebeok, Thomas A., ed. **Encyclopedic Dictionary of Semiotics**. Berlin: Mouton de Gruyter, 1986. 3 vols. (Approaches to Semiotics, no. 73). LC 86-18714. ISBN 0-89925-137-4.

Communication's most theoretical aspects and approaches (as a system of signs and meanings) are examined and discussed in entries in this dictionary. Brief entries trace the historical theoretical backgrounds and the range of present meanings of such terms as *argumentative inference, competence/performance, message*, and *mass communication*. Extended essays survey the historical and critical approaches to advertising, cinema, language, news, nonverbal communication, and philosophy of language. Particular attention is given to biographies of critics and theorists. All entries include citations to bibliographic sources that are listed alphabetically in the cumulative bibliography in volume 3. This dictionary is most useful to researchers in communication theory, language, and rhetoric. For less comprehensive discussions of language, meaning, and communication, researchers can consult David Crystal's *The Cambridge Encyclopedia of Language* (Cambridge: Cambridge University Press, 1987) as well as the *International Encyclopedia of Communications* (entry 127).

144.   Sterling, Christopher H., and Timothy R. Haight. **The Mass Media: Aspen Institute Guide to Communication Industry Trends**. New York: Praeger, 1978. 457p. (Praeger Special Studies in U.S. Economic, Social, and Political Issues). LC 76-24370. ISBN 0275-24020-7.

How many hours each day do Americans watch television? Was there much sex and violence in television programming in the 1970s? What is the average educational level of viewers of public broadcasting programs? These are just a sampling of questions that can be answered by this compilation. Sterling and Haight have done media scholars a great favor by assembling data available in the widest variety of government, academic, professional, and industry sources into some 300 readily usable tables supported by brief discussions. Statistics represent the growth of the specific media industries, ownership and control, economics, professional education and employment, trends in the content of programming, audience demographics, and U.S. media activities in other countries. Recorded data cover 1900 through 1978 and reflect both printed and electronic media. Information regarding electronic media is supplemented by Sterling's *Electronic Media: A Guide to Trends in Broadcasting and Newer Technologies, 1920-1983* (New York: Praeger, 1983). This volume presents statistics for similar subjects and adds data regarding regulation of electronic media. Sources of statistics are identified. No indexes are provided in either volume. Users must rely on the detailed tables of contents.

145.   **Study of Media and Markets**. New York: Simmons Market Research Bureau, 1979- . Annual. ISSN 0737-2000.

The annual publications of Simmons Market Research Bureau, more commonly referred to as *Simmons Reports*, are a very important resource for media analysis, particularly for advertising media planners and marketers. Based on interviews with thousands of adults, the reports present findings on the uses and purchases of 500 products or services and on the reading or viewership of specific media broadcasts or publications. Published in almost 50 separate volumes accompanied by a separately bound *Technical Guide*, the set consists of the *Product Series* and the *Media Series*. *Media Series* volumes provide classified statistical data on publication audiences. Categories are very specific: For example, data are provided for total audiences and in-home audiences; adults, males, females, mothers, and female homemakers; attentiveness; special events; and the reach of broadcast, outdoor, and television media. A very expensive and, of course, absolutely essential professional resource, *Simmons Reports* are sold directly to academic institutions on a one-year delay basis. Online and CD ROM versions are also available (entry 329). The best descriptions of the uses and applications of Simmons studies and other similar resources are contained in *Advertising Media Sourcebook* (entry 107).

146.   Swanson, David L., and Dan Nimmo. **New Directions in Political Communication: A Resource Book**. Newbury Park, CA: Sage, 1990. 413p. LC 89-10711. ISBN 0-8039-3334-7.

Updating Nimmo and Sanders's handbook (entry 136), Swanson and Nimmo offer a collection of essays by different specialists that survey research in the extraordinarily broad area of political communication. Mainly focusing on the creating and processing of political messages within the contexts of institutions, systems, and cultures, essays cover the linguistics of politics; the social and educational roles (political learning) of the democratic processes (debates, television advertising, negative campaigns, and the like); politics and popular culture, the media, and the news; the rhetoric of American governmental institutions; political communication in decision-making groups; and research opportunities employing comparative methods. Anne Johnston's topically organized survey essay, "Trends in Political Communication: A Selective Review of Research," and a supporting bibliography (pp. 329-89) conclude the volume. Excellent subject index-ing references discussions of topics in other areas of the broad field of communication, such as public relations in crisis management, media ethics and responsibility, political advertising, presidential rhetoric, and agenda-setting in groups. Students in many areas of communication will find incredibly valuable the handbook's comprehensive access to a very applied and limited kind of communication.

147.   Tardy, Charles H. **A Handbook for the Study of Human Communication: Methods and Instruments for Observing, Measuring, and Assessing Communication Processes.** Norwood, NJ: Ablex, 1988. 407p. (Communication and Information Science). LC 87-14317. ISBN 0-89391-424-x.

The focus of this handbook is on "methodological problems and solutions unique to the study of communication" (p. xiii). Contributing scholars offer the pros and cons associated with general and specific methods and instruments used in observing, measuring, and assessing interpersonal, small group, and organizational communication. Chapters cover such areas as cognitive complexity and processes, communication compe-tence, networks, communication style, conversational structure, dyadic personal relation-ships, interpersonal interaction, group decision making, attraction and trust, language, self-disclosure, social support, and social anxiety. Author and subject indexes provide access. This handbook supplements the methodological discussions in other research handbooks featured in this section.

148.   Urdang, Laurence. **Dictionary of Advertising**. 3d ed. Lincolnwood, IL: NTC Business Books, 1988. 209p. LC 76-45506. ISBN 0-8442-3040-5.

Urdang offers the broadest coverage of advertising's general terminology. The comprehensive dictionary includes about 4,000 terms from other areas of "marketing plan-ning, copyright, art direction, graphic supply, print production, commercial production, program production, media planning, media research, media analysis, media buying, marketing research, consumer research, field interviewing, statistical analysis, merchandising and promotion planning, public relations counseling, data processing, and advertising finance" (preface). The brief entries provide synonyms and cross-references to other terms. Urdang's dictionary can be supplemented by Jane Imber and Betsy-Ann Toffler's *Dictionary of Advertising and Direct Mail Terms* (Hauppauge, NY: Barron's Educational Series, 1987), which contains nearly 3,000 terms related to television, radio, and print advertising and direct mail.

Urdang's coverage of current advertising terminology supersedes that in Irvin Graham's *Encyclopedia of Advertising: An Encyclopedia Containing More Than 1100 Entries Relating to Advertising, Marketing, Publishing, Law, Research, Public Relations, Publicity and the Graphic Arts*, 2d ed. (New York: Fairchild, 1969). Graham's volume focuses mainly on graphic design and production. A new edition of Graham's work, the only encyclopedia of advertising, is certainly needed. Identifications of 15,000 advertising slogans are provided in Harold S. Sharp's *Advertising Slogans of America* (Metuchen, NJ: Scarecrow Press, 1984). For British advertising terminology, researchers should consult Michael J. Baker's *Macmillan Dictionary of Marketing & Advertising* (New York: Nichols Publishing, 1985).

149.   Weik, Martin H. **Communications Standard Dictionary**. New York: Van Nostrand Reinhold, 1989. 1,219p. LC 87-31582. ISBN 0-442-20556-2.

This is the most comprehensive and authoritative dictionary of communication's tech-nical terminology. Definitions are oriented toward the scientific and technical fields and professions. Emphasis is on standards; hence, definitions are highly technical and very precise. For example, five definitions are provided for *signal*, with nearly a page of cross-references. Only the most advanced scholars in telecommunication and new communication technologies will use this dictionary. Supplemental coverage of about 12,000 terms is provided by Jerry M. Rosenberg's *Dictionary of Computers, Information Processing, and Telecommunications*, 2d ed. (New York: John Wiley & Sons, 1987). Researchers should recognize, however, that Weik's standard compilation is merely the most comprehensive of several equally important technical handbooks and dictionaries that are available. A representative selection of more specialized compilations includes K. Blair Benson's *Television Engineering Handbook* (New York: McGraw-Hill, 1986); Roger L. Freeman's *Reference Manual for Telecommunications Engineering* (New York: John Wiley & Sons, 1985); *IEEE Standard Dictionary of Electrical and Electronics Terms*, 4th ed. (New York: Institute of Electrical and Electronics Engineers, 1988); and *Reference Data for Engineers: Radio, Electronics, Computer, and Communications* (Indianapolis, IN: Howard W. Sams, 1985-).

150.   Weiner, Richard. **Webster's New World Dictionary of Media and Communications**. New York: Simon and Schuster, 1990. 533p. LC 90-31012. ISBN 0-13-969759-4.

What was intended as a "basic glossary and primer" for public relations professionals, according to Weiner, became "the most extensive collection of words in a variety of media and communication fields—including advertising, book production, broadcasting, computers and computer graphics, direct marketing, exhibitions, film, graphic arts, journalism, library science, mail, marketing, market research, newspapers, photography, printing, public relations, publishing, radio, recording, sales promotion, telecommunications, telephone, television, theater, typography, videotex, and writing." The volume attempts far too much to do more than briefly identify a wide selection of general and industry-specific terms (both generally accepted terms and slang) as well as trademarked products, companies, and organizations. Unlike the better dictionaries, such as those by DeVito (entry 115) and Diamant (entry 116), this does not include bibliographic references.

151.   Woodson, Linda. **A Handbook of Modern Rhetorical Terms**. Urbana, IL: National Council of Teachers of English, 1979. 78p. LC 79-17400. ISBN 0-8141-2019-9.

Woodson describes and illustrates about 300 rhetorical terms, such as *deliberative discourse, dyadic argument*, and *mathic function*. In addition, entries typically identify a term's first use and its author and cite its bibliographic source. This feature makes the handbook very useful in research. An appendix lists rhetorical terms by categories. For example, *anaphora* and *zeugma* are listed in "Classical Rhetorical Terms." Two of the terms under "Speech Act Theory" are *communication triangle* and *transactional function*. The index lists the authors cited. Woodson's compilation is strongly oriented toward literary rhetoric rather than specifically toward rhetoric as presently studied in communication or the social sciences. For the practical terminology of formal public speaking and debate, particularly academic debate, Jim Hanson's *NTC's Dictionary of Debate* (Lincolnwood, IL: National Textbook Company, 1989) should be consulted.

152.   **World Communications: A 200 Country Survey of Press, Radio, Television, and Film**. 5th ed. New York: Unipub, 1975. 533p. LC 74-83488. ISBN 92-3-101180-4.

This is a standard source for data on the different national media systems of the world. Although now very badly dated, it remains the recognized cornerstone for the comparative study of national media. Brief tabular data and survey discussions are included for 200 countries. Emphasis is on the place and role of the media in national political and economic development. This work is updated by *World Press Encyclopedia* (entry 131) and other general statistical sources.

3
Indexes and Abstracts

153. **America: History and Life**. Santa Barbara, CA: ABC-Clio, 1964- . 5/year. ISSN 0002-7065.

America: History and Life (AH&L) is the best index to the scholarly literature on historical topics in the broad field of communication in the United States. About 2,000 journals in 40 languages are selectively indexed, including important communication journals like *Journal of Communication* (entry 374), *Media, Culture, and Society* (entry 397), and *Journalism Quarterly* (entry 390). Its primary value, however, is the indexing of journals in history, economics, law, political science, literature, and other specific disciplines as well as major interdisciplinary journals, such as *Technology and Culture* and *Science and Society*, that publish research on topics in communication.

AH&L is published in several sections. For many topics in communication research, the most important sections are *Part A: Article Abstracts and Citations* and *Part D: Annual Index*. Part A appears in three issues per year. The table of contents identifies listings for communication in "Part IV: United States of America, 1945 to Present" in the subsection "Economic Affairs: Transportation and Communication." In addition, issues include separate author and subject indexes. The subject headings employ "generic and specific terms." Those relevant to communication include "Advertising," "Broadcasting," "Communications," "Computers," "Rhetoric," "Public Relations," "Speeches," "Technology Transfer," "Telephones," and "Television." Subject and author listings cumulate annually in part D. In addition, this annual index lists the sources indexed. Cumulative subject indexes for volumes 1-10 (1964-1973) and volumes 11-15 (1974-1978) are available. *Part B: Index to Book Reviews* (published twice per year) lists citations for book reviews. *Part C: American History Bibliography (Books, Articles, and Dissertations)* (published twice per year) lists (without abstracts) all relevant articles (cited in part A), books and book reviews (cited in part B), and dissertations. This coverage of dissertations complements that offered by *Journalism Abstracts* (entry 174) and *Dissertation Abstracts International* (entry 166).

AH&L is the most convenient, current, and comprehensive indexing resource for identifying historical treatments of such topics as the speeches of Abraham Lincoln and Martin Luther King, Jr.; freedom of the press in the United States; and the histories of particular American advertising, public relations, and media organizations and companies. Complementary coverage of the scholarly literature on the history of communication outside the United States is provided by *Historical Abstracts* (Santa Barbara, CA: ABC-Clio, 1955-).

America: History and Life is available online (entry 262).

154. **Applied Science and Technology Index**. New York: H. W. Wilson, 1958- . Monthly. LC 14-5408. ISSN 0003-6986.

Applied Science and Technology Index (AS&TI) offers author and subject indexing of the English-language periodical literature of the field of computer technology and applications and electrical and telecommunications engineering. It is particularly valuable for coverage of the technical literature of telecommunications and new communication technologies. A number of the journals indexed in *AS&TI* publish the most significant and important documentation on research in these areas. These include *Telecommunications Journal* (entry 412) as well as the publications of the ACM and IEEE (entry 463). Other journals indexed include *Journal of the Acoustical Society of America, Artificial Intelligence, Electrical Communication, Electronics and Wireless World, Radio-Electronics,* and *Technology Review.* The most productive listings are found under such broad headings as "Communications Satellites," "Computer Networks," "Optical Communication Systems," "Signal Processing," "Telecommunication," "Telephone," and "Television."

AS&TI is available online and on CD ROM (entry 263).

155. **Arts and Humanities Citation Index**. Philadelphia, PA: Institute for Scientific Information, 1976- . 3/year. LC 79-642953. ISSN 0162-8445.

The possible uses of the *Arts and Humanities Citation Index (A&HCI)* in communication research are numerous. Like the *Science Citation Index (SCI)* (Philadelphia, PA: Institute for Scientific Information, 1961-) and *Social Sciences Citation Index (SSCI)* (entry 185) on which it is modeled, *A&HCI* employs several interrelated indexes to analyze a wide range of scholarly and professional journals. *A&HCI* indexes about 1,300 journals in the humanities and arts, including a significant number of core journals in communication. Coverage is particularly strong in the areas of speech, language, rhetoric, and the media (as a performing art). Indexed journals include *American Film*; *American Speech* (entry 334); *Communication, Communication and Cognition*; *Communication Education* (enty 345); *Communication Monographs* (entry 346); *Communication Research* (entry 348); *Film Criticism*; *Historical Journal of Film, Radio, and Television* (entry 357); *Journal of Communication* (entry 374); *Journal of Communication Disorders* (entry 375); *Journal of Film and Video*; *Journal of Broadcasting and Electronic Media* (entry 370); *Language*; *Literature-Film Quarterly*; *Soviet Film*; and *Wide Angle*. Coverage here complements that offered by *Communication Abstracts* (entry 163) and *Humanities Index* (entry 171).

Key to the effective use of *A&HCI* is understanding exactly what each of the three main indexes does. Briefly, *A&HCI* uses three separate indexes to analyze periodical articles by authors ("Source Index"), cited authors ("Citation Index"), and keywords ("Permuterm Index"). The most important index is the "Source Index," which lists the articles published in the indexed journals alphabetically by author. In short, the "Source Index" is a relatively straightforward bibliography of a year's humanities scholarship, arranged by author, in a significant selection of journals. Use the "Source Index" to discover if a particular scholar published an article in a specific year. In addition to providing complete bibliographic information for the publication, the "Source Index" also notes whom that particular scholar cited to produce the publication.

These "cited authors" are in turn listed alphabetically in *A&HCI*'s "Citation Index." The cited authors, of course, represent all varieties and dates of publications. Their entries in the "Citation Index" identify the writers who cited them (who are listed in the "Source Index"). The "Citation Index" can be used to discover if a particular work—book, article, or otherwise—has been cited in a particular year. This is extremely useful in tracing the influence of a particular communication theorist on later theorists and professionals. Lists of the names of individuals who cite the likes of Aristotle, Sigmund Freud, and Albert Einstein as well as Harold Lasswell, Paul Lazarsfeld, Kenneth Burke, and Jacques Derrida fill numerous columns in the "Citation Index."

The third index in *A&HCI* is the "Permuterm Index." In this index, "every significant word that has appeared in the title of a current article (source item) indexed ... is listed and paired with significant words that appear with it in the title." In the "Permuterm Index," for example, Aristotle, Freud, and Burke can be referenced to *rhetoric, ego,* and *dramatism* to identify titles of articles in which these words appear that are listed in the "Source Index." Similarly, broad topics such as advertising can be cross-referenced to other relevant topics, such as video, to identify articles (in the "Source Index"). In short, by means of the "Permuterm Index," articles represented in the "Source Index" can be identified by discovering any of the significant words in their titles.

Like *SCI* and *SSCI,* physical complexity and microscopic print make *A&HCI* appear even more intimidating than *Communication Abstracts* (entry 163) and Matlon (entry 177). *A&HCI* is not always easy to use. A shortcoming common to all three of the Institute for Scientific Information's citation indexes is the reference to sources and cited authors by initials rather than by proper names. Not every one of the numerous listings for "Jones, T." or "Smith, J." can be the same individual.

A&HCI is available online (entry 264).

156. **Bibliographic Index.** New York: H. W. Wilson, 1937- . 3/year. ISSN 0006-1255.

Bibliographic Index (BibI) provides author and subject access to bibliographies published separately as books and articles or as parts of books. It selectively indexes about 2,600 journals, including core journals in communication like *Communication Quarterly* (entry 347), *Journal of Broadcasting and Electronic Media* (entry 370), and *Journal of Communication* (entry 374). Coverage of books is international, based on Wilson's *Cumulative Book Index* database. Particularly valuable is the indexing of volumes in monograph series, such as Greenwood Press's *Contributions to the Study of Mass Media and Communications* (Westport, CT: Greenwood Press, 1983-). To be included a bibliography must contain 50 or more citations. Some typical bibliographic items identified in *BibI* include Emelda L. Williams and Donald W. Hendon's annotated *American Advertising: A Reference Guide* (entry 18); the bibliography on pages 129-36 in Philip H. Bornstein and Marcy T. Bornstein's *Marital Therapy: A Behavioral-Communications Approach* (New York: Pergamon Press, 1986); and the list of sources in A. M. Rubin and E. M. Perse's "Audience Activity and Television News Gratification," *Communication Research* (entry 348), 14 (February 1987): 81-84. Monitoring *BibI* potentially can prevent needlessly duplicating a bibliography that already exists.

An online version of *BibI* is also available (entry 265).

157. **Biography Index: A Quarterly Index to Biographical Material in Books and Magazines.** New York: H. W. Wilson, 1946- . Quarterly, with annual and three-year cumulations. LC 47-6532. ISSN 0006-3053.

Biography Index (BioI) identifies biographical materials published in books and journals. It is particularly helpful for identifying biographies published as chapters or parts of books, like those featured in biographical collections such as the *New York Times* and volumes of the *Dictionary of Literary Biography* (mentioned in entry 203) as well as other sources like *Current Biography* (entry 197). In addition, *BioI* cites references to biographical articles featured in several thousand popular magazines and scholarly and professional journals covered by the wide-ranging members of the H. W. Wilson family of indexes, like *Readers' Guide* (entry 184), *Humanities Index* (entry 171), *Social Sciences Index* (entry 186), *Essay and General Literature Index* (entry 168), *Applied Science and Technology Index* (entry 154), *Index to Legal Periodicals* (entry 172), *General Science Index* (entry 170), *Art Index, Education Index,* and *Library Literature,* among others. These journals are as disparate as *Vogue, Playboy, National Geographic, Datamation, Department of State Bulletin,* and *Animal Production.* Selected additional periodicals not indexed elsewhere by Wilson are also covered by *BioI.* Two typical entries cite W. Ross Winterowd's article on Kenneth Burke in *Dictionary of Literary Biography,* 45 (1986): 74-79, and L. J. Einhorn's article on Carroll C. Arnold in *Communication Quarterly* (entry 347), 34 (Fall 1986): 344-48. A main listing in each volume arranges the biographees alphabetically. Entries provide dates for each biographee and note the nationalities of non-Americans. Lists of collections analyzed and an "Index of Professions and Occupations" of the biographees conclude each volume. The index is particularly valuable for biographical research in communications. Among the relevant subject headings are "Advertising," "Communications Industries," "Journalists," "News Agencies," "Public Relations," "Radio and Television Advertising," "Reporters," "Speech Educators," "Speech Therapists," and "Telephone Companies."

BioI is available online (entry 266).

158. **Book Review Digest**. New York: H. W. Wilson, 1905- . Monthly, with annual cumulations. LC 6-244490. ISSN 0006-7326.

Reviews of new books on subjects in the field of communications are frequently difficult to locate. Few indexes of book reviews offer comprehensive coverage of journals in communication. Although the most general of several book review indexes, *Book Review Digest* (*BRD*) is nevertheless useful for research in communication because of its long uninterrupted service. Other book review indexing sources, such as *Book Review Index* (entry 159), *Index to Book Reviews in the Humanities*, and *Humanities Index* (entry 171), for example, cite more comprehensive selections of reviewing journals but lack *BRD*'s historical coverage. The focus of the review journal *Communication Booknotes* (entry 344), on the other hand, is limited to mass media and mass communication. For quick identification of reviews of new books on computers, language, rhetoric, and television (particularly popular media personalities), for example, *BRD* is the obvious practical choice. The bulk of each volume is an author index of both "current fiction and non-fiction in the English language," with "excerpted citations to reviews" from a selection of journals. *BRD* indexes the major general and library-oriented reviewing journals like *New York Times Book Review, Publishers Weekly, Choice, Booklist*, and *Library Journal*, as well as selected reviewing journals for several subject disciplines, such as *American Historical Review, English Historical Review, Annals of the American Academy of Political and Social Science*, and *American Journal of Sociology*, among others. Communication journals covered include *Columbia Journalism Review* (entry 342), *Film Quarterly*, and *Sight & Sound*. Issues conclude with a combined subject and title index.

BRD is available online (entry 268).

159. **Book Review Index**. Detroit, MI: Gale, 1965- . Bimonthly. ISSN 0524-0581.

Book Review Index's coverage of reviews of new communication books complements that offered by *Book Review Digest* (entry 158). While coverage of communication journals that publish book reviews is superior in *Book Review Index*, the indexing only by authors and titles significantly reduces its value. In addition, unlike *Book Review Digest*, *Book Review Index* does not include summaries of the reviews. Among the nearly 500 journals indexed are *American Film, Byte, Columbia Journalism Review* (entry 342), *Computers and the Humanities, Film Comment, Film Criticism, Journal of Communication* (entry 374), *Journalism Quarterly* (entry 390), *Language in Society, Public Opinion Quarterly* (entry 404), *Quarterly Journal of Speech* (entry 407), *Quarterly Review of Film and Video*, and *Technology and Culture*. *Book Review Index: Master Cumulation, 1965-1984* (Detroit, MI: Gale, 1985) cumulates 1,600,000 citations for reviews in 10 volumes.

Book Review Index is available online (entry 269). This access allows title keyword searching and increases the index's value.

160. **Business Periodicals Index**. New York: H. W. Wilson, 1958- . Monthly. ISSN 0007-6961.

Business Periodicals Index, usually referred to as *BPI*, is one of the most generally useful resources for identifying literature relevant to the broad field of communications. It provides monthly subject indexing to over 300 English-language periodicals in the fields of business and commerce, including advertising, broadcasting, communications, computer technologies and applications, industrial relations, international business, marketing, printing, publishing, public utilities, regulation of industry, and public relations. The indexed titles include trade publications, popular literature, and scholarly journals devoted to advanced research. Among the journals indexed are *Advertising Age* (entry 330), *AdWeek's Marketing Magazine, Broadcasting* (entry 338), *Communications News, Computer & Communications Decisions, Data Communications, Editor and Publisher, Graphic Arts Monthly and the Printing Industry, Journal of Advertising* (entry 367), *Journal of Advertising Research* (entry 368), *Journal of Business Communication* (entry 372), *Madison Avenue, Marketing & Media Decisions, Public Relations Journal* (entry 405), *Public Relations Quarterly, Public Relations Review* (entry 406), *Technical Communications, Telecommunications* (entry 413), *Telephony*, and *Television/Radio Age* (entry 416). In addition to indexing these important communication journals, *BPI* indexes other major economic and business journals, such as *American Economic Review* and *Harvard Business Review*, that frequently discuss communication topics.

The subject headings used in *Business Periodicals Index* are similar to those used in *Readers' Guide to Periodical Literature* (entry 184) and other Wilson indexes. They generally present no real difficulties for users. A sampling of useful headings relevant to interpersonal and organizational communication includes "Conflict Management," "Leadership," "Group Decision Making," "Interviewing," "Questioning," "Negotiation," "Arbitration," and "Training." Abundant *see* and *see also* references as well as a significant number of alternative subject headings and subheadings are provided. Relevant articles on the topic of, for example, women in the media, appear under such headings as "Women Journalists," "Women in Public Relations," "Women in Broadcasting," "Women in the Advertising Industry," and "Women in Publishing." As in *Readers' Guide*, these subject headings are *see also* referenced from the broader subjects of "Journalists," "Public Relations," "Broadcasting," "Publishing," and "Advertising Industry," among others. Furthermore, these headings also cross-reference each other, ensuring the comprehensiveness of the user's search on this topic.

BPI's strongest coverage in the field of communication is in the area of mass communication, particularly the mass communication industries. Headings for telephones, television, and telecommunications are thoroughly subdivided. "Television Broadcasting," for example, includes the subdivisions "Animated Cartoons," "Awards," "Baseball," "Business and Economic News," "Censorship," "Conversation Programs," "History," "Motion Pictures," "Social Aspects," and "Study and Teaching," to name only a sampling. *BPI*'s coverage of literature on new communication technologies and products, such as facsimile transmission, electronic mail, and local area networks, is also very important. Finally, *BPI*'s coverage of individual communications and media organizations is most significant. The names of private companies and of governmental and quasi-governmental agencies, like AT&T, Cable News Network (CNN), National Broadcasting Company (NBC), Federal Communications Commission (FCC), International Telecommunications Union (ITU), and International Telecommunications Satellite Organization (Intelsat), are treated as subject headings. This coverage makes *BPI* indispensable for research on mass communications from the perspectives of business, economics, and law.

BPI is available online (entry 270).

161.   **Child Development Abstracts and Bibliography**. Chicago, IL: University of Chicago Press, 1927- . 3/year. ISSN 0009-3939.

   Child Development Abstracts and Bibliography (*CDA*) provides abstracts of the professional literature (both books and articles) "related to the growth and development of children." Among the journals indexed are *Child Language Teaching and Therapy, First Language, Journal of Child Language* (entry 373), *Journal of Speech & Hearing Disorders, Journal of Speech & Hearing Research*, and *Language, Speech, and Hearing Services in Schools*. Abstracts are arranged by topic. Lists of studies related to language and communication are included in the section titled "Cognition, Learning, Perception." Author and subject indexes are provided. Useful subject headings include "Communication," "Language," "Speech," "Television," and "Writing."

162.   **CIS Index to Publications of the United States Congress**. Washington, DC: Adler, 1970- . Monthly. ISSN 0007-8514.

   CIS Index indexes a wide selection of congressional publications, including committee hearings and prints; House and Senate reports, documents, and special publications; Senate executive reports; and Senate treaty documents. These total about 800,000 pages per year and cover topics ranging from advertising and telecommunications regulation through language teaching.

   Separate complementary abstract and index issues are published monthly. Abstracts of documents are arranged under Senate and House committees or subcommittees. Each item is assigned a unique number. The cross-referenced indexing for these documents is very detailed. "Index of Subjects and Names" cross-references the subjects of documents and hearings. In addition, the index also incorporates subjects discussed by witnesses; names of individuals and corporations; affiliations of witnesses; names of subcommittees; and official and popular names of bills and laws. The heading "Telecommunication," for example, supplies *see also* references for "Communications Satellites," "Educational Broadcasting," "Public Broadcasting," "Radio," "Telephone and Telephone Industry," and "Television," among other topics. Indexing by personal and corporate names, in addition, makes it possible to monitor the activities of particular communications-related groups. An item is identifiable under cable television, the House Subcommittee on Telecommunication and Finance, and TeleCable Corporation, for example. Separate annual *Indexes* and *Abstracts* volumes cumulate the monthly indexes and abstracts and add several supplemental indexes — for titles of documents; bill numbers; report numbers; document numbers; Senate hearing numbers; Senate print numbers; Superintendent of Documents numbers; and the names of committee and subcommittee chairs (a very valuable feature). In addition, a third volume conveniently rearranges entries that arc related to laws made within a particular year. The *Legislative Histories* volume for 1988, for example, cumulates references for the hearings, debates, and reports on Public Law 100-584, which authorized the National Telecommunications and Information Administration.

   CIS Index is most valuable for identifying the stuff of government — that is, the primary materials — related to the business, legal, and regulatory aspects of the broad field of communications. Just as the subject of communications is everywhere, so is the United States government.

   CIS Index is available online and on CD ROM (entry 271).

163.   **Communication Abstracts**. Beverly Hills, CA: Sage, 1978- . 6/year. ISSN 0162-2811.

   Communication Abstracts (*CA*) is the most important indexing service in the broad field of communication. This recognition of significance, however, must be qualified by the fact that *CA* is also the *only* serially published index in the field. Few librarians or scholars are absolutely satisfied with either the scope, coverage, or format of *CA*. Complaints to its publisher have not yet induced substantial changes, with the exception of the addition of indexing of several valuable titles.

The most significant assets of *CA* are that it attempts to cover the entire field, it offers solid abstracts, it uses straightforward subject headings, and it is easy to use. In comparison to Matlon (entry 177), these features must be regarded as attributes. Each issue of *CA* includes numbered abstracts for about 200 articles from a pool of about 250 journals (most of these are included in chapter 8 of this book, "Core Periodicals") and 50 books and book chapters. These book summaries make *CA* a useful reviewing source, complementing the indexing offered by *Book Review Index* (entry 159), *Book Review Digest* (entry 158), and *Communication Booknotes* (entry 344). In addition, coverage of parts of books makes *CA* a useful supplement to the *Essay and General Literature Index* (entry 168). Separate author and subject indexes in each issue cross-reference the numbered abstracts. The citations provide full bibliographic data and the abstracts are thoroughly descriptive rather than evaluative. One useful feature in the abstracts is the identification of all subject headings that appear in the subject index for individual items. This allows thorough cross-referencing—provided one finds the desired subject in the first place. The author and subject indexes are cumulated in the last issue of each volume. A complete list of the journals covered concludes the third issue of each volume. This is the only place where the list appears.

The liabilities of *CA* are obvious. Historical coverage is insignificant for traditional topics, such as Aristotle, propaganda, or even public relations. The field of communication simply antedates the coverage that begins in 1978. For historical coverage of journals like *Quarterly Journal of Speech* (entry 407) and *Journal of Communication* (entry 374), either Matlon (entry 177) or *Humanities Index* (entry 171) is a better choice. Equally debilitating is *CA*'s rather shallow coverage of the necessarily broad literature of a very broad field. The pool of about 250 journals indexed by *CA* must be regarded as representative rather than exhaustive. At best, only *many* of the major journals in the main areas of communication are covered by *CA*. As a result, supplemental coverage of the literature of rhetoric and language is provided by *HI, LLBA* (entry 175), and *MLA* (entry 178). Similarly, *RG* (entry 184) and *BPI* (entry 160) offer more comprehensive coverage of the professional literature of telecommunication and new communication technologies. For example, *CA*'s 1988 volume listed only one item about electronic mail. While *CA*'s strongest coverage is in the areas of interpersonal and small group communication, even this is exceeded by the likes of *PA* (entry 183) and *SA* (entry 187).

What *CA* does, it does adequately. It seems that the field has simply outgrown *CA*'s coverage, however. It remains a resource that all undergraduate communication students should know and use. As a convenient quick reference tool, it also remains useful for graduate and postgraduate researchers. Here both groups of users can easily identify some relevant studies in major journals on most communication topics. For thorough advanced research, however, *CA*'s coverage must be fortified by consulting a wide variety of more comprehensive discipline-specific and interdisciplinary resources.

That *CA* is not available online, is, indeed, lamentable.

164. **Current Contents**. Philadelphia, PA: Institute for Scientific Information, 1961- . Weekly.

Current Contents (*CC*) reprints the tables of contents of recent issues from a pool of about 6,600 journals and selected "new, multi-authored books." It claims to identify well over 100,000 journal and book articles per year. The journals covered by this unique service are those analyzed by ISI's *Science Citation Index* (Philadelphia, PA: Institute for Scientific Information, 1961-), *Social Sciences Citation Index* (entry 185), and *Arts &*

Humanities Citation Index (entry 155), including important core journals like *Communication Quarterly* (entry 347) and *Journal of Communication* (entry 374). Author and title word indexes conclude each issue. The latter, modeled on the "Permuterm Index" feature of ISI's indexes, is an alphabetical list of "significant words in every article and book title." An article is referenced, first, by the *Current Contents* page that reproduces the table of contents of the journal in which it appears, then by its page number cited in the particular table of contents.

The several *Current Contents* products relevant to communication research include:

164.1.   **Current Contents: Arts & Humanities**. Philadelphia, PA: ISI, 1978- . Weekly. ISSN 0163-3155.

164.2.   **Current Contents: Engineering, Technology, & Applied Sciences**. Philadelphia, PA: ISI, 1970- . Weekly. ISSN 0095-7919.

164.3.   **Current Contents: Social and Behavioral Sciences**. Philadelphia, PA: ISI, 1969- . Weekly. ISSN 0092-6361.

CC is available online (entry 273).

165.   **Current Index to Journals in Education (CIJE)**. Phoenix, AZ: Oryx Press, 1969- . Monthly. ISSN 0011-3565.

Sponsored by the Educational Resources Information Center, *CIJE* provides abstracts of articles, with author and subject indexes, that are published in about 750 "major educational and education-related journals." These include *Argumentative and Alternative Communication, Canadian Journal of Educational Communication, Communication: Journal of Education Today, Communication Education* (entry 345), *Communication Quarterly* (entry 347), *Discourse Processes* (entry 352), *Human Communication Research* (entry 358), *Journal of Child Language* (entry 373), *Journal of Communication* (entry 374), *Journalism Quarterly* (entry 390), *Merrill-Palmer Quarterly, Public Relations Review* (entry 406), *Quarterly Journal of Speech* (entry 407), and *Technical Writing Teacher*, among others.

Monthly issues provide full bibliographic citations (with ERIC's "EJ" numbers) and abstracts that cross-reference the author and subject lists. The most detailed indexing of communications subjects is provided in the areas of language learning and teaching and the uses of media and new communication technologies in education. A sampling of the subject headings for speech includes "Speech Acts," "Speech Curriculum," "Speech Discrimination," "Speech Evaluation," "Speech Habits," "Speech Handicaps," "Speech Improvement," "Speech Pathology," "Speech Perception," "Speech Rate," "Speech Tests," "Speech Therapy," and "Speech Writing." In addition, a "Source Journal List" offers table-of-contents analysis of each journal issue indexed. This makes it possible to scan individual issues of each title for relevant articles. Annual volumes cumulate the author and subject indexes. The source list is cumulated in a "Journal Contents Index."

CIJE's educational interest in communication (that is, communication as an acquired or learned skill) makes it a basic indexing resource in the field. Coverage of other ERIC documents is provided by *Resources in Education (RIE)* (Washington, DC: GPO, 1966-). Both *CIJE* and *RIE* and available online and on CD ROM (entry 276).

166.   **Dissertation Abstracts International**. Ann Arbor, MI: University Microfilms, 1938- . Monthly. ISSN 0419-4209 (Section A); 0419-4217 (Section B); 0307-6075 (Section C).

Dissertation Abstracts International (DAI) provides monthly lists of doctoral dissertations, with abstracts of up to 350 words by the candidates, deposited for microfilming and sale by University Microfilms International. Coverage of Ph.D. dissertations supplements that offered by *Journalism Abstracts* (entry 174). Section A is devoted to the humanities and social sciences; section B to sciences and engineering; and section C (published quarterly) to European dissertations. The contents of section A are divided by subject disciplines. "Communications and the Arts" includes the subdivisions "Information Science," "Journalism," "Mass Communications," and "Speech Communication," among others. "Education" includes the subdivision "Language and Literature." "Language, Literature, and Linguistics" is also appropriately subdivided. The contents of section B, on the other hand, contains divisions for both pure and applied science disciplines. "Physics" includes the subdivisions "Acoustics" and "Electronics and Electricity." "Engineering" includes "Electronics and Electrical." Other divisions provided in section B are "Computer Science" and "Psychology." Section C follows the model of both sections A and B. The monthly issues include separate author and keyword (title words only) indexes. Research in communication requires use of sections A, B, and C. Dissertations on automatic speech recognition, interpersonal communication, or telecommunications are as likely to be found in one section as in the others.

DAI is also available online and on CD ROM (entry 274). Annual volumes of *DAI* and its several predecessors have been cumulated in:

166.1 **Comprehensive Dissertation Index, 1861-1972**. Ann Arbor, MI: Xerox University Microfilms, 1973. 376 vols. LC 73-89046.

This claims to include "virtually every doctoral dissertation accepted in North America since 1961." Multivolume annual supplements (Ann Arbor, MI: Xerox University Microfilms, 1974-) keep *Comprehensive Dissertation Index*, usually referred to as *CDI*, up-to-date. Arrangement by subject discipline with keyword and cumulative author indexing parallels *DAI*. In effect, the up-to-date coverage and thorough subject indexing provided by *DAI* and *CDI* largely supersede several bibliographies of doctoral dissertations.

167. **Engineering Index Monthly**. New York: Engineering Information, Inc., 1934- . Monthly. ISSN 0742-1974.

As its subtitle claims, *Engineering Index Monthly (EI)* is the preeminent "index to the world's engineering developments." *EI* provides abstracts, with subject and author indexing, for over 3,000 scholarly, technical, and professional journals; technical reports; monographs; conference proceedings; and other materials. Its primary value in communication research is as a definitive source of international technical studies in the area of telecommunication and new communication technologies. Among the core journals indexed by *EI* are *Telematics and Informatics* (entry 415), *Telecommunication Journal* (entry 412), and *Telecommunications Policy* (entry 414). *EI*'s coverage of international technical literature of telecommunication is definitive. *British Telecommunications Engineering*; *Japan Telecommunications Review*; *Annales des Telecommunications*; *Telecommunication Journal of Australia*; *Elektrotechnika*; *Alta Frequenza*; *Technische Mitteilungen PTT (Post-, Telephon-, und Telegrafenbetrieben)*; and *Radioelectronics and Communications Systems* (the English version of *Izvestiya Vysshikh Uchebnykh Zavedenii Radioelektronika*) are a small sampling of the international titles in telecommunication that are included. Few communication researchers will ever need to access research of this kind. All, however, should be sophisticated enough to appreciate that it is accessible through resources like *EI*.

Relevant citations and abstracts in *EI* can be identified in several ways. In both the monthly issues and the annual cumulations, the main section of *EI* consists of bibliographic citations and abstracts that are listed under alphabetically arranged subjects. These subjects are actually headings and subheading combinations based on a comprehensive authority, *SHE: Subject Headings for Engineering* (New York: Engineering Information, Inc., 1972-). Major headings provided include "Communication Satellites," "Speech," "Telecommunications," "Telephones," and "Television," for example. The heading "Technology" contains the subheadings "Developing Countries," "Economic and Sociological Effects," and "Philosophical Aspects," as well as subheadings for particular countries. To locate studies related to more specific subjects, researchers should consult the subject index. This cumulates the headings and subheadings used in the main section and incorporates "free language terms," including acronyms, popular terms, names of software programs, trademarks, and the like. Among these terms are *high definition television (HDTV), FCC,* and *ITU.* The subject index cross-references the abstracts by number. Both the monthly issues and the annual cumulations include author indexes. In addition, the annual cumulations provide a useful index by authors' affiliations.

EI is available online and on CD ROM (entry 272).

168. Essay and General Literature Index: An Index to Collections of Essays and Works of a Composite Nature That Have Reference Value. New York: H. W. Wilson, 1931- . Semiannual, with annual and various cumulations. LC 34-14581. ISSN 0014-083x.

Essay and General Literature Index (E&GLI) indexes book chapters or parts of collections, such as published proceedings or symposia papers. In this, *E&GLI* supplements the coverage of parts of books provided by *Communication Abstracts* (entry 163). Few alternative indexes do this. Communication researchers will find this most useful when they need to identify critical and scholarly analyses or commentaries on any area in the field. Essays covered include critical, biographical, and topical materials. Among the collections regularly indexed by this standard reference work is *Harvard Studies in Classical Philology*, which features critical studies of rhetoric. A typical item is M. Linsky's "The Media and Public Deliberation," pp. 205-27, in R. B. Reich's *The Power of Public Ideas* (New York: Ballinger, 1987). Useful subject headings include the names of prominent figures, such as Aristotle, Cicero, and Kenneth Burke, as well as broad topics like "Conversation," "Language and Languages," "Mass Media," "Popular Culture," "Psycholinguistics," and "Semiotics." It is not surprising that a significant number of comments and criticisms have been directed in the area of new communication technologies. A recent issue of *E&GLI* included such headings as "Automatic Speech Recognition," "Computer Vision," "Optoelectrical Devices," "Technological Innovations," and "Telecommunications."

Several cumulations published by H. W. Wilson facilitate retrospective searching of this comprehensive index. In addition, the set also includes:

168.1. Essay and General Literature Index: Works Indexed 1900-1969. New York: H. W. Wilson, 1972. 437p. LC 34-14581. ISBN 0-8242-0503-0.

This is a main entry and title listing of nearly 10,000 collections indexed during the period.

Essay and General Literature Index is available online and on CD ROM (entry 277).

169. Film Literature Index: A Quarterly Author-Subject Index to the International Periodical Literature of Film and Television/Video. Albany, NY: State University of New York at Albany, Film and Television Documentation Center, 1973- . Quarterly. ISSN 0093-6758.

Film Literature Index offers comprehensive subject indexing, in separate sections, of the international periodical literature of film in addition to substantial coverage of the literature of television and video. Among the 150 major film journals indexed are *American Cinematographer, Sight & Sound*; and *Historical Journal of Film, Radio, and Television* (entry 357), as well as significant critical, professional, and technical journals such as *Wide Angle*; *Literature/Film Quarterly*; *Variety*; and *SMPTE Journal*. Coverage of international journals, like *Cahiers du Cinema, Monthly Film Bulletin*, and *Soviet Film*, is also noteworthy. Among the 100 journals selectively indexed in the television and video section are *Cardozo Arts & Entertainment Law Journal* (entry 339), *Columbia Journalism Review* (entry 342), and *Journal of Communication* (entry 374); other major humanities journals, such as *American Scholar, Journal of Modern Literature*, and *New Literary History*; and national newspapers, including the *New York Times* and *USA Today*. In both sections, subject listings are provided for film, television, and video personalities (screenwriters, performers, directors, cinematographers, and the like); institutions (societies, organizations, and companies); film and program titles; and topics. Researchers should check under titles for reviews. Extensive listings are provided for topics like HDTV, families in television/video, and the FCC. Coverage of literature on music videos is more extensive than that offered in *The Music Index* (Detroit, MI: Information Coordinators, 1949-), for example. Sublistings include "Distribution," "Gender Roles," and "Political Analyses," among others. The annual cumulations preserve the separate listings for film and television/video.

Film Literature Index is not available online.

170. **General Science Index**. New York: H. W. Wilson, 1978- . Monthly. LC 79-2592. ISSN 0162-1963.

General Science Index (GSI) frequently provides the sole source of general science indexing in undergraduate collections in small college libraries as well as in the undergraduate library units of major academic research library systems. Though it is no real substitute for the more comprehensive indexing of technical literature provided by *Applied Science and Technology Index* (entry 154), *Telecommunication Abstracts* (entry 188), or *Engineering Index* (entry 167), *GSI* nonetheless offers quick and specific access to scientific literature on the full range of topics in the field of communication that appears in a core of basic and, more significantly, authoritative science journals. Listings for telecommunication and new communication technologies are notable. *GSI* indexes *High Technology Business*, among other new technology journals. Articles on the topics of advertising, information theory, and television and children, for example, are identified from journals like *Nature, Science, American Journal of Public Health*, and *New England Journal of Medicine*. Here the researcher can conveniently identify those studies on such perennially current issues as tobacco and advertising, television's impact on children, and popular opinions about AIDS that were cited in the previous night's news broadcast.

GSI is available online and on CD ROM (entry 278).

171. **Humanities Index**. New York: H. W. Wilson, 1974- . Quarterly, with annual cumulations. LC 75-648836. ISSN 0095-5981.

Originally published as *International Index* (1907-1965) and, later, *Social Sciences and Humanities Index* (1965-1974), *Humanities Index (HI)* today provides a convenient starting point for research in the areas of language, rhetoric, and the media. Students who need to locate recent critical studies on any topic in the broad field of communications, however, can be steered with confidence toward this index. Its coverage compares favorably with both *Communication Abstracts* (entry 163) and Matlon (entry 177). Likewise, advanced scholars should be advised that *HI* provides timely indexing of core journals that are most likely to publish articles on topics (the major ones, at least) of their areas of expertise as well as those areas with which they are perhaps less conversant.

HI provides author and title indexing to articles, including reviews of books (listed separately after the main index), motion pictures, radio programs, television programs, and videotapes, published in a significant number of core and otherwise important communication journals. These include *American Film, American Speech* (entry 334), *Columbia Journalism Review* (entry 342), *Communication Quarterly* (entry 347), *Communication Research* (entry 348), *Computers and the Humanities, ETC, Film Comment, Film Quarterly, Journal of Broadcasting and Electronic Media* (entry 370), *Journal of Communication* (entry 374), *Journal of Linguistics, Journal of Popular Culture* (entry 385), *Journalism History* (entry 388), *Journalism Quarterly* (entry 390), *Language, Literature/Film Quarterly, Mass Comm Review* (entry 395), *Quarterly Journal of Speech* (entry 407), *Quarterly Review of Film & Video, The Quill, Sight & Sound*, and *WJR*. Coverage of rhetoric is particularly strong. Headings are provided for a variety of specific aspects and figures, including "Accusation," "Apologetics," "Closure," "Comparison," "Description," "Dialogue," "Digression," "Discourse Analysis," and "Narrative," among others. Useful subject headings for other communication topics include "Advertising" (cross-referenced to headings like "Folklore and Advertising," interestingly), "Automatic Speech Recognition," "Conversation," "Electronic Data Publishing," "Facsimile Transmission," "Freedom of Information," "General Semantics," "High Definition Television," "Information Theory," "Intercultural Communication," "Nonverbal Communication," "Semantics," and "Teleconferencing." Among the alternative headings for television are "Communism and Television," "Mythology and Television," and "Theatre and Television."

HI is an essential resource for communication research at all levels. *HI* is available online and on CD ROM (entry 280).

172. **Index to Legal Periodicals**. New York: H. W. Wilson, 1908- . Monthly. LC 41-21689. ISSN 0019-4077.

Index to Legal Periodicals (ILP) is generally useful for research in all areas of communications. It is particularly valuable, however, for topics related to the communications industries on all levels — internationally, nationally, and locally. *ILP* provides author and subject indexing of a broad range of legal periodicals published in the United States, Canada, Great Britain, Ireland, Australia, and New Zealand, as well as of legal yearbooks and annual institutes and reviews. Among the journals indexed are several core communication journals in addition to others that specifically focus on the legal issues related to the entertainment industry and the performing arts. These include *Cardozo Arts & Entertainment Law Journal* (entry 339), *Columbia/VLA Journal of Law & Entertainment, Comm/Ent* (entry 343), *Communications and the Law* (entry 350), *Computer/Law Journal, Federal Communications Law Journal* (entry 355), *High Technology Law Journal, Journal of Space Law, Journal of the Copyright Society, Loyola Entertainment Law Journal*, and *Rutgers Computer and Technology Law Journal*. Other important general journals that publish studies relevant to communication and are indexed by *ILP* include *Duke Law Journal, Iowa Law Review, UCLA Law Review*, and *Southern California Law Review*.

ILP employs a strictly controlled list of subject headings. Useful headings for communication research include "Advertising," "Cable Television," "Carriers," "Censorship," "Commercial Speech," "Communications," "Computer Crime," "Freedom of Speech," "Freedom of the Press," "Language," "Libel and Slander," "News Media," "Propaganda," "Public Relations," "Radio and Television," "Telecommunications," "Telephones and Telegraphs," and "Videotapes." Perhaps the most productive heading, however, is "Obscenity." The list of subject headings is published in the index's annual cumulations. In addition, the names of individuals and organizations are used as subject headings. Articles treating the FCC are indexed under "United States. Federal Communications Commission." In addition to subject indexing, *ILP* includes supplementary indexes. The "Table of Cases" index identifies articles by litigants, such as the FCC or the Pacifica Foundation. The "Table of Statutes" index cross-references articles by both the popular and official names of the laws.

ILP is available online and on CD ROM (entry 281).

173. **Index to the Times**. Reading, England: Research Publications, 1906- . Monthly. ISSN 0260-0668.

Index to the Times — the *Times* of London — provides significant coverage of world events complementing that offered by *The New York Times Index* (entry 180). It is particularly valuable for news and other accounts of events and developments in the global communication and information industry. Subject headings, provided for relevant topics, include "Computers," "Electronics and Electronics Industry," "Telecommunications," "Telephones," and "Television." The index's historical coverage of communication and other "media" events — wars, inventions and discoveries, social and cultural changes, and historical personalities — is also important. *Palmer's Index to the Times* (1868-1943; reprint, New York: Kraus Reprints, 1965) extends indexing for the years 1790 through 1905.

Indexing to the London *Times* is also available online (entry 319).

174. **Journalism Abstracts**. Columbia, SC: Association for Education in Journalism and Mass Communication, 1963- . Annual. ISSN 0075-4412.

Journalism Abstracts indexes and abstracts Ph.D. dissertations and master's theses in journalism and mass communication from universities in the United States and Canada. The citations and abstracts (written by the degree candidates) are arranged alphabetically by author in separate sections for Ph.D. dissertations and master's theses. Indexes are provided for authors, degree-granting institutions, and subjects. Subject headings are derived from keywords in titles and abstracts, including names of individuals and organizations. All areas of the broad field of communication are represented. A recent volume identified dissertations or theses under the headings "Arts Criticism," "Communication Theory," "Educational Media," "Forensics," "Graphics," "Group Communication," "Information Seeking," "Interviewing," "Language Translation," "Organizational Communication," "Satellite Communication," "Speech Education," and "Telephones," among other topics. Despite the fact that the subject index is somewhat cluttered by "index terms without numbers" (that is, terms used in previous indexes), *Journalism Abstracts'* only real deficiency is its lack of comprehensiveness. Not all programs in communications submit abstracts of completed dissertations and theses, although a list of dissertations in mass communication from institutions that do not send abstracts to *Journalism Abstracts* was recently included. Nonetheless, a comprehensive search for dissertations in the field demands consulting *Dissertation Abstracts International* (entry 166) in addition to *Journalism Abstracts*.

175. **LLBA: Linguistics and Language Behavior Abstracts**. San Diego, CA: Sociological Abstracts, 1967- . Quarterly. ISSN 0023-8295.

Other indexes, such as *Psychological Abstracts* (entry 183), *MLA* (entry 178), and *CIJE* (entry 165), offer solid coverage of the scholarly and professional literature of language and linguistics. *LLBA*, on the other hand, is the best index to this literature. It describes itself as "a collection of nonevaluative abstracts which reflects the world's literature in language behavior, linguistics, and related disciplines." These disciplines include anthropology, applied linguistics, audiology, clinical psychology, communication sciences, education, gerontology, laryngology, linguistics, neurology, otology, pediatrics, pharmacology, philosophy, phonetics, physiology, psychiatry, psycholinguistics, psychology, rhetoric, semiotics, sociolinguistics, sociology, speech, speech pathology, acoustics, comparative literature, ethology, and information science. Among the journals indexed are *American Speech* (entry 334), *Argumentation* (entry 335), *Brain and Language, Communication and Cognition, Communication Quarterly* (entry 347), *Communication Reports, Discourse Processes* (entry 352), *ETC, First Language, Journal of Business Communication* (entry 372), *Journal of Communiction Disorders* (entry 375), *Journal of Language and Social Psychology, Language, Language and Communication* (entry 392), *Language and Society, Language and Speech* (entry 393), *Southern Communication Journal* (entry 411), and *Speech Communication*.

Entries and abstracts are arranged in topical chapters. A detailed table of contents identifies several sections relevant to research in communications. Separate chapters include "Discourse Analysis/Text Linguistics"; "Interpersonal Behavior and Communication," with the subdivisions "Interpersonal Communication," "Communication in Groups," and "Mass Media"; and "Nonverbal Communication." The subsection "Child Language Acquisition" is included in the section titled "Psycholinguistics." Separate author and subject indexes cross-reference the citations. The subject index uses a controlled vocabulary of 800 words and phrases. These are linked with title keywords. Useful headings for communication research include "Communication in Groups," "Communication Theory," "Dyadic Interaction," "Discourse Analysis," "Language and Culture," and "Mass Media." Coverage of communicative disorders and disabilities is particularly strong.

LLBA is available online (entry 282).

176. **Management Contents**. New York: Find-SVP, 1975- . Semimonthly. ISSN 0360-2400.

This is another "current contents" service of ISI, similar to the several *Current Contents* series (entry 164). *Management Contents (MC)* provides facsimile tables of contents for a selection of about 320 professional and scholarly journals in the fields of management, finance, economics, accounting, marketing, business operations, organizational behavior, and public administration. Coverage of core or otherwise important journals in the areas of advertising; public relations; organizational communication; and the electronics, telecommunication, and new communication technologies industries is particularly strong. Among the journals regularly indexed are *ASQ* (entry 337), *California Management Review, Columbia Journal of World Business, European Journal of Marketing, Information Age* (entry 361), *Journal of Advertising Research* (entry 368), *Journal of Business Communication* (entry 372), *Journal of Economic Psychology*, and *Journal of Marketing* (entry 380). Basic business and economic journals such as *Business Week, Forbes*, and *Harvard Business Review* are also indexed. Indexing by selected subjects is provided. Among the headings relevant to communication are "Advertising," "Artificial Intelligence," "Communications Industry," and "Organizational Structure." In addition, indexing is provided for the names of corporations, such as British Telecom, AT&T, and IBM, that are included in article titles. Timeliness and specificity make *Management Contents* very useful for identifying the current literature of organizational communication and telecommunication.

177. Matlon, Ronald J., ed. **Index to Journals in Communication Studies through 1985**. 3d ed. Annandale, VA: Speech Communication Association, 1987. 645p. LC 87-61400.

This index, frequently referred to as the Matlon Index or simply Matlon, although somewhat difficult to use, is nevertheless an important source for identifying articles in all fields of communication as well as journalism. It indexes 15 of the most important English-language journals in these fields, including *Association for Communication Administration*

Bulletin; *Communication Quarterly* (entry 347); *Critical Studies in Mass Communication* (entry 351); *Journal of the American Forensic Association*, now *Argumentation and Advocacy* (entry 336); *Journal of Broadcasting and Electronic Media* (entry 370); *Journal of Communication* (entry 374); and *Philosophy and Rhetoric* (entry 401). Now in its third edition, the index is arranged in a format that centers on the tables of contents of each issue of the 15 journals rather than on alphabetically arranged subject headings, such as those used in the Wilson indexes like *Readers' Guide to Periodical Literature* (entry 184) and *Business Periodicals Index* (entry 160) or in *PAIS* (entry 181).

Separate sections are provided for each journal. Every primary article published in these journals is listed in this issue-by-issue, volume-by-volume arrangement, with a unique number assigned to each one. Articles are cited by title, author, and pagination. Book reviews, editorial remarks, letters to the editors, and the like are not indexed.

Three different types of indexes provide access to the reproduced tables of contents. The *Key-word Index of Subjects* provides an alphabetical list of keywords in the article titles. Resembling a standard subject heading list, it is the easiest to use and understand of all the indexes. A student looking for studies of, say, women in the media, might search under such headings as "Women — Electronic Journalism," "Women in the Print Media," and "Women in Television," which are used as keywords in this index. A code number that follows each of the terms refers to the coded classification scheme used in a second index, *Index to Subject Matter in Communication Study Journals*. These subject classifications have been adopted from the National Center for Educational Statistics. Only the five major classifications relevant to communication and journalism have been retained. "Communication," designated as "05," is the category more applicable to journalism. Related or narrower subheadings such as "Advertising Media," "Electronic Journalism," "Journalism History," "News Reporting and Writing," and "Photographic Journalism" are included in this category and arranged in descending hierarchical levels. An index of authors is also provided.

All of the keyword references to articles that deal with the subject of women in the media, to continue with the previous example, are listed in the "05" classification. Code "05.07," the subgroup for print media, offers an extensive list of more specific subdivisions, including "Women." Cross-references from this subject identify the unique numbers assigned to approximately 30 articles cited in the table-of-contents lists. Many of these articles are also included in other classifications in the index.

Matlon is not available online, unfortunately. It would seem to be an ideal candidate for reformatting on CD ROM.

178.   Modern Language Association of America. **MLA International Bibliography of Books and Articles on the Modern Languages and Literatures**. New York: Modern Language Association, 1921- . Annual. ISSN 0024-8215.

The most important reference work for advanced study of English and American language and literature, the *MLA International Bibliography* (hereafter referred to as *MLA*) is also very useful for communication research in the areas of language and rhetoric as well as television as a performing arts and aesthetic medium. Among the journals indexed are *Communication Quarterly* (entry 347), *Journal of Communication* (entry 374), *Journalism Quarterly* (entry 390), and *Quarterly Journal of Speech* (entry 407).

Since major restructuring in 1981, *MLA* has been published in two physically massive tomes. The first, *Classified Listings*, includes five individual sections ("volumes") for (1) British, American, Australian, and other English-language literatures; (2) European, Asian, African, and Latin American literatures; (3) linguistics; (4) general literature and related subjects; and (5) folklore. Each volume includes a detailed table of contents. The linguistics volume includes a section titled "Psycholinguistics," with the subheadings

"Speech Disorders" and "Speech Pathology." The general literature volume includes separate listings for film, radio, television, semiotic criticism, and rhetorical literary theory. Listings of studies on particular individuals, such as Kenneth Burke, Jacques Derrida, and Paul De Man, are included in their respective national literatures.

The second physically massive tome of the restructured *MLA* is the *Subject Index*. (Subject indexing was not provided previous to the revision.) This cross-references the five classified listings in the first volume. Veteran researchers will find this new access to the *MLA* quite luxurious; novices, of course, will wonder how research was accomplished without it. Alternative headings for "Communication" include "Adult-Child Communication," "Animal Communication," "Cross-Cultural Communication," "Nonverbal Communication," "Prelinguistic Communication," and "Referential Communication." Related terms are *communication apprehension, communication skills, communication technology, communication theory, communicative acts, communicative competence, communicative development*, and *communicative strategy*, among others. Alternative headings for "Rhetoric" include "Classical Rhetoric," "Political Rhetoric," "Rhetorical Devices," "Rhetorical Theory," and "Stylistics." Among headings related to speech are "Speech Accommodation," "Speech Disorders," "Speech Intelligibility," "Speech Pathology," "Speech Perception," and "Speech Rate."

MLA is available online and on CD ROM (entry 283).

A companion list of the serials indexed by *MLA* is published in:

178.1. MLA Directory of Periodicals: A Guide to Journals and Series in Language and Literature. New York: Modern Language Association of America, 1979- . Biennial. ISSN 0197-0380.

This directory provides basic data (such as addresses of editorial offices and ISSNs) as well as subscription, advertising, and editorial information for the journals included in *MLA*. This is a good place to obtain manuscript requirements for particular journals.

179. Monthly Catalog of United States Government Publications. Washington, DC: GPO, 1895- . Monthly. ISSN 0362-6830.

This is the most comprehensive bibliography of literature produced by the United States government, the producer of the greatest amount of literature relevant to communication. The coverage of *Monthly Catalog* complements that provided by *CIS/Index* (entry 271).

Issues arrange entries for documents by issuing department, office, or agency—for example, the Department of Education, Corporation for Public Broadcasting, House Subcommittee on Telecommunications and Finance, National Technical Information Service (NTIS), or FCC. Here the introductory list of government authors is very helpful. Semiannual indexes of authors, titles, subjects, series/reports, contract numbers, stock numbers, and title-keywords are provided. In general, the title-keyword indexes are the most useful. For example this permits cross-referencing *high* with *definition television* to identify hearings that would be otherwise hopelessly entangled and lost under the issuing author—"United States. Congress. House. Committee on Energy and Commerce. Subcommittee...." *ad nauseam*.

Monthly Catalog is available online and on CD ROM (entry 279).

180. The New York Times Index. New York: New York Times, 1913- . Semimonthly. ISSN 0147-538x.

The New York Times Index is the best known and most widely available newspaper index. Coverage extends back to 1851, making it particularly valuable in historical research in speech and political communication on such topics as contemporary coverage of

Abraham Lincoln's *Gettysburg Address*, the First World War, or the civil rights movement. Current coverage of the communication and media industries is also notable. *The New York Times Index* is a likely source for accounts of developments in new communication technologies. Useful headings in this area include "Astronautics," "Automated Language Processing Systems," "Cellular Telephones," "Compact Disks," "Data Processing (Computers)," "Electronic Information Systems," "Electronic Mail," "Facsimile Systems," "Optical Character Recognition," and "Optical Disks," among others. In addition to the indexing by subject, headings are provided for individuals and organizations, such as CBS, FCC, and ITU.

Indexing of the *New York Times* is available online (entry 284).

181. **PAIS Bulletin**. New York: Public Affairs Information Service, 1915- . Monthly. ISSN 0731-0110.

PAIS Bulletin is among the most useful indexes for identifying scholarly and professional literature in the areas of organizational communication; advertising, public relations, mass media, and information management, policy, and regulation; and intercultural and international communication. *PAIS Bulletin* provides broad coverage of "worldwide English-language public policy literature"—the literature of law, political science, economic and social conditions, public administration, and international relations. One of its main strengths is the coverage of a wide variety of formats. The bulletin indexes about 1,400 journals; books; domestic and foreign federal, state, and local government documents; organizational publications; and the *Wall Street Journal*. Among the journals indexed are *Adweek, Gannett Center Journal, Gazette* (entry 356), *Government Information Quarterly, Index on Censorship, Information Society* (entry 363), *International Journal of Advertising* (entry 364), *Journal of Advertising* (entry 367), *Journal of Broadcasting and Electronic Media* (entry 370), *Journalism Quarterly* (entry 390), *Political Communication and Persuasion* (entry 402), *Public Opinion Quarterly* (entry 404), *Public Relations Review* (entry 406), *Public Utilities Fortnightly, Space Policy, Telecommunications Policy* (entry 414), and *Transnational Data and Communications Report*. *PAIS Bulletin* also indexes publications of recognized social sciences trade publishers like Artech, Lawrence Erlbaum, Jossey-Bass, JAI Press, Computer Science Press, Sage, and John Wiley & Sons as well as those from agencies and organizations like the FCC, ITU, Unesco, Organization for Economic Cooperation and Development (OECD), and NTIS.

Indexing in the monthly issues is by subject only. Annual volumes include a cumulative author index. Coverage of telecommunication and new communication technologies is especially strong. Useful subject headings in this area include "Communication Systems" (this includes telecommunications), "Remote Sensing Systems," "Optical Storage Devices," "Radio Telephones," "Electronic Mail," "Electronic Publishing," "Satellites—Communication Uses," "Teletext," "Teleconferencing," "Videotex," and "Digital Audio/Optical Discs." Other useful subject headings are "Advertising," "Communication in Management," "Communication in Politics," "Mass Media," "Propaganda," "Publicity, Government," and "Public Relations." *PAIS Bulletin*'s extensive systems of *see* and *see also* cross-referencing and subheadings are very valuable. The heading "Broadcasting," for example, references relevant literature under more specific topical headings, like "Acid Rain—Broadcasting" and "Trade Unions—Broadcasting." Similarly, literature under broad communication topics is subdivided into "Economic Aspects," "Legal Aspects," "Statistics," and the like.

PAIS Bulletin is available online and on CD ROM (entry 285).

182. **Philosopher's Index: An International Index to Philosophical Periodicals.** Bowling Green, OH: Bowling Green State University, Philosophy Documentation Center, 1967- . Quarterly. ISSN 0031-7993.

It is safe to say that scholarly literature on topics in communication will be found in every subject discipline. Its prominence in philosophical research reflects the fact (frequently quickly skimmed over in the communication textbooks) that communication did not begin with the invention of electronic broadcasting. *Philosopher's Index (PI)* is especially important for identifying studies on the more abstract (theoretical, moral, ethical, and asethetic) topics and issues of communication. *PI* indexes about 450 international journals, only a few of which are also indexed by other major communication indexes. Among the indexed journals are *Communication and Cognition, Mind & Language, Critical Inquiry, Science, Technology & Human Values*, and *Philosophy & Rhetoric* (entry 401). Issues of *PI* include a main "Author Index with Abstracts." Titles are cross-referenced within this list. A separate subject index references the author index. In addition, a "Book Review Index" is provided. Coverage of information and communication theory is particularly important. Other relevant subject headings include the names of prominent theorists (Aristotle, Immanuel, Kant, Kenneth Burke), "Language," "Linguistics," "Rhetoric," and "Semantics."

PI is available online (entry 286).

183. **Psychological Abstracts.** Arlington, VA: American Psychological Association, 1927- . Monthly. ISSN 0033-2887.

Psychological Abstracts (PA) is the major index in the field of psychology. It is particularly valuable in communication research for coverage of the literature in the areas of interpersonal, small group, and organizational communication; mass media uses and effects; and language, linguistics, and nonverbal communication. In addition to indexing books and journals in the field, *PA* also indexes a significant number of core or otherwise important communication journals, including *Communication and Cognition, Communication Education* (entry 345), *Communication Monographs* (entry 346), *Communication Research* (entry 348), *First Language, Journal of Communication* (entry 374), *Journal of Communication Disorders* (entry 375), *Quarterly Journal of Speech* (entry 407) and *Western Journal of Speech Communication* (entry 418).

Monthly issues include a detailed table of contents that identifies several useful major categories and subsections relevant to specific areas of communication research. "Communication Systems" includes the sections "Language & Speech" and "Literature & Art." "Human Experimental Psychology" includes "Auditory & Speech Perception." "Physical and Psychological Disorders" includes "Speech & Language Disorders." "Treatment and Prevention" includes "Speech Therapy." Entries and abstracts are assigned unique volume and item numbers within each section. Monthly issues conclude with an author index and a brief subject index. Subject indexing is limited to specific terms or phrases, like *arguments, body language, coversation, eye contact, group discussion, interpersonal communication, interviewing*, and *parent-child communication*. More detailed subject indexing is provided in the annual subject indexes. The annual index uses "major terms" ("the main focus of the article") and "index phrases" ("a concise statement of the article's content or, when appropriate, ... the independent and dependent variable described in the material as well as in the subject population") to describe each item. For example, an article under the heading "Conversation" is described as follows: "gender identity, conversational overlaps & interruptions during same sex dyadic role play, collect students, application of symbolic interactionism approach." Similarly, an entry under "Persuasive Communication" is described as: "forewarning of communicator's persuasive & fear arousing intentions, psychological reactance & defense avoidance & behavioral intentions before vs during vs after communication, college students." The result is a very specific indexing that saves substantial time. Useful subject headings include "Animal Communication," "Censorship," "Communication Systems," "Communication Theory," "Communications Media," "Content Analysis," "Interpersonal Communication," "Messages," "Nonverbal Communication," "Persuasive Communication," "Symbolism," "Verbal Communication," and "Vocalization." Specifically identified communications media include audiotapes, closed circuit television, radio, television, and telephone systems. Subject headings for telecommunication and new communication technologies include "Automated Information Processing," "Computer Assisted Diagnosis," "Speech Processing (Mechanical)," "Synthetic Speech," and "Telecommunications Media."

PA is available online and on CD ROM (entry 287).

184. **Readers' Guide to Periodical Literature**. New York: H. W. Wilson, 1900- . Monthly. ISSN 0034-0464.

Readers' Guide to Periodical Literature (RG) is among the most useful indexes for identifying materials for research in communication, if not actually communication research literature. *RG* offers author and subject indexing of a wide variety of popular (that is, not scholarly) and professional journals. It is particularly valuable for identifying primary materials and other documentation that reflect communication-related concerns, such as assessments of the image of women in advertising from the women's press, the television industry's views of current events, or popular attitudes toward social, economic, or political issues of the day.

In addition, *RG* indexes a number of journals that regularly publish state-of-the-art information on communication topics. These include *Aviation Week & Space Technology, Business Week, Byte, Channels* (entry 340), *Fortune, High Fidelity, High Technology Business, Radio-Electronics, Science, Scientific American, Technology Review, TV Guide* (entry 417), *Video*, and *Vital Speeches of the Day*. Coverage of current topics in telecommunication and new communication technologies is particularly strong. Subject headings include "Cellular Radio," "Compact Discs," "Digital Audio Tape Recorders and Recording," "Direct Broadcast Satellite Services," "Electronic Mail Systems," "Fax Machines," "High Definition Television," "Local Area Networks," and "Teleconferencing," among others. Useful headings for other areas of communication include "Communication," "Communication in Management," "Communication in Politics," "Conversation," "Language and Languages," and "Mass Media." On the other hand, coverage of interpersonal communication topics generally identifies a weaker, more popular variety of literature published in journals like *Psychology Today*, for example.

RG is available online and on CD ROM (entry 288).

185. **Social Sciences Citation Index**. Philadelphia, PA: Institute for Scientific Information, 1970- . 3/year. ISSN 0091-3707.

Like the *Science Citation Index* (Philadelphia, PA: Institute for Scientific Information, 1961-) and *Arts & Humanities Citation Index* (entry 155), the possible uses of the *Social Sciences Citation Index (SSCI)* are numerous. *SSCI* employs several interrelated indexes to analyze a wide range of scholarly and professional journals in the disciplines of the social sciences. Indexing is both comprehensive and selective. Among the journals indexed are a significant number of core journals in communication. Coverage is particularly strong in the areas of advertising, public relations, marketing, and management; political, organizational, and interpersonal communication; and media uses and effects. Indexed journals include *Central States Speech Journal* (mentioned in entry 349); *Communication Education* (entry 345); *Communication Monographs* (entry 346); *Communication Research* (entry 348); *Critical Studies in Mass Communication* (entry 351); *EC&TJ* (entry

353); *Human Communication Research* (entry 358); *Information Age* (entry 361); *Journal of Advertising* (entry 367); *Journal of Advertising Research* (entry 368); *Journal of Broadcasting and Electronic Media* (entry 370); *Journal of Communication* (entry 374); *Journalism Quarterly* (entry 390); *Language and Communication* (entry 392); *Media, Culture and Society* (entry 397); *Public Opinion Quarterly* (entry 404); *Public Relations Review* (entry 406); *Quarterly Journal of Speech* (entry 407); *Telecommunications Policy* (entry 414); and *Written Communication* (entry 420). Coverage here complements that offered by *Communication Abstracts* (entry 163) and *Humanities Index* (entry 171) as well as by *Arts and Humanities Citation Index* (entry 155).

As with its counterparts, the key to the effective use of *SSCI* is understanding exactly what each of the three main indexes does. *SSCI* uses three separate indexes to analyze periodical articles by authors ("Source Index"), cited authors ("Citation Index"), and keywords ("Permuterm Index"). The most important index is the "Source Index," which lists the articles published in the indexed journals alphabetically by author. It amounts to a bibliography of a year's scholarship, arranged by author, in a significant selection of major social science journals. Use the "Source Index" to discover if a particular scholar published an article in a specific year. In addition to providing complete bibliographic information for the publication, the "Source Index" also notes whom that particular scholar cited to produce the publication.

These "cited authors" are in turn listed alphabetically in *SSCI*'s "Citation Index." The cited authors, of course, represent all varieties and dates of publications. Their entries in the "Citation Index" identify the writers who cited them, who are listed in the "Source Index." The "Citation Index" can be used to discover if a particular work — book, article, or otherwise — has been cited in a particular year. It is especially useful for tracing the influence of specific communication theorists. For example, to identify recent scholarship that cited Harold D. Lasswell and Abraham Kaplan's *Power and Society* (New Haven, CT: Yale University Press, 1950), researchers can check under the names "Lasswell, H." and "Lasswell, H. D." Under the subentry "50 Power Soc" (that is, the 1950 publication *Power and Society* are listed abbreviated names of authors and their journal citations for articles that cited Lasswell and Kaplan's important work. Bibliographic entries for these citations are then located in the "Source Index." By doing this, researchers can identify other cited works, in addition to Lasswell and Kaplan's, that might be relevant to their topic.

The third index in *SSCI* is the "Permuterm Index." In this index, "every significant word that has appeared in the title of a current article (source item) indexed ... is listed and paired with significant words that appear with it in the title." In the "Permuterm Index," broad topics like advertising can be cross-referenced to other relevant topics, such as art, newspapers, and stereotypes. This cross-referencing index is extremely valuable for identifying studies of very specific communication theories, for example, the "hypodermic needle" model of mass communication. The term *hypodermic* is cross-referenced to *mass commu.* or *model* to indicate articles that are then found in the "Source Index."

Coverage of *SSCI* is particularly strong in the areas of communication most closely related to psychology, sociology, political science, and economics. Relevant terms cross-referenced to *small group* include *behavior, communication, discussions, feedback, interaction, language, speaking*, and *talking*. Those for *telecommunication* include *advantages, development, economics, impacts*, and *regulations*, among others. It is generally safe to say that a literature search is incomplete until the *SSCI* has been consulted in depth.

SSCI is available online and on CD ROM (entry 290).

186. **Social Sciences Index**. New York: H. W. Wilson, 1974- . Quarterly. ISSN 0094-4920.

Social Sciences Index (*SSI*) and *Humanities Index* (*HI*) (entry 171) were originally published as *International Index* (1907-1965) and, later, *Social Sciences and Humanities*

Index (1965-1974). Today *SSI* complements *HI* for coverage of topics in interpersonal communication as well as of others related to the media, particularly from the perspectives of the disciplines of psychology, sociology, economics, political science, and education. Coverage of the media industries from the perspectives of current events and business, however, is stronger in *HI*. On the other hand, given its focus, *SSI*'s attention to new communication technologies with educational, psychological, political, and sociological applications is also useful.

Like *HI, SSI* offers author and subject indexing for a number of core communication journals and other journals that regularly feature communication research, including *ASQ* (entry 337); *American Economic Review*; *Communication Research* (entry 348); *Economist*; *Journal of Applied Behavioral Science*; *Journal of Business Ethics*; *Journal of Communication* (entry 374); *Journal of Nonverbal Behavior* (entry 383); *Journal of Personality and Social Psychology*; *Media, Culture and Society* (entry 397); *Perceptual and Motor Skills*; *Public Management*; *Public Opinion Quarterly* (entry 404); *Social Forces*; *Social Problems*; and *Technology and Culture*. Book reviews are listed separately at the end of each issue.

SSI provides thorough topical coverage and cross-referencing. *Interpersonal communication* is indexed under "Communication." On the other hand, a significant number of studies relevant to communication research appear under the headings "Interpersonal Attraction" and "Interpersonal Relations." "Communication, Nonverbal" cross-references alternative headings, like "Facial Expression," "Gaze—Psychological," "Gesture," and "Touch," among others. Likewise, the heading "Advertising" references related headings for specific products: "Alcoholic Beverages—Advertising," "Cigarette Industry—Advertising," "Drug Industry—Advertising," and "Telephone Companies—Advertising." Headings for new communication technologies include "Automatic Speech Recognition," "Cellular Radio," "Direct Broadcasting Satellite Television," "Electronic Mail Systems," "Facsimile Transmission," "Imaging Systems," "Optical Storage Devices," and "Videotelephones."

SSI is available online and on CD ROM (entry 289).

187. **Sociological Abstracts**. San Diego, CA: Sociological Abstracts, 1952- . 5/year. ISSN 0038-0202.

Like *Psychological Abstracts* (entry 183), *Sociological Abstracts* (*SA*) provides significant coverage of the scholarly literature relevant to research in the areas of interpersonal, small group, and organizational communication as well as mass media effects and the roles of mass media in society and culture. *SA* provides detailed author and subject indexing for a significant number of core or otherwise important communication journals, including *Communication and Cognition, Communication Monographs* (entry 346), *Communication, Critical Studies in Mass Communication* (entry 351), *Journal of Broadcasting and Electronic Media* (entry 370), *Journal of Advertising* (entry 367), *Language and Communication* (entry 392), *Language and Society, Quarterly Journal of Speech* (entry 407), and *Technology and Culture*.

Issues of *SA* include a detailed table of contents that identifies several chapters or categories relevant to communication. Category 0800, "Mass Phenomena," includes the subsections "Public Opinion," "Communication," and "Mass Culture." Category 1300, "Sociology of Language & the Arts," includes the section "Sociology of Language/Socio-linguistics." Other relevant categories include 0400, "Group Interactions"; 0500, "Culture and Social Structure"; and 0900, "Political Interactions." The main section of each issue consists of entries and abstracts. These are cross-referenced by separate author and subject indexes. Subject indexing employs 5,000 "descriptors or key terms." As in *PA*, these terms are crossed with "phrases composed of ... the dependent variable; the independent variable; tests (measures); population; type of study"; and other significant words. For example, an article under the heading "Telecommunication" is described as follows: "language/culture maintenance, northern California Portuguese-speaking community, electronic media's role; interviewers; broadcaster, community leaders." A unique reference number, consisting of the volume, issue, and item numbers, cross-references the entry and abstract. Useful subject headings in the area of telecommunication and new communication technologies include "Automation," "Computers," "Electronic Technology," "Information Technology," "Networks," "Technological Innovations," "Technological Progress," "Telecommunications," and "Telephone Communications." A source list is also included in each issue. In addition, issues of *SA* include the "IRPS," or "International Review of Publications in Sociology." This lists and abstracts book publications in the field as well as relevant book reviews. "IRPS" includes separate author and source indexes.

SA is available online and on CD ROM (entry 291).

188. **Telecommunication Abstracts**. New York: R. R. Bowker, Bowker A&I Publishing, 1985-1989. 5 vols. ISSN 0882-1429.

This *was* the index of choice for telecommunication professionals who could afford its industry-specific services. Researchers must now consult the more comprehensive and complex *Engineering Index* (entry 167). *Telecommunication Abstracts* focused "on research and development, business trends, new products, and regulatory issues in the telecommunications field," providing monthly indexing and abstracting of scientific, technical, and professional journals; conference and symposium proceedings; government, corporate, and academic reports; and patents. Among the approximately 200 journals that received either comprehensive or selective indexing were the numerous ACM and IEEE (see entry 360) journals, *Advertising Age* (entry 330), *AT&T Technical Journal, Broadcasting* (entry 338), *Computer Networks and ISDN Systems, Federal Communications Law Journal* (entry 355), *Network World, OECD Observer, Space Policy, Telecommunication Journal* (entry 412), *Telematics & Informatics* (entry 415), *Telephony, Wall Street Journal*, and *Yale Journal on Regulation*. Issues of *Telecommunication Abstracts* cumulated annually and served as the finding aid for a microfiche collection that reproduced the full text of a significant portion of the abstracted literature.

189. **Topicator: Classified Article Guide to the Advertising/Communications/Marketing Periodical Press**. Clackamas, OR: Lakemoor, 1965- . Bimonthly. ISSN 0040-9340.

Topicator is a convenient index to a selected core of the professional literature of marketing and the media. This is the place to look for quick reports of current events and developments and hot products and programs from the business perspective. It is not the place for theory, aesthetics, or language. *Topicator* indexes 18 major communication journals, including *Advertising Age* (entry 330), *Broadcasting* (entry 338), *Channels* (entry 340), *Columbia Journalism Review* (entry 342), *Direct Marketing, Educational Technology Research & Development, Editor & Publisher, Folio, Graphic Arts Monthly, Journal of Advertising* (entry 367), *Journal of Broadcasting and Electronic Media* (entry 370), *Journal of Communication* (entry 374), *Marketing & Media Decisions, Packaging, Sales & Marketing Management, Television/Radio Age* (entry 416), *TV Guide* (entry 417), and *Variety*.

Topicator is not an easy resource to use. Despite the use of a tightly controlled (but growing) vocabulary of subject headings, or "categories," and subheadings, locating everything on a particular topic requires a lot of digging. "Federal Communication Commsn." is a specific category, for example. On the other hand, "FCC" is a subheading in the category "Cable Television." The subject of television is ubiquitous. Categories and headings provided include "High Definition Television," "Advertising—Television," "Audience," "Commercials—Television," "Independent Television," "International Broadcasting—Programming—Television," and "Pay Television," among others. If the subject or topic of interest is specific enough and readily identifiable (such as videotext, station ownership, or public service advertising), using *Topicator* is immediately rewarding. The category "Convention Reports" (from the American Newspaper Publishers Association, National Association of Broadcasters, Radio Association of Broadcasters, National Cable Television Association, and the like) is very valuable for quick reference. Finding literature on other topics, however, such as those above or children's programming (possibly located under the heading "Programming—Television—Network—Children's Shows"), is more difficult and rather frustrating. All references are by page numbers. Bimonthly issues are consecutively paginated. The annual index simply cumulates the tables of contents from the bimonthly issues.

The usefulness of *Topicator*, like that of Matlon (entry 177), would be greatly improved if it was converted into an appropriate electronic format. *Topicator* is not available online.

190. **Wall Street Journal Index**. New York: Dow Jones, 1957- . Monthly. ISSN 0099-9660.

The *Wall Street Journal Index* is mainly useful for identifying news reports and other features in the *Wall Street Journal* about the media and communication industries. Useful subject headings include "Automation," "Communications," "Computers," "Electronics," "Facsimile Transmission," "Telecommunications," and "Video Equipment." In addition, the *Wall Street Journal Index*, like *The New York Times Index* (entry 180) and *Index to the Times* (entry 173), offers indexing for the names of individuals and organizations in the news. Relevant features in the *Wall Street Journal* are indexed in *PAIS Bulletin* (entry 181).

Indexing of the *Wall Street Journal* is available online (entries 275 and 284).

4

Biographical Sources

191.   **American Men and Women of Science: Social and Behavioral Sciences**. 13th ed. New York: R. R. Bowker, 1978. 1,545p. LC 82-7219. ISSN 0065-9363.

The individuals covered in this supplemental volume of *American Men and Women of Science* (New York: R. R. Bowker, 1906-) represent areas of the social and behavioral sciences—including communication, information science, psychology, and sociology—that are not covered in other volumes in this series. About 24,000 individuals are profiled in one-paragraph entries that cite date and place of birth, professional memberships, areas of research and teaching, awards and prizes, education, and present position and address. Publications are not listed. The emphasis is on men and women in the United States and Canada, although representatives from abroad are also cited. The "Discipline Index" divides communication and information science into the subcategories of communication, information science, information systems, journalism, library science, mass communication, speech, speech communication, speech pathology, and audiology. Among the biographees are Phillip J. Tichenor, George Gerbner, Elihu Katz, and Curtis MacDougall. While now somewhat out of date, the volume remains useful for locating and identifying social science scholars, including many whose expertise is communication theory and research. Biographical sketches provided in the *Biographical Supplement* of the *International Encyclopedia of the Social Sciences*, David L. Sills, ed. (New York: Free Press, 1979), offer similar coverage of the social sciences. That volume includes substantially longer entries for 215 deceased and living individuals born previous to 1891 whose areas of research include linguistics, psychology, sociology, economics, human biology, anthropology, criminology, and other social science fields. These essays compare favorably with those included in the *International Encyclopedia of Communications* (entry 127).

192.   **Biography and Genealogy Master Index**. Detroit, MI: Gale, 1980- . Annual. LC 82-15700. ISSN 0730-1316.

Researchers will save vast amounts of time and effort if they use this source as the starting point to locate biographical information on individuals of any kind, either dead or alive. The index is a cumulative listing of English-language biographical profiles included in biographical dictionaries, subject encyclopedias, and volumes of literary criticism. Most are current and/or standard sources; however, some important retrospective dictionaries are also represented. To date, the most recent edition and its supplements cite almost seven million biographies in several hundred sources. Among the more important sources indexed are *Contemporary Authors* (entry 195), *Biography Index* (entry 157), *Newsmakers* (entry 204), and *Who's Who in Finance and Industry*, 25th ed. (Wilmette, IL: Marquis Who's Who, 1987). Doubtless, the recently published *Who's Who in Advertising* (Wilmette, IL: Marquis Who's Who, 1990-1991), providing brief entries for 17,500 advertising professionals, will be indexed in a subsequent annual volume. Coverage of less well known sources is also significant, such as James W. Cortada's *Historical Dictionary of Data Processing: Biographies* (New York: Greenwood Press, 1987) and Robert Slater's *Portraits in Silicon* (Cambridge, MA: MIT Press, 1987). As a result, *Biography and*

Genealogy Master Index is particularly useful for locating information about obscure individuals as well as serving as a cross-referencing index to a wide variety of sources.

The index debuted as *Biographical Dictionaries Master Index* (Detroit, MI: Gale, 1975-1976). The second edition, published in 1980, appeared under the current title. Publication of annual supplements commenced in 1981. The current pattern is five-year cumulations of the annual supplements. In addition, Gale has published several spinoffs from the original collection that are relevant to research in communication. Barbara McNeil's *Performing Arts Biography Master Index*, 2d ed. (Detroit, MI: Gale, 1981) was an expanded revision of Dennis La Beau's *Theatre, Film, and Television Biographies Master Index* (Detroit, MI: Gale, 1979). Both of these indexes, as well as Alan E. Abrams's *Journalists Biographies Master Index: A Guide to 90,000 References to Historical and Contemporary Journalists in 200 Biographical Directories and Other Sources* (Detroit, MI: Gale, 1979), are now superseded by *Biography and Genealogy Master Index.*

It is worth noting that *Biography and Genealogy Master Index* is also available online (entry 267).

193.   Bogle, Donald. **Blacks in American Film and Television: An Encyclopedia**. New York: Garland, 1988. 510p. LC 87-29241. ISBN 0-8240-8715-1.

Although this compilation is devoted to a special segment of performers, it also serves as an important supplement to more general biographical dictionaries of television and film personalities. Author of *Toms, Coons, Mullatoes, Mammies, and Bucks: An Interpretive History of Blacks in American Films* (New York: Viking, 1973, 1989), a definitive study on the role of blacks in American cinema, Bogle provides detailed information on television credits and filmographies for both major and minor black performers, directors, choreographers, producers, and others active in either television or film since the beginnings of both industries. Coverage of less well known individuals makes the encyclopedia particularly valuable. About one-third of the volume consists of profiles ranging in length from one-half page to six full pages, with photographs. The rest of the volume is annotated lists of films and television programs (classified as television series, television movies, miniseries, and specials) in which at least one African-American has been involved.

194.   Bronstein, Arthur J., Lawrence J. Raphael, and C. I. Stevens, eds. **A Biographical Dictionary of the Phonetic Sciences**. New York: Press of the Lehman College, 1977. 255p. LC 77-87592.

Biographies of historical and present-day phoneticists, phonologists, philologists, dialecticians, linguists, and other phonetic scientists specializing in such related activities as speech synthesis, analysis of speech, and acoustics are included in this dictionary. Signed entries are arranged in columnar format. Information includes date and place of birth, areas of specialization, highest academic degree and date awarded, professional title, academic affiliation, major publications, and areas of current research or scholarly interest. Bibliographies of additional biographical references are also provided. Coverage of historically significant biographees distinguishes this work. Among the prominent individuals included are Noah Webster, for greatly influencing American English spelling and pronunciation; George Bernard Shaw, for his interest in reforming English phonetics and spelling; and Jacob and Wilhelm Grimm (the Brothers Grimm of fairy tale fame), for the cooperative work that led to the development of the *Deutscher Wörterbuch*, the great German etymological dictionary begun in 1852 and finally completed by others in 1954.

195.   **Contemporary Authors**. Detroit, MI: Gale, 1981- . Irregular. (New Revision Series). LC 81-640179. ISSN 0275-7176.

Contemporary Authors describes itself as a "biobibliographical guide to current writers in fiction, general nonfiction, poetry, journalism, drama, motion pictures, television, and other fields." Irregularly published volumes include brief (one-quarter page to three pages) profiles of both professional an academic published authors, newspaper and broadcast reporters, correspondents, newspaper and magazine editors, photojournalists, television screenwriters, print journalists, radio personalities, and many other types of active media professionals. Writers from other countries are also included. This wide coverage makes *Contemporary Authors* a good place to start to locate information about the author of a popular work as well as the author of a work aimed at a scholarly audience. Entries provide personal data (including current address), career highlights, works in progress, published works, and personal sidelights. Entries occasionally include autobiographical comments. Brief checklists of additional biographical sources are also included. To date, over 93,000 authors have been covered. Among the individuals included are communication theorists Erik Barnouw, Noam Chomsky, and Robert Sklar; broadcast journalists Walter Cronkite and Jane Pauley; and print journalists Mike Royko and Carl Bernstein. Successive updated profiles are likely to have appeared for prominent or otherwise prolific authors.

Contemporary Authors is not the easiest biographical source to use. Coverage has varied. The earliest volumes cited only living writers. With volume 104, authors who died after 1900 are included. Changes in coverage since its first appearance in 1962 and an interest in including updated profiles have compelled Gale to alter the series on numerous occasions. Fortunately, the most recently published volume includes a cumulative index to all previous volumes.

196.   **Contemporary Theatre, Film, and Television.** Detroit, MI: Gale, 1984- . Irregular. LC 84-649371. ISSN 0749-064x.

Contemporary Theatre, Film, and Television represents both a new title and a significant expansion of the coverage of its predecessor, the venerable *Who's Who in the Theatre* (1912-1983). In addition to theatrical personalities, the new publication also features biographical sketches of film and television personalities as well as of other individuals no longer professionally active but who may be of popular interest. Uniform, alphabetically arranged entries include personal data (including addresses of offices and agents), career highlights, lists of publications, additional personal sidelights, and selected references to other biographical sources. Coverage is limited to individuals professionally active in either the United States or Great Britain. A cumulative index to the series also includes individuals who were covered in the seventeenth edition of *Who's Who in the Theatre*. For biographies of less well known current and historical personalities, particularly from the early days of television, researchers should consult Brown's *Encyclopedia of Television* (entry 111) and more specialized compilations, such as Vincent Terrace's *Encyclopedia of Television Series, Pilots, and Specials* (New York: New York Zoetrope, 1985) and Tim Brooks's *The Complete Directory to Prime Time TV Stars, 1946-Present* (New York, Ballantine Books, 1987), in addition to *Biography and Genealogy Master Index* (entry 192) and *Biography Index* (entry 157).

197.   **Current Biography Yearbook.** New York: H. W. Wilson, 1940- . Monthly, with annual cumulations. LC 40-27432. ISSN 0084-9499.

Now in its fiftieth year of publication, *Current Biography Yearbook* remains among the most comprehensive, well-written, and informative sources of biographical information on living individuals in all areas of endeavor from anywhere in the world. It offers the fullest range of individuals from a variety of countries and disciplines. This is a particularly useful place to look for biographical sketches of present-day personalities in the fine and performing arts (including radio, television, theater, and motion pictures), literature, journalism, business, politics and government, sports, and the like. Among individuals recently covered are religious broadcaster Pat Robertson; Michael Eisner, chief executive officer of Walt Disney Productions; journalists Sam Donaldson and Pierre Salinger; and Christie Hefner, publisher of *Playboy*. The three- to five-page biographies provide personal and career data; autobiographical comments and other information by and about the biographee culled from interviews and the media; black-and-white photographs; and selected bibliographies of additional biographical references from magazines, biographical dictionaries, and books. Volumes contain both new articles and many that are substantially updated and revised. In addition, obituary notices appear for persons who were profiled in earlier issues. The "Classification by Profession" list cross-references biographees with the particular fields in which they are most widely known. *Current Biography Yearbook*'s coverage complements that offered by *Newsmakers* (entry 204).

198. **Directory of American Scholars: A Biographical Directory**. New York: R. R. Bowker, 1942- . Irregular. LC 57-9125. ISSN 0070-5101.

First published in 1942 as a component of *American Men of Science*, which is now *American Men and Women of Science* (New York: R. R. Bowker, 1973-), the *Directory of American Scholars* is among the foremost educational biographical sources. In general, researchers should consult this source when they need information about a communication theorist or scholar whose interests are oriented toward the humanities. Now in its eighth edition (1982), the directory arranged profiles of American scholars in four volumes, covering history (volume 1); speech and drama (volume 2); foreign languages, linguistics, and philology (volume 3); and philosophy, religion, and law (volume 4). In all, some 37,500 scholars active in teaching, research, and writing are briefly profiled. Volume 2 includes 11,000 scholars of English, speech, drama, and film studies. Uniform one-paragraph entries note date and place of birth, scholarly specialties (highlighted in bold print), education, present position, honors and awards, major publications, and current address. Each volume includes a geographical index. A cumulative alphabetical name index is included in volume 4 only. For information on communication scholars whose research is oriented toward the social sciences (including journalism scholars) and sciences (including telecommunications, acoustics, speech pathology, and audiology), researchers should consult *American Men and Women of Science: Social and Behavioral Sciences* (entry 191) and *American Men and Women of Science*. For the most timely information on the positions and addresses of current scholars, researchers should consult the *National Faculty Directory* (Detroit, MI: Gale, 1970-) or the various specialized membership directories of appropriate national organizations.

199. Dziki, Sylwester, Janina Maczuga, and Walery Pisarek, eds. **World Directory of Mass Communication Researchers**. Cracow, Poland: O'srodec Bada'n Prasoznawczych RSW "Prasa-ksiazka-Ruch," 1984. ca. 300p. (Library of Knowledge of the Press, vol. 17). OCLC 12661086.

Based on questionnaires sent to members of various international and national organizations, universities, and research institutions, the editors developed this biographical directory of individuals currently involved in research in a broad range of areas in mass communication, such as media and society, media theory, language of mass media, sociology of mass communication, mass communication economics, and the like. Entries are all in English. The editors acknowledge that the list is far from complete. Despite any deficiencies, however, the directory covers many researchers not included in other biographical sources, most of which focus on Americans, Canadians, and Western Europeans. Alphabetically arranged half-page entries include personal data (including home address and telephone), university degree and title, career information, research interests, memberships and associations, awards and distinctions, honorary degrees, and major publications. Broader supplemental information for other selected scholars and researchers, including those in communication fields, from around the world is available in *The World of Learning* (London: Europa, 1947-).

200. **Foremost Women in Communication: A Biographical Reference Work on Accomplished Women in Broadcasting, Publishing, Advertising, Public Relations, and Allied Professions.** New York: Foremost Americans Publishing, 1970. 788p. LC 79-125936. ISBN 0-8352-0414-6.

Although out of print and badly dated, this volume remains a classic biographical source in the field. An updated and revised edition is much needed. The nearly 8,000 women profiled represent a variety of areas and professions, including radio and television directors, reporters, editors, librarians, publicity officers, advertising and public relations executives, media directors, public relations consultants, cartoonists, literary agents, and related positions. Alphabetically arranged entries include data such as job title, address, career highlights, education, professional memberships, awards, residence, selected family information, and major publications. Separate geographical and occupational indexes (with categories for 15 different industries or careers) are included.

201. Ingham, John N. **Biographical Dictionary of American Business Leaders**. Westport, CT: Greenwood Press, 1983. 4 vols. LC 82-6113. ISBN 0-313-21362-3.

Information on the "historically most significant business leaders from colonial times to present" is provided here. In all, some 1,159 individuals are featured in 835 biographical sketches. Some sketches cite more than one individual. Entries, ranging from one to three pages, provide personal data, major accomplishments, publications, and bibliographies of additional biographical information in sources such as *Who Was Who*, the *New York Times*, *Who's Who in America*, and *Dictionary of American Biography*. Eight appendixes in volume 4—by industry, company, birthplace, principal place of business, religion, ethnicity, and year of birth, as well as one titled "American Women Business Leaders"— enhance the collection's usefulness in communication research. The industry index includes subdivisions for communications, advertising, public relations, and publicity. Among the individuals featured are Ivy Ledbetter Lee (1877-1934), "the father of public relations"; James Walter Thompson (1847-1928), founder of J. Walter Thompson, one of America's premier advertising agencies; Theodore Newton Vail (1845-1920), an executive of the Bell Telephone Company; and Gene Orvon Autry, television station entrepreneur (yes, that's Gene Autry in one of his other guises). Since the dictionary focuses primarily on individuals born previous to the second quarter of the twentieth century, information on more current figures will be more easily found in sources such as *Newsmakers* (entry 204), *Current Biography* (entry 197), and the like.

202. **Journalism and Mass Communication Directory**. Columbia, SC: Association for Education in Journalism and Mass Communication, 1983- . Annual. LC 87-655726. ISSN 0895-6545.

The bulk of this work is the membership roster of the Association for Education in Journalism and Mass Communication (AEJMC) (entry 460). For each member the roster provides name, title, current position, academic degrees, years of experience, teaching areas, division memberships, office and home addresses, and office telephone number. The directory also features descriptions of the major course sequences, faculty, degrees conferred, and special facilities for AEJMC-affiliated colleges and departments of journalism and mass communication in the United States. Other sections present classified lists of relevant associations, institutions, information centers, special interest groups, professional and student societies, foundations, and sources of funds and fellowships in journalism.

203. McKerns, Joseph P. **Biographical Dictionary of American Journalism**. New York: Greenwood Press, 1989. 820p. LC 88-25098. ISBN 0-313-23818-9.

A recent significant spurt in the publication of journalism biographical works has attempted to fill what had been a virtual dearth of publications before the mid-1980s. With the notable exception of *Who Was Who in Journalism, 1925-1928* (Detroit, MI: Gale, 1978), no separate biographical dictionary of journalists was available. In fact, that volume was actually a cumulation of brief entries for active American and Canadian journalists from the 1925 and 1928 editions of *Who's Who in Journalism*. McKerns's dictionary is among the most recent as well as the most comprehensive journalism biographical sources, offering profiles of some 500 individuals who have been active in the development of American journalism from 1690 to the present. These include reporters, editors, correspondents, commentators, documentary film and television producers, sports journalists, and publishers, among others. Individuals associated with ethnic, minority, and women's media are also covered. Entries of two to four pages typically focus on the biographee's contributions and importance to American journalism. Personal and educational data as well as career information are also cited. Brief bibliographies of works by and about the biographees, including references in biographical dictionaries and obituaries in the *New York Times*, conclude the entries. An appendix lists the biographees in categories for specific news media and professional fields as well as in more topical groups, such as women in journalism, minority and ethnic journalism, and winners of the DuPont, Peabody, and Pulitzer prizes.

Other biographical sources of note for historical personalities in American journalism include Loren Ghiglione's *Gentlemen of the Press: Profiles of American Newspaper Editors: Selections from the Bulletin of the American Society of Newspaper Editors* (Indianapolis, IN: R. J. Berg, 1984) and William H. Taft's *Encyclopedia of Twentieth-Century Journalists* (New York: Garland, 1986). Additionally, several volumes of the *Dictionary of Literary Biography* (Detroit, MI: Gale, 1978-) have covered newspaper and magazine journalists, including Perry J. Ashley's *American Newspaper Journalists, 1690-1872* (Detroit, MI: Gale, 1985), *American Newspaper Journalists, 1873-1900* (Detroit, MI: Gale, 1983), *American Newspaper Journalists, 1901-1925* (Detroit, MI: Gale, 1984), and *American Newspaper Journalists, 1926-1950* (Detroit, MI: Gale, 1984); and Sam G. Riley's *American Magazine Journalists, 1741-1850* (Detroit, MI: Gale, 1988), *American Magazine Journalists, 1850-1900* (Detroit, MI: Gale, 1989), and *American Magazine Journalists, 1900-1960: First Series* (Detroit, MI: Gale, 1990). *Journalists Biographies Master Index*, now subsumed in *Biography and Genealogy Master Index* (entry 192), and *Biography Index* (entry 157) — both of which, incidentally, index these volumes in the *Dictionary of Literary Biography* — should be consulted for other biographical materials on journalists.

204. **Newsmakers**. Detroit, MI: Gale, 1988- . 3/year; annual cumulations. LC 89-646490. ISSN 0899-0417.

Begun in 1985 as *Contemporary Newsmakers* (1985-1987), this relatively new source provides detailed information on present-day individuals who have appeared in the media. Similar in style to *Current Biography* (entry 197), each quarfterly issue covers about 200 newsmakers, with annual cumulations including 50 additional profiles. Two- to four-page sketches provide personal data (date and place of birth, parents, marital status, children, current address, information about education, awards, honors, and so forth). In addition, career information, extensive sidelights, and bibliographical references to biographical information in other sources are included. Typical sources cited are *Forbes, People, Saturday Review, Wall Street Journal, Sports Illustrated, TV Guide* (entry 417), and *Los Angeles Times*. Many entries include autobiographical and other information from first-person interviews. All include black-and-white photographs. In addition to a cumulative personal name index, annual volumes include a cumulative subject index that offers headings for broadcasting, advertising, cable television, telecommunications, and radio and television, as well as for specific media organizations, such as MCI Communications and Fox Broadcasting Company. An occupation index is also provided. An obituary section has been featured since 1988. *Newsmakers* is among the first places to check for biographical information on individuals who have gained media recognition in such areas as telecommunication, advertising, and television within the last decade. Among those profiled are George Gillet, telecommunication entrepreneur; John C. Malone, president of Tele-Communications, Inc.; and Hal Rincy, prominent advertising executive and winner of numerous Clio awards.

205. **O'Dwyer's Directory of Public Relations Executives**. New York: J. R. O'Dwyer, 1979- . Annual. LC 80-643238. ISSN 0191-0051.

Editor Jack O'Dwyer annually compiles this biographical directory of over 5,000 executives involved in corporate or association public relations or employed in public relations firms. Coverage is limited to executives with at least five years of business experience who are in the positions of manager (in a corporation or association), account supervisor (in an agency), or higher. Entries list current firm or affiliation, date of appointment, career highlights, education, awards, memberships, business address, and telephone number. Some entries include home address. A corporation/association index identifies the executives of specific institutions, agencies, and associations, such as Ashland Oil, Harvard University, Lyric Opera of Kansas City, Ketchum Public Relations, or MCI Communications. O'Dwyer is a name commonly associated with public relations directories and related publications. O'Dwyer also publishes *O'Dwyer's Directory of Corporate Communications* (entry 245) and *O'Dwyer's Directory of Public Relations Firms* (entry 246), both of which are basic and valuable public relations reference sources. More extensive lists of public relations professionals can be found in the annual membership list of the Public Relations Society of America (entry 479) and the International Association of Business Communicators (entry 467).

206. **Public Relations Register**. New York: Public Relations Society of America, 1981- . Annual. ISSN 0033-3670.

This annual directory of the membership of the Public Relations Society of America (entry 479) is published in the June issue of *Public Relations Journal* (entry 405). Appearing under variant titles, such as *Public Relations Handbook and Register, PRSA Directory*, and *PRSA/Directory*, the directory provides name, corporate office, address, and telephone number for each of the association's members. Separate geographical and organizational listings are also included. In addition, a service directory (consisting of about 75 classifications of products and services of interest to public relations professionals) and lists of major public relations award winners, professional codes, and PRSA officers are featured. A complementary publication is *World Book of IABC Communicators*, published annually in the second issue (in January) of *Communication World* (San Francisco, CA: International Association of Business Communicators, 1970-). The brief profiles offered in both membership directories provide information on a broader range of public relations and business communication practitioners than that found in *O'Dwyer's Directory of Public Relations Executives* (entry 205).

207. Scheur, Steven H., Robert Pardi, and Charles Witbeck, eds. **Who's Who in Television and Cable**. New York: Facts on File, 1983. 579p. LC 82-12045. ISBN 0-87196-747-2.

This directory provides information on over 2,000 individuals associated with the television, video, and cable industries. Although its biographical data is very superficial, the work includes many biographees not treated elsewhere. Among the biographees are the major executives of commercial networks, public television, and major cable services, as well as producers, writers, actors, broadcast producers, meteorologists, personnel officers, satellite communication broadcasters, advertising officers, communication lawyers, and others: in short, the broadest range of professionals currently involved in the broadcast field at the network level and the local stations in New York, Washington, and Los Angeles. Alphabetically arranged one-quarter-page entries include personal data, current business address, education, career highlights, achievements, and awards. Black-and-white photographs accompany selected entries. A corporation index references biographees by names of major networks, such as Cox Cable Communications, VIACOM, Turner Broadcasting, ESPN, and the like. A job title, or position, index includes 17 classifications, such as chief executive officers, producers, and TV/communication lawyers. Already a bit dated, this compilation complements coverage of television professionals offered in Tim Brooks's *The Complete Directory of Prime Time TV Stars, 1946-Present* (New York: Ballantine Books, 1987) and the third volume of Vincent Terrace's *Encyclopedia of Television: Series, Pilots, and Specials, 1974-1984* (mentioned in entry 111).

208. **Speech Communication Directory**. Annandale, VA: Speech Communication Association, 1981- . Annual. LC 81-64956. ISSN 0190-2075.

This is the annual directory of the membership of the Speech Communication Association (entry 482) and its cooperative associations. The bulk of the work consists of alphabetically arranged entries that provide name, address, professional position, highest degree attained (with year and conferring institution), and professional memberships. In addition, the directory features a list of the association's current and past officers, publications, board members, award recipients, constitution, and laws and regulations.

5

Library Catalogs

209. ATAS/UCLA Television Archives Study Collection. **ATAS/UCLA Television Archives Catalog: Holdings in the Study Collection of the Academy of Television Arts & Sciences/University of California, Los Angeles Television Archives.** Los Angeles, CA: Department of Theater Arts, University of California; Pleasantville, NY: Redgrave Publishing, 1981. 200p. LC 82-146642. ISBN 0-913178-69-1.

This catalog lists the holdings of recorded television programs in the collection of the Los Angeles Television Archives at the University of California. The collection includes the significant holdings of the Academy of Television Arts and Sciences, the institution that awards the Emmys. Part 1 of the catalog presents an alphabetical list of programs followed by individual episodes in chronological order. Entries indicate episode and series titles, networks on which first aired, air dates, producers, directors, cast credits, storage locations, formats, and viewing times. In addition to tapes of television series, the archive contains footage of speeches, political campaigns, commercials, and other program genres, including news specials, sports, musicals and dramas. Part 2 lists materials uncataloged at the time of publication. A similar list of programs that the collection preserves only on audiotapes appears in part 3. Almost all of the materials in the archive are U.S. productions. Scholars should take careful note of the catalog's 1981 publication date. Only holdings through 1979 are reported.

210. **British National Film & Video Catalogue.** London: British Film Institute, 1984- . Quarterly, with annual cumulations. ISSN 0266-805x.

This authoritative quarterly "aims to provide details on all films and videos released for non-theatrical loan, or if British, for loan or purchase within the U.K." The catalog provides access to productions of both the British film and television industries. British film and television productions, documentaries, independent productions, educational or training films, and feature films are included in two main sequences: the first, for nonfiction videos and films, is arranged by Universal Decimal Classification subjects; the second, for fiction films, is alphabetically arranged by title. Entries indicate subject, distributor, production title, availability, technical details, credits, length, format, intended audience, and the like. Some entries list alternate language versions, original title, and theatrical release date. Production, subject, title, and corporate name (for distributors, producers, and the like) indexes provide access. The British Film Institute's three-volume *Catalogue of the Book Library of the British Film Institute, London, England* (Boston, MA: G. K. Hall, 1975) offers an excellent record of British broadcasting archival materials in addition to the library's collection of cinematic materials.

211. Center for Applied Linguistics Library. **Dictionary Catalog of the Library of the Center for Applied Linguistics, Washington, DC.** Boston, MA: G. K. Hall, 1974. 4 vols. LC 75-301806.

The Center for Applied Linguistics is primarily concerned with language and linguistics. Although dated, this catalog reflects materials held by the center through the mid-1970s. The collection's strengths include languages and communication, the origins of speech, human communication, and the linguistic aspects of communication, as well as language acquisition and animal communication. The catalog covers books in English, French, Arabic, and Russian and excludes periodical holdings.

212. Library of Congress. **Radio Broadcasts in the Library of Congress, 1924-1941: A Catalog of Recordings**. James R. Smart, ed. Washington, DC: Library of Congress, 1982. 149p. LC 81-607136. ISBN 0-8444-0385-7.

As a result of the 1976 revision of the copyright law, the Motion Picture, Broadcasting, and Recorded Sound Division of the Library of Congress was established to provide greater access to the library's holdings in these areas. Largely the work of James R. Smart, the division's librarian, the catalog identifies and describes about 5,100 broadcasts, dating from 1924 through 1941, that are preserved on audio recordings in the collection. Entries for the broadcasts, chronologically arranged by air date, include program title, a brief description, location codes, call letters of the recording station, program length, and major participants. Programs with unknown broadcast dates are listed separately. Indexing by performers and program title provides access. A companion volume for the Library of Congress's television holdings is *3 Decades of Television* (entry 213).

213. Library of Congress. Motion Picture, Broadcasting, and Recorded Sound Division. **3 Decades of Television: A Catalog of Television Programs Acquired by the Library of Congress, 1949-1979**. Sarah Rouse and Katharine Loughney, eds. Washington, DC: Library of Congress, 1989. 688p. LC 86-20098. ISBN 0-8444-0544-2.

Although a number of institutions around the world now collect recordings of television programs, the Library of Congress has collected films made for television since 1949, making it the "granddaddy" of television archives. The library's collection now numbers over 100,000 titles. It is unfortunate that the library did not acquire many early shows because these were not registered for copyright due to a quirk of law. Others were simply never recorded during the era of live television. This new catalog lists only those titles acquired by the library from 1949 through 1979, of which about 85 percent were copyright deposits. The remaining titles were received as gifts. Included in the catalog are series (a group of programs with a collective title), serials (programs with a continued story line), telefeatures, speeches, documentaries, and network, local, and primetime programs. Television commercials and regular network news broadcasts are excluded. Entries identify title, copyright status, production company and date, telecast date, copy description, shelf number, plot summary, format, credits, and content descriptor. A "Content Descriptor Index" references the titles in 41 subject and genre categories. The library has also published a similar catalog for radio programs, *Radio Broadcasts in the Library of Congress, 1924-1941* (entry 212).

214. Mass Communications History Center. **Sources for Mass Communications, Film, and Theater Research: A Guide**. Madison, WI: State Historical Society of Wisconsin, 1982. 176p. LC 81-13569. ISBN 0-87020-211-1.

Manuscript holdings in mass communication through August 1979 of both the Mass Communications History Center of the State Historical Society of Wisconsin and the Wisconsin Center for Film and Theater Research of the University of Wisconsin, Madison, are combined in this guide. Describing some 547 collections that include materials relevant to advertising, public relations, broadcasting, motion pictures, press, theater, and journalism, entries identify each collection's contents, formats, donors, subjects, ownership, chronological coverage, size, and accompanying documentation. Holdings acquired previous to World War I are excluded. Appendix A lists the collections by broad subjects; appendix B cites related resources. This is a revision of *The Collections of the Mass*

Communications History Center of the State Historical Society of Wisconsin and the Collections of the Wisconsin Center for Film and Theater Research of the University of Wisconsin and the State Historical Society of Wisconsin (Madison, WI: State Historical Society of Wisconsin, 1979).

215. Mehr, Linda Harris. **Motion Pictures, Television, and Radio: A Union Catalogue of Manuscript and Special Collections in the Western United States**. Boston, MA: G. K. Hall, 1977. 201p. (Reference Publication in Film). LC 77-13117. ISBN 0-8161-8089-x.

Mehr profiles special collections with holdings in film, television, and radio located in universities, libraries, historical societies, and research centers in Arizona, California (home to 58 of the 73 collections covered), Colorado, Idaho, New Mexico, Oregon, Utah, and Washington. The "Institutional Listing of Collections" identifies collections, addresses, curators, hours, and subjects. Despite the narrow geographical coverage, the catalog cites useful data on collections of records, books, scrapbooks, oral histories, radio and television scripts, and radio and television broadcast recordings (such as the CBS Radio Master Tape held by the Pacific Pioneer Broadcasters in Hollywood). Access is provided by a general index and an "Index to Occupations," which references the collections by the occupations of the persons included in them. Although badly dated, the catalog offers a solid starting point for research.

216. Murphy, James Jerome. **Renaissance Rhetoric: A Short-Title Catalogue of Works on Rhetorical Theory from the Beginnings of Printing to A.D. 1700, with Special Attention to the Holdings of the Bodleian Library, Oxford: With a Select Basic Bibliography of Secondary Works on Renaissance Rhetoric**. New York: Garland, 1981. 353p. (Garland Reference Library of the Humanities, vol. 237). LC 80-8501. ISBN 0-8240-9487-5.

Murphy began this project in 1975 when a National Endowment for the Humanities grant allowed him to visit a number of European libraries with substantial holdings in Renaissance rhetoric. He soon decided that his catalog would record rhetoric holdings of Oxford's Bodleian Library (for the most part) since its major collection was not described in any printed catalog (unlike those of the British Library, the Library of Congress, and the Bibliotheque Nationale). The resulting catalog identifies works dealing with rhetoric by 867 authors published from 1455 through 1700 and located in seven major and six secondary archival sources. In addition to entries for these holdings, the volume includes an extensive selective bibliography of modern books and articles on rhetoric.

217. Public Affairs Video Archives. School of Humanities, Social Science, and Education, Purdue University. **Public Affairs Video Archives Catalog**. West Lafayette, IN: The Archives, 1988- . Irregular. OCLC 18932523.

Created in 1986 to house and disseminate all C-SPAN programs, Purdue University's Public Affairs Video Archives publishes this looseleaf catalog of its holdings. Videotapes cover House and Senate floor and committee and subcommittee hearings, National Press Club newsmaker luncheons, State Department and Pentagon briefings, White House special events, interviews with important and newsworthy individuals, and occasional sessions of the Canadian Parliament. The catalog arranges entries for the videotapes (all available for purchase) in 29 subject categories. In addition to title and identification number, entries include name, location, and date of event; date of airing; program length and viewing time; and the names and affiliations of major participants. The collection of the Public Affairs Video Archives provides significant opportunities and materials for historical research in political communication. The materials included do not duplicate the coverage of network evening news programs available in the Vanderbilt Television News Archives's *Television News Index and Abstracts* (entry 218).

218.   **Television News Index and Abstracts: A Guide to the Videotape Collection of the Network Evening News Programs in the Vanderbilt Television News Archives**. Nashville, TN: Vanderbilt Television News Archives, 1968- . Monthly. ISSN 0085-7157.

This serves as an index to the collections of the Television News Archives (entry 445) located at Vanderbilt University. Issues provide entries that consist of "descriptive abstracts of items on the evening news, presented in the format of the broadcast according to network, date, and time of each item" (within 10 seconds). Abstracts are indexed by name and subject.

219.   Television Script Archive, Annenberg School of Communications, University of Pennsylvania. **Index to the Annenberg Television Script Archive: Volume I: 1976-1977**. Sharon Black and Elizabeth Sue Moresh, eds. Phoenix, AZ: Oryx Press, 1990- . Irregular. LC 89-16199.

This is the first of what promises to be an extensive series of catalogs intended to describe the University of Pennsylvania's collection of over 28,000 American television scripts of series and unsold pilots. The collection's scripts of movies made for television, television specials, and soap operas have been excluded. In volume I, Black and Moresh, both associates of the archive, profile 2,477 records representing 127 series and 30 unsold pilots that were developed or aired in 1976-1977. The number of individual records far exceeds the show titles because episodes are separately profiled; 21 entries, for example, appear under the title "Mary Tyler Moore." Series are listed alphabetically, with episodes subarranged chronologically. Detailed entries identify accession number, series title, episode title, authors, draft stages, script dates, air date, notables appearing in the script, places, types of places, times, pagination, adaptations, and other data. Over 400 subject headings are used to describe and classify script contents. This will be the most comprehensive script catalog available. Nancy Allen's *An Annotated Catalog of Unpublished Film and Television Scripts* (Champaign, IL: University of Illinois Library and the Graduate School of Library and Information Science, 1983) offers similar information on a small number of television scripts.

220.   University of Illinois, Urbana-Champaign. **Catalog of the Communications Library**. Boston, MA: G. K. Hall, 1975. 3 vols. ISBN 0-8161-1174-x.

This catalog continues to represent the standard in the field. Edited by Eleanor Blum, then head of the Communications Library at the University of Illinois, the catalog photographically reproduces the library's card catalog, representing over 10,500 books and 200 periodical titles. Then (1975) and almost certainly now, the Communications Library of the University of Illinois "is probably the largest collection of English-language books on the subject assembled as a single unit." Established as a reading room in 1933, the collection is comprehensive and international in scope in the areas of mass communication, communication theory, advertising, freedom of the press, and popular culture. Materials on film, television, postal services, graphic arts, telephony, and copyright are also included. The Communications Library's quarterly new acquisitions list, *New Books in the Communications Library* (Urbana-Champaign, IL: Communications Library, University of Illinois, 1975-), updates the printed catalog. The quarterly list is currently edited by Diane Foxhill Carothers, head of the Communications Library, and is available to libraries and scholars on request.

6
Directories and Yearbooks

221. **Adweek Agency Directory**. (National Edition). New York: Adweek, 1983- . Annual. OCLC 10434498.

Adweek, a major advertising publisher, provides this guide to over 8,000 American agencies. Alphabetically arranged entries within geographical classifications (New England, East, Southeast, Midwest, Southwest, and West) include addresses, telephone numbers, number of employees, worldwide billings, key personnel, branch offices, and products/services, in addition to agencies' specialties and major accounts. Many entries describe an agency's capabilities and separate figures of billings by medium. The directory also offers brief information on regional advertising clubs and associations. All of the information in the agency listings is provided by the agencies. Adweek also publishes separate regional agency directories. Researchers should consult the more frequently updated *Standard Directory of Advertisers* (entry 249) for additional coverage of American agencies.

222. **Bacon's Radio/TV Directory**. Chicago, IL: Bacon's PR and Media Information Systems, 1987- . LC 87-640075. ISSN 0891-0103.

Publicity specialists will find this a useful guide to more than 10,000 commercial and noncommercial broadcast stations in the United States. Separate listings cover television, radio, cable, and network stations, arranged geographically and then by call letters. Brief entries include call numbers, addresses, telephone numbers, national affiliation, and major programs that are willing to accept publicity. The program notes list contacts, type of program (news, interviews, panels, and the like), and key personnel. Indexes to programs and call letters and maps of the top 30 U.S. radio and television markets enhance access. Bacon also annually publishes *Bacon's Media Alert* (Chicago, IL: Bacon's Publishing, 1982-) and *Bacon's Publicity Checker* (Chicago, IL: Bacon's Publishing, 1952-), with the latter issued in parts for newspapers and magazines.

223. **Broadcasting Yearbook**. Washington, DC: Broadcasting Publications, 1935- . Annual. LC 89-29741. ISSN 0732-7196.

Recognized since 1935 as one of the staples of the U.S. broadcasting and cablecasting industries, this yearbook has appeared under several different titles, including *Broadcasting Cable Yearbook* (1989), *Broadcasting Cablecasting Yearbook* (1982-1988), *Broadcast Cable Yearbook* (1980-1981), and *Broadcasting Yearbook* (1935-1979). The directory remains an important and basic guide to broadcasting and cablecasting products and services in the United States and Canada. Its main section geographically arranges profiles of radio, television, and cable television stations, as well as Armed Forces Radio, Radio Free Europe, and low-power stations. Among other features are current analyses of the television marketplace, market status, FCC regulations, cable regulations, multiple systems operations, and group ownership. Also included are directories of relevant goods and services, satellite ownership and operators, news services, consultants, special program providers, associations, and the like; maps of markets; and lists of media rankings and awards.

224. **Cable Yellow Pages**. Englewood, CO: Media Image Corporation, 1989/90- . Annual. OCLC 20808121.

Media Image calls this new annual "the telephone directory for and about the cable television industry." One of the few available sources that covers this industry exclusively, *Cable Yellow Pages* offers data on 3,000 U.S. cable television and multiple system operations (MSO) vendors and organizations that provide a variety of products and services, such as fiber optic systems, low-power television equipment, satellite hardware, mobile satellite uplink services, and testing. The directory's white pages geographically arrange vendors and organizations. Home, regional, and overseas offices of MSOs are also listed.

225. Caruba, Alan, and Mitchell P. Davis. **Power Media Selects: The Nation's Most Influential Media Elite: A Media Directory**. Washington, DC: Broadcast Interview Source, 1989. 216 leaves. ISBN 0-93433-06-8.

Public relations professionals and other communicators will find this a revealing glimpse at what the authors call the "power elite." Caruba and Davis identify, subjectively evaluate, and provide basic information (addresses, telephone and fax number, and the like) for the American media's "most influential" individuals and groups, including newswire services, syndicates, columnists, newspapers, newsletters, radio and television talk shows, and the like. For those whose game (or business) is publicity, this is an excellent source of insider information on who or what to contact to get it.

226. **The Corporate Fund Raising Directory**. Washington, DC: Public Service Materials Center, 1980/81- . Irregular. LC 83-1082. ISSN 0736-8615.

For those working in areas of public relations who need to solicit monies for charitable uses, this work is very helpful. Arranged alphabetically by company, entries provide the names and titles of contact persons within the organization as well as information on applications and grants, the areas of funding in which the corporation is most interested, geographic preferences, and other useful data. Corporations described in the directory are national, rather than state or local. Although no specific criteria for inclusion are noted, the corporations described range in assets from $50,000 annually upward to multimillions. Separate indexes by location of corporate headquarters, geographic preferences, areas of interest, and contact persons are provided. *National Directory of Corporate Public Affairs* (entry 244) offers some of the same information, although it is not as detailed. Likewise, *Fund Raiser's Guide to Capital Grants* (Washington, DC: Taft Group, 1988) offers similar information for 600 corporations and foundations that provide funds, equipment, or buildings or that otherwise support nonprofit organizations or institutions. Data is largely based on grants provided in 1986.

227. **CPB Public Broadcasting Directory**. Washington, DC: Corporation for Public Broadcasting, 1982- . Annual. LC 87-640327.

The Corporation for Public Broadcasting annually provides the names, addresses, telephone numbers, and principal officers of national, regional, and state public broadcasting organizations, networks, and related agencies. Geographical, personal name, and station indexes provide access.

228. DiPrima-LeConche, Patricia. **The National Directory of Product Publicity Sources**. Westbury, NY: Asher-Gallant, 1987. 167p. LC 87-17542. ISBN 0-87280-157-8.

Identified in this directory are about 1,000 magazines and trade publications that accept publicity for new services, developments, or products. The alphabetically arranged main section provides basic information for the periodicals (such as address, telephone number, contact, circulation, target audience, and the like) as well as information about editorial policies related to publicity, including methods of handling press releases, release formats, and photographic specifications. This guide is intended to identify the most potentially rewarding sources or audiences for publicity.

229. **Directory of Women's Media**. Washington, DC: Women's Institute for Freedom of the Press, 1988- . Annual. LC 88-2258. ISSN 0198-3401.

Providing access to areas of the media not easily found elsewhere, *Directory of Women's Media* is both a directory and a biographical information source on women in the worldwide mass media industry. Groups and individuals voluntarily submit information, making coverage rather uneven. Women's media are arranged in two primary sections, the first devoted to media groups arranged in 20 subject areas, such as broadcasting, video and cable production, speakers bureaus, and the women's press. Entries give address, telephone number, contact, and brief description. The second section features a "Directory of Media Women and Media-Concerned Women." Alphabetically arranged profiles give biographical and career data for about 600 women from throughout the world, including freelance writers, performers, radio producers, educators, editors, publishers, photographers, correspondents, and journalists. Asterisks indicate members of the Women's Institute for Freedom of the Press. Inclusion in this directory is voluntary and some of the individuals' work in media seems tenuous at best. Nevertheless, coverage updates the dated listings in *Foremost Women in Communication* (entry 200). The directory formerly appeared as the *Index/Directory of Women's Media* (1975-1987). Similar coverage of media directed at particular groups is included in *National Black Media Directory: For Business/ Civic/Charitable Organizations* (Ft. Lauderdale, FL: Alliance Publishers, 1989) and in Ana Veciana-Suarez's *Hispanic Media USA: A Narrative Guide to Print and Electronic Hispanic News Media in the United States* (Washington, DC: Media Institute, 1987).

230. Duncan, James H. **American Radio Report**. Indianapolis, IN: Duncan's American Radio, 1976- . Quarterly. LC 78-642306. ISSN 0738-8675.

James H. Duncan is a leader in the field of radio market information in the United States. His *American Radio Report* provides excellent information on each radio market in this country. The bulk of each volume profiles individual radio stations within a particular market by time of day, identifies listeners by age and sex, and so forth. Other charts list the leading stations by format. National ratings appear in the spring and summer issues. Fall issues, also called the *Small Market Edition*, analyze an additional 125 small radio markets not included in other issues. Duncan also publishes *Duncan's Radio Market Guide* (Indianapolis, IN: Duncan's American Radio, 1984-), an annual that provides radio revenue information. In addition, Duncan provides a historical résumé of radio broadcast rating and market statistics from 1976 through 1982 in *Radio in the United States, 1976-1982: A Statistical History* (Kalamazoo, MI: Duncan Media Enterprises, 1982).

231. **Editor and Publisher International Yearbook**. New York: Editor and Publisher, 1920/21- . Annual. ISSN 0424-4923.

Although numerous newspaper directories are now in print, *Editor and Publisher* is undoubtedly the classic in its field, offering comprehensive classified information on dailies and weeklies published worldwide. Primary sections arrange data (such as address, telephone number, advertising notes, editors and other personnel, publishing history, political orientation, circulation, and the like) for U.S. dailies, U.S. weeklies, and Canadian newspapers, these three constituting the bulk of each volume. As well, coverage is provided for foreign newspapers, syndicates and news services, mechanical equipment, and organizations. Volumes also list newspaper trade unions, foreign press associations, action/hotline editors, and the like. This is the preferred directory for current information on newspapers, particularly those published in the United States and Canada.

232.   Elmore, Garland C. **Communication Media in Higher Education: A Directory of Academic Programs and Faculty in Radio-Television-Film and Related Media**. Annandale, VA: Association for Communication Administration, 1987. 529p. LC 87-159380.

Elmore describes graduate and undergraduate media studies programs in radio, television, motion pictures, new communication technologies, and other areas offered by nearly 600 departments or programs in American universities and colleges. Arranged by state in part 1, entries for institutions give addresses, telephone numbers, names of chief administrators, and descriptions of programs (course titles, enrollment, numbers of degrees granted, full-time faculty, and the like). Part 2 classifies degrees by academic level. Part 3 is a directory of 1,700 communication media faculty. Despite glaring omissions (which Elmore attributes to lack of responses to his questionnaires), this is a good place to begin for information on academic communication programs.

For information on opportunities for professional educational experiences, students should consult Ronald H. Claxton and Biddie Lorenzen's annual *Student Guide to Mass Media Internships* (San Marcos, TX: Labor Research Group, Department of Journalism, Southwest Texas State University, 1975-), which describes programs in both print and electronic media.

233.   Elving, Bruce F. **FM Atlas and Station Directory**. 10th ed. Adolph, MN: FM Atlas, 1986. 164p. LC 85-82619. ISBN 0-917170-05-9.

Like several other directories included here, the *FM Atlas and Station Directory* offers reliable information on North American radio broadcasting. This guide is unique, however, in that the focus is exclusively FM stations. Separate information for stations in the United States, Canada, Mexico, Puerto Rico, and the Virgin Islands is subarranged by city, with maps to help locate the stations. A useful list of FM translators (broadcasting devices that use frequencies differing from those used by stations to originate the transmissions) is also included. This list may be unique to Elving's directory.

234.   Epler-Wood, Gregory, and Paul D'Ari. **Cable Programming Resource Directory**. Washington, DC: Communication Press, Broadcasting Publications, 1987- . Irregular. ISSN 0898-8668.

The bulk of this directory, sponsored by the National Federation of Local Cable Programmers, contains a geographically arranged list of cable companies, corporations, organizations, government agencies, and educational institutions that can provide public access to public cable television facilities in the United States. Entries include addresses, telephone numbers, contacts, descriptions of the organizations, channels, services, staffing, training, equipment, formats, budgets, number of subscribers, and hours of cablecasts. Other chapters offer analyses and tabular data for community programming and lists of organizations and businesses that provide full-length programming at little or no cost, distribute material in conjunction with public information campaigns, and produce international crosscultural programming. Public cable broadcasters will find this information of immense value in their searches for useful and low-budget program selections.

235.   Fishman, Joshua A., Esther G. Lowry, William G. Milam, and Michael H. Gertner. **Guide to Non-English Language Broadcasting**. Rosslyn, VA: National Clearinghouse for Bilingual Education, 1982. 115p. (Language Resources in the United States, vol. 2). LC 83-125794. ISBN 0-89763-070-x.

Radio and television broadcast stations that transmit programs in languages other than English are profiled in this now somewhat dated resource. Entries for 1,400 stations include call letters, addresses, contacts, and language programming, including program lengths and the number of hours of language programming.

236. Fry, Ronald W. **Career Directory Series**. Hawthorne, NJ: Career Press, 1986- . Annual. OCLC 13048354.

The primary business of the six different titles that are part of this annual series is to assist media job hunters in the search for employment, internships, and training programs in agencies, corporations, associations, television and radio stations, and in newspaper, book, and magazine publishing houses. Volumes include:

236.1. **Advertising Career Directory**. Hawthorne, NJ: Career Press, 1986- . ISSN 0882-8253.

236.2. **Book Publishing Career Directory**. Hawthorne, NJ: Career Press, 1986- . ISSN 0882-8261.

236.3. **Magazine Publishing Career Directory**. Hawthorne, NJ: Career Press, 1986- . ISSN 0889-8502.

236.4. **Marketing & Sales Career Directory**. Hawthorne, NJ: Career Press, 1987- . ISSN 0889-8510.

236.5. **Newspaper Career Directory**. Hawthorne, NJ: Career Press, 1987- . ISSN 0889-8499.

236.6. **Public Relations Career Directory**. Hawthorne, NJ: Career Press, 1986- . ISSN 0882-8288.

More career guides than directories, the tenor and style of the contents are clearly aimed at recent college graduates and other relative newcomers to the media professions. Actual jobs are not listed, only likely job openings. The job listings identify potential employers, including addresses, types of firms or publications, specializations, contacts, revenue figures, types of jobs, and the like. Prominent professionals in each area offer essays on where jobs are, particular specializations, the best methods of securing employment, and personal tips and advice. The advice is sound, but communication majors will probably skip directly to the job listings. Job seekers will be better served by checking the trade magazines for real job openings.

237. **Grants for Film, Media, and Communications: Foundation Center**. New York: The Foundation Center, 1987. 106p. ISBN 0-87954-219-5.

Researchers for whom grant seeking is an eternal quest should consult this specialized directory that identifies 1,951 grants of $5,000 or more made by 299 foundations (in 1985 and 1986) to support projects in television, radio, documentaries, general media, communication technologies, journalism, publishing, and film. Arranged by state, entries cite recipients and amounts awarded and describe the funded activities. Indexes for recipients, locations, and subjects provide access.

238. **Handbook of Advertising & Marketing Services**. New York: Executive Communications, 1985- . Annual. LC 84-4004. ISSN 0749-2243.

Like Weiner's *Professional's Guide to Public Relations Services* (entry 257), this handbook describes services that are of interest to advertisers, advertising agencies, and marketers, particularly those who wish to advertise in publications and brochures. The handbook is not an advertising rate or specification resource; rather, it gives addresses, telephone numbers, and brief descriptions of organizations that provide creative, product development, design, promotion, advertising, and sales services as well as marketing consultants, specialized agencies, broadcast services, direct marketing services, and the like. Information includes key contacts, fees, current clients, areas of expertise, major successes, and awards.

239. **International Television & Video Almanac**. New York: Quigley Publishing, 1955- . Annual. LC 87-644123. ISSN 0539-0761.

Like its predecessor, *International Television Almanac* (1955-1986), this respected source offers broad but somewhat superficial coverage of the domestic and international television and video industries. Each volume, with separate sections for television and home video, is a compendium of the most prominent or important individuals, organizations, places, and services (manufacturers, distributors, publishers, and the like), with emphasis on the United States. Approximately half of each volume contains a who's who of actors, executives, exhibitors, and filmmakers that functions as a quick source of identification. One interesting feature is an analysis of the previous year of television in the United States, with statistics. With the notable exception of *Broadcasting Yearbook* (entry 223), *International Television & Video Almanac* is the most widely available resource of its kind. It is an excellent source for information, provided one remembers that its strength is broad rather than deep coverage.

240. Jones, Vane A. **North American Radio-TV Station Guide**. Indianapolis, IN: Howard W. Sams, 1963- . Annual. LC 63-23371. ISSN 0078-1347.

The main purpose of this directory is to provide brief identifying information for AM and FM radio and television stations in the United States, Canada, Cuba, Mexico, and the West Indies. Stations currently on the air, temporarily suspended, or with construction permits are included. Entries are arranged by geographic locations, channels, frequencies, and call letters—an arrangement that makes use both convenient and timely. Researchers might also wish to consult *Broadcasting Yearbook* (entry 223) for more detailed information on personnel, addresses, ownership, and broadcasting power.

241. Kelly, Kevin. **Signal: Communication Tools for the Information Age: A Whole Earth Catalog**. New York: Harmony Books/Crown, 1988. 226p. LC 88-13165. ISBN 0-517-57084-x.

Those familiar with the style of the famed *Whole Earth* catalogs will immediately recognize the usefulness of this eclectic collection of descriptions, complete with ordering information, of "information age" books, journals, equipment and other mechanical devices, and general supplies of interest to communicators in the most comprehensive sense of the word. As in other volumes in the series, the listings seem to be secondary to graphics and text—photographs, illustrations, charts, maps, essays, reviews, and the like. Few communication industry purchasing agents will find the catalog of great professional use. On the other hand, the catalog is an excellent tool for locating a wide range of items not commonly found at the neighborhood Radio Shack, such as backyard satellite television components, robot supplies, and spying devices. Beyond purely utilitarian purposes, the catalog is a good read.

242. **The Knowledge Industry Publications 200**. White Plains, NY: Knowledge Industry, 1987. LC 88-21425. ISBN 0-8103-4254-5.

The Knowledge Industry Publications 200 profiles 200 of the United States' largest media and information companies, including newspaper and magazine publishers, television broadcasters, motion picture distributors, book publishers, and radio broadcasters. Entries provide the numbers of media and total employees, media revenues by types, corporate officers, and organizational descriptions (with divisions), balance sheet data, and lists of newspaper, magazine, television, and radio station ownership. The volume also includes media ranking and revenue tables. Indexes of executives and subsidiaries provide access. Although much of the financial data is available (and more up-to-date) in other more comprehensive business resources, *The Knowledge Industry Publications 200*'s specific coverage is most convenient for communication researchers.

243. McClendon, Natalie. **Go Public: The Traveler's Guide to Non-Commercial Radio**. Lincoln, NE: Wakerobin Communications, 1987. 219p. LC 87-50064. ISBN 0-9617-9890-4.

While *CPB Public Broadcasting Directory* (entry 227) focuses on public television stations, *Go Public* describes about 1,000 U.S. public, noncommercial radio stations that are either controlled by nonprofit organizations or government agencies or funded by taxes, direct listener donations, or private donations. Stations with an exclusively religious focus are specifically excluded. Arranged in sections for geographical regions, entries give station power, broadcast range, city of license, frequency, major broadcast sources, program types and formats, selected personalities and reporters, and day-by-day programming schedule. A geographical index of frequencies and a list of noncommercial classical music stations are also included. An interesting overview of the development of public radio completes the volume.

244. **National Directory of Corporate Public Affairs**. Washington, DC: Columbia Books, 1983- . Annual. LC 83-643539. ISSN 0749-9736.

The corporate public relations profession in the U.S. is profiled in this annual. The "Companies" section alphabetically lists about 1,500 companies that maintain a public affairs program, providing addresses and telephone numbers of corporate and Washington, D.C., offices and brief company descriptions, with data on grant recipients, preferences, and areas of interest. The "People" section identifies nearly 12,000 corporate employees involved in public affairs activities, such as lobbying, community relations, political action groups, and distributing grants and other contributions. This directory is mainly valuable for information on corporate support in American politics.

245. O'Dwyer, Jack. **O'Dwyer's Directory of Corporate Communications**. New York: J. R. O'Dwyer, 1976- . Annual. LC 75-23562. ISSN 0149-1091.

Along with other directories in this series, including *O'Dwyer's Directory of Public Relations Firms* (entry 246) and *O'Dwyer's Directory of Public Relations Executives* (entry 205), *O'Dwyer's Directory of Corporate Communications* is a valuable and informative guide to a particular segment of the U.S. public relations industry, giving names of individuals associated with public relations or corporate communications offices and departments in nearly 4,500 companies, 1,000 associations, and over 100 federal agencies, bureaus, or commissions. This particular directory excludes employees of public relations agencies. Alphabetically arranged in seven classified lists (with the most extensive for corporations), entries identify addresses, telephone numbers, subsidiaries, and executive officers and other key corporate communications personnel. Data is also rearranged in geographic, industry, and type of services lists. Users interested in advertising should consult the *Standard Directory of Advertising Agencies* (entry 250) and *Standard Directory of Advertisers* (entry 249) for more detailed data. As for public relations information, *O'Dwyer's Directory of Corporate Communications* is the place to begin.

246.   O'Dwyer, Jack. **O'Dwyer's Directory of Public Relations Firms**. New York: J. R. O'Dwyer, 1969- . Annual. LC 83-10671. ISSN 0078-3374.

Public relations firms and public relations departments in advertising agencies are the major focuses of this important directory. Entries give addresses, telephone numbers, areas of public relations specialization, corporate officers and other personnel, and major accounts. An important feature is an index to firms with specialized skills in over a dozen categories, such as agri-business, political campaigns, health, home furnishings, and the like. Also included is an index to firms by location in the U.S. and to those with foreign offices.

247.   Roberts, Steven, and Tony Hay. **International Directory of Telecommunications: Market Trends, Companies, Statistics, and Personnel**. 2d ed. London: Longman, 1986. 345p. (Companion for Industry). LC 86-5438. ISBN 0-582-90207-x.

Mobile telecommunications equipment, electronic mail, electronic document transfer, and data communications are just a few of the many services and goods described in this British publication whose greatest strength is its coverage of telecommunications governmental agencies, manufacturers, and service providers throughout the world. The nations of the world have been divided into regional groupings, each of which is covered in separate chapters that include tables of statistics, narrative descriptions of telecommunications in the regions, and directories. Directories (the bulk of each chapter) alphabetically arrange entries for operators; government commissions; equipment manufacturers, services, and vendors; broadcasters; telecommunications project designers; regional holding companies; regulatory agencies; and trade associations. Entries provide addresses, telephone numbers, and descriptions of each organization, including activities, operating territory, products, personnel, trade names, publications, and the like. Although Great Britain and Europe receive the most coverage, all countries are covered to some degree. Indexes for companies and organizations, product areas, registered trade names, and personnel provide access.

248.   Sapolsky, Barry S., and Deborah Wool. **Directory of Communication Research Centers in U.S. Universities, 1984-1985**. Tallahassee, FL: Communication Research Center, College of Communications, Florida State University, 1985. 48p. OCLC 13039513.

During the 1983-1984 academic year, Sapolsky and Wool conducted a mail survey of communication research centers and ultimately compiled information on about 40 centers that responded fully or partially. Although now aged a few years, the information provides a relatively comprehensive overview of U.S. centers, institutions, and laboratories devoted to mass communication research, in such areas as public opinion, audience reaction, media content or effects, medical communication, censorship, televison and film analysis, interactive cablecasting, and the like. Brief profiles give addresses, telephone numbers, personnel, years in operation, funding sources, publications, short- and long-term goals, and the like. Information is spotty and ultimately dependent on survey responses.

Information on other mass communication research centers and resources is contained in Donald G. Godfrey's *A Directory of Broadcast Archives* (Washington, DC: Broadcast Education Association, 1983), which includes data for 70 radio and television archives in universities, institutions, museums, and private or commercial associations in the United States and Canada.

249.   **Standard Directory of Advertisers**. Wilmette, IL: National Register Publishing, 1915- . Annual, with 5/year cumulative supplements. LC 15-21147. ISSN 0081-4229.

Over 25,000 companies that allocate over $75,000 annually for national or regional advertising are profiled in separate classified (published in April) and geographically arranged (published in May) editions of this long-published work. The classified edition arranges company data (such as addresses, telephone numbers, personnel, type of business, subsidiaries, sales figures, and trade names) under 51 different product classifications. Advertising professionals and researchers should note that the names of advertising firms used by companies are listed along with the types of media used and billing figures by media. This is a companion to the *Standard Directory of Advertising Agencies* (entry 250).

250. **Standard Directory of Advertising Agencies**. Wilmette, IL: National Register Publishing 1964- . Annual, with 3/year cumulative updates. LC 88-649207. ISSN 0085-6614.

This companion to the *Standard Directory of Advertisers* (entry 249) is known throughout the advertising profession as the "Agency Red Book." (Its cover is red.) The directory provides invaluable information on national and regional advertising agencies in the United States. Alphabetically arranged entries — updated in February, June, and October — note addresses, personnel, national agency affiliations, association memberships, approximate annual billings, gross billings by media types, and major accounts. About one-quarter of each annual volume contains a "Who's Where in Advertising," locating and providing professional titles and affiliations of individuals cited in the main directory. A monthly looseleaf service, *Agency News* (Wilmette, IL: National Register Publishing, 1977-), supplements the annual and triennial listings.

251. **Standard Rate and Data Service**. Wilmette, IL: Standard Rate and Data Service, 1919- .

Publications of the *Standard Rate and Data Service*, frequently cited as *SRDS*, include:

251.1. **Business Publication Rates & Data**. Wilmette, IL: SRDS, 1919- . Monthly. ISSN 0038-948x.

251.2. **Consumer Magazine and Agri-Media Rates and Data**. Wilmette, IL: SRDS, 1919- . Monthly. ISSN 0038-9595.

251.3. **Direct Mail List**. Wilmette, IL: SRDS, 1967- . Bimonthly. ISSN 0038-9463.

251.4. **Newspaper Rates & Data**. Wilmette, IL: SRDS, 1919- . Monthly. ISSN 0038-9544.

251.5. **Print Media & Production Rates & Data**. Wilmette, IL: SRDS, 1968- . Quarterly. ISSN 0038-9455.

251.6. **Spot Radio Rates & Data**. Wilmette, IL: SRDS, 1929- . Monthly. ISSN 0038-9560.

251.7. **Spot Television Rates & Data**. Wilmette, IL: SRDS, 1947- . Monthly. ISSN 0038-9552.

These telephone-book-like publications feature standard, authoritative, and timely information on media advertising rates and marketing rankings. Although amounts of specific information in particular rate tables and specifications vary (since data are provided by different sources), all entries generally identify general rates and specifications, contacts, key personnel, advertising representatives, and the like. In addition, issues feature market maps and relevant statistics. For several reasons, researchers will find that using *SRDS* publications is challenging and often difficult to interpret. Foremost is the absence of a description of any sort about using or analyzing *SRDS*'s various rate tables and specifications. The publishers assume that users begin with some basic knowledge. In addition, the very act of locating *SRDS* publications is typically frustrating because of the similar titles in the series. Researchers must find the correct index and/or classification table before proceeding. Nonetheless, *SRDS* publications are the standards in the field. Publication frequency ensures the best possible accuracy on rates and data. Similar coverage of international advertising and advertisers is offered by *International Media Guides* (South Norwalk, CT: International Media Enterprises, 1972-).

252. **Telecom Factbook**. Washington, DC: Television Digest (Warren Publishing), 1985-1987. Annual. LC 84-7078. ISSN 0749-5668.

Television Digest, known for its newsletters and guides in telecommunication (entry 254), also published this directory whose primary asset was comprehensive coverage of the worldwide telecommunication industry. Geographically arranged entries gave addresses, telephone numbers, chief officials, and brief descriptions of services in separate sections for carriers; satellite systems; electronic mail and video operators and services; manufacturers and suppliers; international and domestic national, regional, state, and local governmental departments and agencies; and trade and professional associations. A final section was devoted to an annual ranking, with statistics, of the top 125 telecommunications services.

Another similar directory, *Telecommunications Systems and Services Directory: An International Descriptive Guide to Telecommunications, Systems, and Services*, 2d ed. (Detroit, MI: Gale, 1983) and its supplements, offer information supplied by the organizations themselves. More important are the numerous directories of specialized telecommunications services that are also available. Phillips Publishing produces several directories that offer similar information for different telecommunication industries. The annual *Satellite Directory* (Bethesda, MD: Phillips Publishing, 1979-) focuses on U.S. manufacturers and distributors of satellite receivers, system operators, consultants, regulatory agencies, communication attorneys, and the like. It also features an extensive list of ships and offshore facilities in the INMART system. *The Long-Distance Telephone Sourcebook: A Guide to Alternative Products and Services* (Bethesda, MD: Phillips Publishing, 1985) gives similar kinds of information for long-distance telephone products, services, and systems. *Videotex Marketplace* (Bethesda, MD: Phillips Publishing, 1984) focuses on equipment, suppliers, and services of the North American videotex industry, including a glossary of videotex terms. *The Cellular Marketplace* (Bethesda, MD: Phillips Publishing, 1984) is a guide to the radio telephone industry. Other useful directories include the annual *International Satellite Directory: The Complete Guide to the International Satellite Industry* (Corte Madera, CA: Design Publishers, 1986-), which includes informative maps indicating the names, positions, and owners/operators of satellites; and the annual *Telecommunications Sourcebook* (Washington, DC: North American Telecommunications Association, 1981-), which describes U.S. and international manufacturers or contractors that sell, install, or maintain communication systems. Emphasis is on U.S. and Canadian companies. *How to Find Information about Companies in the Telecommunications, Data Processing, and Office Automation Industries* (Washington, DC: Washington Researchers Publishing, 1987) concentrates on government offices and agencies, associations, publications, and other sources; equipment or product manufacturers or suppliers are excluded. Tom Kieffer and Terry Hansen's *Get Connected: A Guide to Telecommunications* (Culver City, CA: Ashton-Tate, 1984) is a beginners' handbook to telecommunications and directory of relevant services.

253. **Telephony's Directory & Buyers' Guide for the Telecommunications Industry.** Chicago, IL: Intertec Publishing, 1895- . Annual. ISSN 1096-139x.

Although its current title suggests comprehensive coverage, this classic annual focuses exclusively on the telephone industry, giving information for equipment and supply manufacturers and distributors as well as related support services. Sections list firms that lease or sell equipment, independent operating systems, Bell companies, government agencies, trade associations, and the like. Previously published as *Telephony's Directory of the Telephone Industry* and *Telephony's Directory of Telephone Exchanges*, this is a basic tool for current and historical information about the U.S. telephone industry.

254. **Television and Cable Factbook.** Washington, DC: Television Digest, 1944- . Annual (in 2 vols.). LC 83-647864. ISSN 0732-8648.

Two separate volumes, *Stations* and *Cable and Services*, provide current and comprehensive information on commercial television and cable television stations in the U.S. (mainly) as well as in U.S. Territories (Guam, Virgin Islands, the Marianas, Puerto Rico), Canada, and Cuba (selectively). The geographically arranged *Stations* volume subarranges stations by call letters, giving addresses, telephone numbers, network affiliations, licensees, technical facilities, news services, Arbitron rankings, and other data. Data for Cuba and the Marianas is excluded here. No similar source provides more comprehensive information. It also includes briefer data for public and educational television stations; lists of TV applications, construction permits, low-power stations, and foreign language programming on commercial stations, among others; and an international directory of television stations. A "Yellow Pages Buyer Guide" lists services, distributors, and manufacturers. The *Cable and Services* volume is an important source of information on cable systems. Annual volumes are supplemented by *Weekly Television Action Update* (Washington, DC: Television Digest, 1964-).

255. Thorpe, Frances. **International Directory of Film and TV Documentation Centres.** 3d ed. Chicago, IL: St. James Press, 1988. 140p. ISBN 0-912289-29-5.

Originally published in 1976 as the *FIAF* (Federation Internationale des Archives du Film) *Directory of Film and TV Documentation Sources*, the directory offers geographically arranged information for over 100 worldwide film and television institutions, archives, museums, and libraries. Entries provide addresses and descriptions of hours, reproduction services, computer accessibility, and major holdings and special collections. Emphasis is on U.S. and European collections. A subject index to the collections assists access. Researchers interested in locating U.S. and Canadian broadcast centers will also find helpful Donald G. Godfrey's *A Directory of Broadcast Archives* (Washington, DC: Broadcast Education Association, 1983). Equally interesting is Bonnie G. Rowan's *Scholar's Guide to Washington D.C. Film and Video Collections* (Washington, DC: Smithsonian Institution Press, 1980), although it is now somewhat out of date. Elizabeth Oliver's *Researchers Guide to British Film & Television Collections*, 2d ed. (London: British Universities Film & Video Council, 1985) profiles similar collections in Britain.

256. **TV Station & Cable Ownership Directory.** Washington, DC: Warren Publishing, 1990- . 2/year. ISSN 1050-3633.

Other television broadcast directories cited in this guide offer little, if any, detailed information on cable and television station ownership. This important new directory, published in March and September by the publisher of *Television and Cable Factbook* (entry 254) and other newsletters, alphabetically lists both individual and corporate owners of commercial television stations, educational television stations, cable systems, low-power television stations, and others. Entries give basic information (addresses, telephone numbers, ownership and percentages of ownership, officers and representatives, and Arbitron Market TV Households data) and list television, cable, radio, newspaper, and other publications owned. Entries for cable systems list cable communities and total basic subscribers. Lists of recent cable and television systems and stations sold are also featured. A useful "Ownership Category Index" rearranges owners cited in the main listing by specific media types. Although somewhat similar information is provided in *The Knowledge Industry Publications 200* (entry 242), *TV Station & Cable Ownership Directory* covers television and cable ownership in greater detail than any other source now available.

257. Weiner, Richard. **Professional's Guide to Public Relations Services**. 6th ed. New York: American Management Association, 1988. 483p. LC 87-47829. ISBN 0-8144-5932-3.

This is not a directory of public relations agencies; rather, it lists goods and services that public relations services often need to use. Weiner arranges entries for 1,500 companies such as clipping bureaus, image consultants, photographers, animal and prop suppliers, speakers bureaus, skywriters, celebrity escorts, and the like, in 35 categories. Descriptions of the various services range from one line to several pages. Weiner firmly declares that only firms that he would personally recommend are included and he clearly makes recommendations. In addition, Weiner provides a lengthy section on public relations research materials, identifying specific reference works, research collections, databases, and research services. This guide is one of the most useful public relations resources.

A similar but more specialized guide of practical interest and value to public relations professionals is Mitchell P. Davis's *Directory of Experts, Authorities, & Spokespersons: The Talk Show Directory*, 6th ed. (Washington, DC: Broadcast Interview Source, 1989). This identifies hundreds of contacts for associations, corporations, public interest groups, and individuals that have expressed interest in providing speakers or appearing as "experts" on radio and television talk shows.

258. **Working Press of the Nation**. Burlington, IA: National Research Bureau, 1947- . Annual (in 5 vols). LC 46-7041. ISSN 0084-1323.

With the exceptions of *Editor and Publisher International Yearbook* (entry 231) and *Broadcasting Yearbook* (entry 223), no other media guide is as basic or as important as the volumes that comprise this valuable reference source. Over the years it has increased from a single volume to its present five (in 1976), including volume 1, *Newspaper Directory*; volume 2, *Magazine Directory*; volume 3, *TV and Radio Directory*; volume 4, *Feature Writer and Photographer Directory*; and volume 5, *Internal Publications Directory*. Volume 1 lists newspapers, feature syndicates, and news and photo services. A subject index to editorial personnel and an index of newspapers with TV supplements are also useful features. Volumes 2 and 3 profile thousands of U.S. magazines and stations. Writers and photographers are indexed by subject specializations in volume 4. Of special interest is the list of both internal and external publications of almost 3,000 U.S. corporations, associations, clubs, agencies, and other groups in volume 5.

259. **World Radio TV Handbook**. New York: Billboard Publications, 1947- . Annual. LC 48-20385. ISSN 0144-7750.

This classic annual is the most authoritative and comprehensive cumulation of information on worldwide radio broadcasting. Arranged by continents, entries identify long-, medium-, and short-wave broadcasts and regional programs and describe foreign language broadcasts. In addition, the annual features forecast tables for megahertz broadcast bands, articles about prospective solar activity, TV country codes, and the like. Since this type of data is quickly dated, users should be sure to obtain the latest edition of the handbook.

7
Online and CD ROM Databases

Addresses of database service suppliers and vendors are listed in the appendix.

Bibliographic Files

260. **ABI/Inform**. UMI/Data Courier. Online services: American Library Association; BRS; Dialcom; DIALOG; Executive Telecom Systems; Knowledge Index; Mead Data Central; Orbit Search Services; Tech Data. Online coverage: Varies (1970- on BRS). Update frequency: Varies (weekly on American Library Association, Dialcom, DIALOG, Knowledge Index). CD ROM version: *ABI/INFORM ONDISC* (UMI/Data Courier). CD ROM coverage: 1984- . Update frequency: Monthly.

One of the more important databases for research in mass and organizational communication, ABI/INFORM offers coverage superior to that provided by *Business Periodicals Index* (entry 160). Indexing about 800 scholarly and trade journals, it is particularly valuable for analysis of telecommunication literature. Access through the CD ROM version is most convenient. Training or practice online versions are available on BRS and DIALOG services.

261. **Advertising & Marketing Intelligence Services Abstracts**. New York Times Company. Online service: Mead Data Central. Online coverage: 1979- . Update frequency: Daily.

This indexes and abstracts features on the advertising industry, new products, sales, consumer behavior, and the like that appear in about 60 major English-language and international journals, including *Advertising Age* (entry 330), *Journal of Advertising* (entry 367), and *Journal of Advertising Research* (entry 368).

262. **America: History and Life** (entry 153). Online services: DIALOG; Knowledge Index. Online coverage: 1964- . Update frequency: Quarterly.

Online cumulation of the printed version's different sections greatly facilitates access. Use of the printed version, however, is usually adequate for undergraduate research needs.

263. **Applied Science & Technology Index** (entry 154). Online service: WILSONLINE. Online coverage: October 1983- . Update frequency: Twice weekly. CD ROM version: *Applied Science & Technology Index* (Wilsondisc). CD ROM coverage: 1983- . Update frequency: Quarterly.

264. **Arts & Humanities Search** (entry 155). Online services: BRS; DIALOG. Online coverage: 1980- . Update frequency: Varies (weekly on DIALOG).

Searching truncated keywords in the online version permits superior access to the entries in the "Permuterm" section of this index. Use of the printed version, however, is usually adequate for undergraduate research needs. Training or practice online versions are available on both BRS and DIALOG services.

265. **Bibliographic Index** (entry 156). Online service: WILSONLINE. Online coverage: November 1984- . Update frequency: Twice weekly.

266. **Biography Index** (entry 157). Online service: WILSONLINE. Online coverage: August 1984- . Update frequency: Twice weekly. CD ROM version: *Biography Index* (Wilsondisc). CD ROM coverage: 1984- . Update frequency: Quarterly.

267. **Biography Master Index** (entry 192). Online service; DIALOG. Online coverage: Current. Update frequency: Annual.

This cumulates the *Biography and Genealogy Master Index*, including all editions, cumulations, and updates. Despite that updating is annual and that File 287 contains biographees with surnames beginning A-L and File 288 contains M-Z (meaning that some names must be searched in both files), the online version offers superior access to biographical references in over 700 different editions of sources. All extensive biographical research in any field should start with an online search in this file.

268. **Book Review Digest** (entry 158). Online service: WILSONLINE. Online coverage: January 1983- . Update frequency: Twice weekly. CD ROM version: *Book Review Digest* (Wilsondisc). CD ROM coverage: 1983- . Update frequency: Quarterly.

269. **Book Review Index** (entry 159). Online service: DIALOG. Online coverage: 1969- . Update frequency: 3/year.

Cumulative indexing makes the online version more attractive than the printed version.

270. **Business Periodicals Index** (entry 160). Online service: WILSONLINE. Online coverage: June 1982- . Update frequency: Twice weekly. CD ROM version: *Business Periodicals Index* (Wilsondisc). CD ROM coverage: 1982- . Update frequency: Quarterly.

271. **CIS/Index** (entry 162). Online service: DIALOG. Online coverage: 1970- . Update frequency: Monthly. CD ROM version: *Congressional Masterfile 2* (Congressional Information Service). CD ROM coverage: 1970- . Update frequency: Quarterly.

CIS/Index online and *Congressional Masterfile 2* CD ROM versions contain records from 1970 to the present only. In addition to these files, CIS also publishes a separate *Congressional Masterfile* CD ROM that contains retrospective files for the period 1789-1969. This CD ROM corresponds to several CIS printed indexes, including *CIS Unpublished U.S. Senate Committee Hearings Index (1823-1964)* (Bethesda, MD: CIS, 1986); *CIS U.S. Congressional Committee Hearings Index (1833-1969)* (Bethesda, MD: CIS, 1981); *CIS U.S. Congressional Committee Prints Index (1833-1969)* (Washington, DC: CIS, 1980); and *CIS U.S. Serial Set Index (1789-1969)* (Washington, DC: CIS, 1975).

272. **Compendex Plus** (entry 167). Online services: BRS; DIALOG; Knowledge Index; Orbit Search Service; Tech Data. Online coverage: Varies (from 1970 on DIALOG, Orbit). Update frequency: Monthly. CD ROM version: *Compendex Plus CD ROM* (Engineering Information Inc.). CD ROM coverage: 1970- . Update frequency: Monthly.

Where available, the CD ROM version offers very convenient access. Training or practice online versions are available on both BRS and DIALOG services.

273. **Current Contents Search** (entry 164). Online services: BRS; DIALOG. Online coverage: Current 6 months. Update frequency: Weekly.

274.   **Dissertation Abstracts Online** (entry 166). Online services: BRS; DIALOG; Knowledge Index; Tech Data. Online coverage: 1861- . Update frequency: Monthly. CD ROM version: *Dissertation Abstracts ONDISC* (University Microfilms International). CD ROM coverage: 1861- . Update frequency: Quarterly.

Both the online and CD ROM versions cumulate *Dissertation Abstracts International, American Doctoral Dissertations, Comprehensive Dissertation Index*, and *Masters Abstracts* (on BRS and DIALOG). Where available, the CD ROM version offers very convenient access.

275.   **Dow Jones Text-Search Services**. Dow Jones. Online service: Dow Jones News/Retrieval. Online coverage: 1979- . Update frequency: Daily.

In addition to other services, this file provides daily indexing of all editions of the *Wall Street Journal* from 1984 to the present; see entry 190 for other indexing of the *Wall Street Journal*.

276.   **ERIC** (entry 165). Online services: BRS; DIALOG; Knowledge Index. Online coverage: 1966- . Update frequency: Monthly. CD ROM version: *ERIC* (Silver Platter Information Services). CD ROM coverage: 1966- . Update frequency: Quarterly.

Both the online and CD ROM versions cumulate *Current Index to Journals in Education* and *Resources in Education*. Access on CD ROM is very convenient, despite the fact that several different discs contain the database. A training or practice online version is available on the DIALOG service.

277.   **Essay and General Literature Index** (entry 168). Online service: WILSONLINE. Online coverage: January 1985- . Update frequency: Twice weekly. CD ROM version: *Essay and General Literature Index* (Wilsondisc). CD ROM coverage: 1985- . Update frequency: Quarterly.

278.   **General Science Index** (entry 170). Online service: WILSONLINE. Online coverage: May 1984- . Update frequency: Twice weekly. CD ROM version: *General Science Index* (Wilsondisc). CD ROM coverage: 1984- . Update frequency: Quarterly.

279.   **GPO Monthly Catalog** (entry 179). Online services: BRS; DIALOG; Tech Data; WILSONLINE. Online coverage: July 1976- . Update frequency: Monthly. CD ROM versions: *Government Documents Catalog Service* (Autographics, Inc.); *Government Publications and Periodicals* (Wilsondisc); *Government Publications Index* (Information Access Company, Inc.); *GPO on Silver Platter* (Silver Platter Information Services). CD ROM coverage: 1976- . Update frequency: Varies (monthly on Information Access version).

Any of the CD ROM versions offers convenient access.

280.   **Humanities Index** (entry 171). Online service: WILSONLINE. Online coverage: February 1984- . Update frequency: Twice weekly. CD ROM version: *Humanities Index* (Wilsondisc). CD ROM coverage: 1984- . Update frequency: Quarterly.

281.   **Index to Legal Periodicals** (entry 172). Online service: WILSONLINE. Online coverage: August 1981- . Update frequency: Twice weekly. CD ROM version: *Index to Legal Periodicals* (Wilsondisc). CD ROM coverage: 1981- . Update frequency: Quarterly.

282.   **Linguistics and Language Behavior Abstracts (LLBA)** (entry 175). Online services: BRS; DIALOG. Online coverage: 1973- . Update frequency: Quarterly.

Despite its complexity, the printed version is usually adequate for undergraduate research needs. The *MLA Bibliography* on CD ROM (entry 283) somewhat duplicates *LLBA*'s coverage in the areas of language acquisition, discourse, and the like. It is cost effective to consult the MLA's CD ROM version (when it is available) before resorting to (or as a prelude to) *LLBA* online.

283. MLA Bibliography (entry 178). Online services: DIALOG; Knowledge Index; WILSONLINE. Online coverage: 1964- . Update frequency: 9/year. CD ROM version: *MLA International Bibliography* (Wilsondisc). CD ROM coverage: 1981- . Update frequency: Quarterly.

Online access makes this very complex, intimidating, and unwieldy resource quite manageable. The CD ROM version, however, makes using it "child's play." CD ROM coverage from 1981 to the present is adequate for most undergraduate research needs. The browse feature is particularly convenient for quick references on such ubiquitous topics as speech, rhetoric, language, communication theory, and interpersonal communication. Additional access by journal titles and names of organizations is also attractive.

284. Newsearch. Information Access Company. Online services: BRS; DIALOG; Knowledge Index. Online coverage: Current month. Update frequency: Daily.

Among other services, *Newsearch* provides daily indexing of major newspapers, including the *New York Times* and the *Wall Street Journal*; see entries 180 and 190 for other indexes of these titles.

285. PAIS International (entry 181). Online services: BRS; DIALOG; Knowledge Index; Tech Data. Online coverage: 1972- . Update frequency: Monthly. CD ROM version: *PAIS on CD ROM* (PAIS). CD ROM coverage: 1972- . Update frequency: Quarterly.

Both online and CD ROM versions cumulate *PAIS Bulletin* and *PAIS Foreign Language Index.*

286. Philosopher's Index (entry 182). Online services: DIALOG; Knowledge Index. Online coverage: 1940- . Update frequency: Quarterly.

Access to the printed version is generally adequate for most undergraduate research needs. Because its coverage of communication topics (in rhetoric, communication theory, and the like) is duplicated to some degree in CD ROM versions of other files, such as *MLA Bibliography* (entry 283) and *Humanities Index* (entry 280), the online version of the *Philosopher's Index* should be used mainly as a last resort.

287. PsychInfo (entry 183). Online services: BRS; DIALOG; Knowledge Index. Online coverage: 1967- . Update frequency: Monthly. CD ROM version: *PsychLit* (Silver Platter Information Services). CD ROM coverage: 1974- . Update frequency: Quarterly.

Access to the CD ROM version is very convenient, despite the fact that the file is contained on several different discs.

288. Readers' Guide to Periodical Literature (entry 184). Online service: WILSONLINE. Online coverage: January 1983- . Update frequency: Twice weekly. CD ROM version: *Readers' Guide to Periodical Literature* (Wilsondisc). CD ROM coverage: 1983- . Update frequency: Quarterly.

289.   **Social Sciences Index** (entry 186). Online service: WILSONLINE. Online coverage: February 1984- . Update frequency: Twice weekly. CD ROM version: *Social Sciences Index* (Wilsondisc). CD ROM coverage: 1984- . Update frequency: Quarterly.

290.   **Social SciSearch** (entry 185). Online services: BRS; DIALOG. Online coverage: 1972- . Update frequency: Twice monthly. CD ROM version: *Social Sciences Citation Index Compact Disc Edition* (Institute for Scientific Information). CD ROM coverage: 1986- . Update frequency: Quarterly.

Searching truncated keywords in the online version permits superior access to the entries in the "Permuterm" section of this index. Use of the printed version, however, is usually adequate for undergraduate research needs. Training or practice online versions are available on both BRS and DIALOG services.

291.   **Sociological Abstracts** (entry 187). Online services: BRS; DIALOG; Knowledge Index. Online coverage: 1963- . Update frequency: 5/year. CD ROM version: *Sociofile* (Silver Platter Information Services). CD ROM coverage: 1974- . Update frequency: 3/year.

The CD ROM version is preferable to all others.

Full-Text Files

292.   **Advertising Age** (entry 330). Online service: Mead Data Central. Online coverage: 1986- . Update frequency: Weekly.

293.   **Audio Week**. Washington, DC: Warren Publishing, 1989- . Online services: DIALOG; NewsNet. Online coverage: 1989- . Update frequency: Varies (daily on DIALOG).

Audio Week corresponds to a newsletter that features professional information about the consumer electronics industry. Emphasis is on legal activities.

294.   **Common Carrier Week**. Washington, DC: Warren Publishing, 1984- . Online services: DIALOG; NewsNet. Online coverage: Varies (from 1984 on NewsNet). Update frequency: Varies (daily on DIALOG).

This offers the full-text of a newsletter that features business and legal information on the telephone industry.

295.   **Communications Daily**. Washington, DC: Warren Publishing, 1981- . Online services: DIALOG; Mead Data Central; NewsNet. Online coverage: Varies (from 1982 on NewsNet). Update frequency: Daily.

Communications Daily is among the most important and useful newsletters for information about the communication industries in the broadest sense. It features brief notices about business and legal activities relevant to the telephone, broadcasting, cable, video, and telecommunications industries.

296.   **Communications Week**. Manhasset, NY: CPM Publications, 1984- . Online service: DataTimes. Online coverage: 1988- . Update frequency: Weekly.

This includes the full-text of a weekly newspaper that features current trade and legal news relevant to the telecommunication industry in general.

297. **Consumer Electronics**. New York: International Thomson Retail Press, 1972- . Online services: DIALOG; NewsNet. Online coverage: Varies (from 1982 on NewsNet). Update frequency: Varies (daily on DIALOG).

Consumer Electronics contains the full-text of a newsletter that focuses on new consumer electronics product research and development, marketing, and industry information.

298. **Data Broadcasting Report**. Binghamton, NY: Waters Information Services, 1985- . Online service: NewsNet. Online coverage: 1988- . Update frequency: Monthly.

Current news features on research and development in radio and television broadcasting appear in this newsletter.

299. **Data Communications**. New York: McGraw-Hill, 1974- . Online services: DIALOG; Dow Jones News/Retrieval; Mead Data Central. Online coverage: Varies (from 1982 on Mead Data Central). Update frequency: Monthly.

Data Communications corresponds to a newsletter that publishes current information relevant to computer and electronic data transmission.

300. **Electronic Media** (entry 340). Online service: Mead Data Central. Online coverage: 1988- . Update frequency: Weekly.

301. **Enhanced Services Outlook**. Alexandria, VA: Capitol Publications, Telecom Publishing Group, 1988- . Online services: DIALOG; NewsNet. Online coverage: 1988- . Update frequency: Varies (daily on DIALOG).

News features on current research and development activities of the Bell Operating Companies as well as notices of relevant regulatory actions appear in this newsletter.

302. **FCC Daily Digest**. Washington, DC: Warren Publishing, 1985- . Online service: NewsNet. Online coverage: 1985- . Update frequency: Daily.

FCC Daily Digest publishes the official press releases and other notices of FCC actions that affect the communication industry.

303. **FCC Week**. Alexandria, VA: Telecom Publishing Group, 1981- . Online services: DIALOG; NewsNet. Online coverage: Varies (from 1985 on NewsNet). Update frequency: Varies (daily on DIALOG).

This corresponds to a weekly newsletter that relates and comments on the current regulatory activities of the FCC.

304. **Hollywood Hotline**. Eliot Stein. Online services: CompuServe; General Electric Information Services; Networking and World Information, Inc.; NewsNet; Quantum Computer Services; Western Union Telegraph Company. Online coverage: March 1983- . Update frequency: Daily.

Hollywood Hotline provides access to trade news of the motion picture, music, television, and related entertainment industries.

305. **Information Week**. Manhasset, NY: CPM Publications, 1979- . Online service: DataTimes. Online coverage: 1988- . Update frequency: Weekly.

This corresponds to a newsletter that includes current news about the communication and computer industries.

306. **Lexis**. Mead Data Central. Online service: Mead Data Central. Online coverage: Varies. Update frequency: Varies.

Lexis offers superior bibliographic and full-text access to U.S. statutes, regulations, and court decisions, conveniently cumulating countless legal reference works. The system includes a database that specifically focuses on communication law. *Lexis* is typically available only in law libraries and even then, by contractual agreement, it is usually restricted to legal professionals and law students. West Publishing offers a rival service in *Westlaw* (entry 321).

307. **Network World**. Framingham, MA: CW Communications, 1983- . Online service: Mead Data Central. Online coverage: 1986- . Update frequency: Weekly.

This corresponds to a newsletter that contains current information on issues and developments in the data communication industries.

308. **New York Times** (entry 180). Online service: Mead Data Central. Online coverage: June 1980- . Update frequency: Daily.

This offers daily indexing of the *New York Times* (daily editions).

309. **PR Hi-Tech Alert**. Michael Naver. Online service: NewsNet. Online coverage: 1984- . Update frequency: Twice a month.

PR Hi-Tech Alert online newsletter highlights current public relations industry activities employing cable, broadcasting, telecommunication, computer, and similar technologies.

310. **PR Newswire**. PR Newswire, National Press Communications Service. Online services: DIALOG; Dow Jones News/Retrieval; Knowledge Index; Mead Data Central; NewsNet; VU/TEXT. Online coverage: Varies (from 1980 on Mead Data Central). Update frequency: Daily.

This provides the full-text of press releases issued by public relations agencies as well as by other groups.

311. **Public Broadcasting Report**. Washington, DC: Warren Publishing, 1978- . Online services: DIALOG; NewsNet. Online coverage: Varies (from 1982 on NewsNet). Update frequency: Varies (daily on DIALOG).

Public Broadcasting Report corresponds to a newsletter that emphasizes legal developments affecting public radio and television.

312. **Public Relations Journal** (entry 406). Online service: Mead Data Central. Online coverage: 1980- . Update frequency: Monthly.

313. **Satellite News**. Potomac, MD: Phillips Publishing, 1978- . Online services: DIALOG; NewsNet. Online coverage: Varies (from 1982 on NewsNet). Update frequency: Varies (daily on DIALOG).

Current trade news related to the satellite industry appears here.

314. **Satellite Week**. Washington, DC: Warren Publishing, 1979- . Online services: DIALOG; NewsNet. Online coverage: Varies (from 1981 on NewsNet). Update frequency: Varies (daily on DIALOG).

This corresponds to a newsletter that relates activities and developments in the satellite industry. Emphasis is on legal issues affecting the use of outer space.

315. **Telecommunications Alert**. New York: Management Telecommunications Publishing, 1983- . Online service: NewsNet. Online coverage: 1987- . Update frequency: Monthly.

Telecommunications Alert digests news features on telecommunications topics appearing in about 200 other trade newsletters, such as *Communications Daily* (entry 295).

316. **Telecommunications Reports**. Washington, DC: Business Research Publications, 1934- . Online service: NewsNet. Online coverage: 1985- . Update frequency: Weekly.

Emphasis in *Telecommunications Reports*, one of the oldest and most respected trade newsletters, is largely on the FCC and regulation of telecommunication.

317. **Telephone News**. Potomac, MD: Phillips Publishing, 1980- . Online services: DIALOG; NewsNet. Online coverage: Varies (from 1982 on NewsNet). Update frequency: Varies (daily on DIALOG).

This corresponds to a newsletter that focuses specifically on the telephone industry.

318. **Television Digest**. Washington, DC: Warren Publishing, 1945- . Online services: DIALOG; NewsNet. Online coverage: Varies (from 1982 on NewsNet). Update frequency: Varies (daily on DIALOG).

Television Digest contains the full-text of a newsletter that focuses on activities in the cable and broadcast television industries. Emphasis is largely on legal developments and issues.

319. **The Times Newspapers** (entry 173). Online service: Profile Information. Online coverage: 1985- . Update frequency: Daily.

This provides daily indexing to the *Times* of London.

320. **Video Week**. Washington, DC: Warren Publishing, 1980- . Online services: DIALOG; NewsNet. Online coverage: Varies (from 1982 on NewsNet). Update frequency: Varies (daily on DIALOG).

Video Week corresponds to a newsletter that provides current information on the video industry.

321. **Westlaw**. West Publishing. Online service: West Publishing. Online coverage: Varies. Update frequency: Varies.

Similar to *Lexis* (entry 306), *Westlaw* provides comprehensive bibliographic and full-text access to U.S. statutory, regulatory, and case law. The system includes a database that specifically covers communications law. Access is typically limited to law libraries.

Numeric and Data Files

322. **Arbitron Radio and Arbitron TV**. Arbitron Ratings Company. Online services: Interactive Market Systems; Management Science Associates; Telmar Group. Online coverage: Current. Update frequency: Annually.

This service provides categorized audience measurement data for television and radio markets.

323. **Baseline**. Baseline, Inc. Online service: Baseline, Inc. Online coverage: 1900- . Update frequency: Irregular (Newsline file is updated daily).

Baseline's several files provide encyclopedic information on U.S. film, theater, television, and other entertainment industries, including biographical and directory information about personalities and other media professionals, market data on products, descriptions and detailed data for programming, and current industry news.

324. **Billboard Information Network**. Billboard Information Network. Online service: Billboard Information Network. Online coverage: Most recent 3 weeks. Update frequency: Daily.

Directory information for the music, recording, and video industries as well as marketing, sales, and rental data for products are included here.

325. **CODE (Cable Online Data Exchange)**. Nielsen Home Video Index. Online service: A. C. Nielsen. Online coverage: Current. Update frequency: Monthly.

CODE provides directory information and categorized numerical data for U.S. cable television systems.

326. **Nielsen Station Index**. Nielsen Media Research. Online services: Management Science Associates; Market Science Associates; Telmar Group. Online coverage: 1975- . Update frequency: Irregular.

This index provides categorized numeric data on household television viewing habits in selected U.S. metropolitan markets.

327. **Nielsen Television Index**. Nielsen Media Research. Online service: Interactive Market Systems. Online coverage: 1970- . Update frequency: Quarterly.

Nielsen Television Index provides categorized numeric data for national television audience viewing habits.

328. **Roper Reports**. The Roper Organization. Online service: Interactive Market Systems. Online coverage: 1981- . Update frequency: 10/year.

Roper Reports provides data from opinion poll responses on advertising, communication, media, social issues, and the like.

329. **Study of Media and Markets**. Simmons Market Research Bureau, Inc. (entry 145). Online services: Interactive Market Systems; Management Science Associates; Market Science Associates; Telmar Group. Online coverage: Current. Update frequency: Annual. CD ROM version: *Study of Media and Markets* (Simmons Market Research Bureau). CD ROM coverage: Current. Update frequency: Annual.

This is the electronic version of a standard marketing information source. The service provides numerical media audience and market survey data for magazine, cable, television, radio, newspaper, outdoor advertising, and other media usage and consumption, with demographic and psychographic data for the market and individual users sampled.

8
Core Periodicals

330. **Advertising Age**. Chicago, IL: Crain Communications, 1930- . Weekly. ISSN 0001-8899.

A weekly newspaper of the advertising and marketing professions, *Advertising Age* features current news — and "last-minute news" — of interest to industry; commentaries and "viewpoints" by prominent professionals about these developments; and topical features and departments about new products, technologies, media programming, legal and managerial issues, and the like. In addition, each issue typically includes a special report on particular geographic or demographic markets or other current topics, such as sports marketing and business-to-business advertising. It regularly includes a list of top-performing U.S. advertising agencies. *Advertising Age* is indexed in *BPI* (entry 160) and *Topicator* (entry 189).

Other titles aimed at advertising industry professionals that are similar in scope to *Advertising Age* include *Adweek* (New York: ASM Communications, 1960-); *Adweek's Marketing Week* (New York: ASM Communications, 1986-); *Madison Avenue* (New York: Madison Avenue Magazine Corp., 1958-), monthly; and *Marketing & Media Decisions* (New York: Decision Publications, 1966-), 15/year.

331. **American Behavioral Scientist**. Newbury Park, CA: Sage, 1957- . 6/year. ISSN 0002-7642.

A major interdisciplinary journal of the social sciences, nearly every issue of *American Behavioral Scientist* contains features relevant to research in interpersonal and intercultural communication. Volume 32.2 (November-December 1988) focused on the theme "Communication, Technology, and Culture" and included 10 articles on topics like electronic mail and interactive computer searching. Volume 31.3 (January-February 1988), "Communication and Affects," included articles on nonverbal and interpersonal communication and persuasion. Volume 30.5 (May-June 1987), "The VCR Age," featured articles in intercultural and international communication as well as others on the social implications of new communication technologies. Features in other issues have reported on aging, loneliness, and communication; news media coverage of race relations; the measurement of black public opinion; and ritual in family conversation. *American Behavioral Scientist* is indexed in *AH&L* (entry 153), *BibI* (entry 156), *BRI* (entry 159), *CA* (entry 163), *CC* (entry 164), *CIJE* (entry 165), *PA* (entry 183), *SA* (entry 187), *SSCI* (entry 185), and *SSI* (entry 186).

332. **American Journalism**.Tuscaloosa, AL: University of Alabama, School of Communication, 1982- . Quarterly. ISSN 0882-1127.

The exclusive focus of *American Journalism*, which is sponsored by the American Journalism Historians Association, is the history of journalism. Issues typically feature three substantive scholarly studies of wide-ranging topics in the recent and remote history of American journalism as well as in journalism historiography. Despite *American Journalism*'s apparent leaning toward contributions about newspaper journalism and the printed media (only a few articles have discussed electronic media), a significant number of these features are also valuable for research on political communication and advertising. Articles have discussed the passage of the Communications Act of 1934, political party and press relations during the Federalist period, media ethics in the 1890s, nineteenth-century newspaper and magazine advertising, the religious origins of muckraking, and the role of local radio during World War II. Occasional essays on historiography have also appeared. In addition, bibliographical or library-related articles are published. Michael Murray's "Research in Broadcasting: An Overview of Major Resource Centers" (1 [Winter 1984]: 77-80) discussed several private collections. One issue in each volume publishes the winning essays in an annual competition sponsored by the association. Issues include three to four reviews of new books. *American Journalism* is indexed in *CA* (entry 163).

333. **American Political Science Review**. Washington, DC: American Political Science Association, 1906- . Quarterly. ISSN 0003-0554.
    One of the premier American political science journals, *American Political Science Review* has published numerous historically significant studies of political persuasion and propaganda, such as H. D. Lasswell's "Theory of Political Propaganda" (21 [1927]: 627-31) and H. W. Stoke's "Executive Leadership and the Growth of Propaganda" (35 [1941]: 490-500). Today the journal continues to publish research articles, notes, and review essays on topics of international interest in all historical periods. Particular attention has focused on public opinion and communication in political and social movements. Other studies have addressed leadership, power and influence, attitude change, political rhetoric, agenda-setting, and organizational structure. Review essays survey new publications. Issues usually include reviews of several new books on such topics as political theory; American, international, and comparative politics; and political economy. *American Political Science Review* is indexed in *BioI* (entry 157), *BRD* (entry 158), *BRI* (entry 159), *CC* (entry 164), *RG* (entry 184), and *SSI* (entry 186).
    Several other major political science journals are particularly valuable for research on political communication as well as on public policies related to communication and information in general. *American Politics Quarterly* (Newbury Park, CA: Sage, 1973-), a quarterly, offers coverage of topics in political and organizational behavior and communication, public opinion, information policy, and mass media law and regulation. Another major journal in the field of political science, *Journal of Politics* (Austin, TX: University of Texas Press, 1939-), a quarterly, has published a significant number of scholarly contributions in the areas of political communication, public opinion, and the mass media.

334. **American Speech: A Quarterly of Linguistic Usage**. Tuscaloosa, AL: University of Alabama Press, 1926- . Quarterly. ISSN 0003-1283.
    The focus here is on "English language in the Western Hemisphere" and the influences of other languages on English. *American Speech* publishes substantial research articles in semantics, etymology, and dialectology. A particular interest is African-American English. Features have appeared on the influence of scientific terminology on popular language, British and American influences on New Zealand's "media" English, Canadian dialects in the northern United States, scholarly oral and literary communication, and the influence of Chinese, Czech, and West Indian English on English in the United States. In addition, the regular feature "Among the New Words" offers definitions and historical illustrations of new words that can augment such standard sources as the *Oxford English Dictionary* and *Dictionary of American English*. Interestingly enough, this feature provides a very useful index to the influence of the mass media on the English language. Some recently discovered synonyms for *couch potato* include *couch tomato, couch rat, boob tuber*, and *telespud*, for example. Selections of three to five reviews of new publications are also published. The journal is most valuable as a source of research on language, speech, and rhetoric.

American Speech is indexed in *AH&L* (entry 153), *CC* (entry 164), *HI* (entry 171), and *LLBA* (entry 175).

335. **Argumentation**. Dordrecht, The Netherlands: Kluwer Academic Publishing Group, 1987- . Quarterly. ISSN 0920-427x.

Important for the study of rhetoric, *Argumentation* is an international journal that gathers "contributions from all schools of thought — ranging from literary rhetoric to linguistics, from history to logic, from theological argument to legal reasoning, from natural inference to the argumentative structures of science." Issues focus on specific themes or topics, such as "North American Perspectives on Teaching Critical Thinking," "Argumentation and Logic," and "Lying." Contributions are assembled by guest editors; features in all languages are published. Most issues include a useful bibliography on the focus topic. A few book reviews are occasionally published. *Argumentation* is unindexed at this time.

336. **Argumentation and Advocacy: The Journal of the American Forensic Association**. Columbia, MO: American Forensic Association, 1988- . Quarterly. ISSN 0002-8533.

Formerly *Journal of the American Forensic Association* (1964-1988), *Argumentation and Advocacy* publishes scholarly articles in "all areas of communication theory and practice relevant to forensics," which is defined as "an argumentative perspective on communication" that involves "the study of reason given by people as justification for acts, beliefs, attitudes, and values." These include "theoretical, critical, and pedagogical studies of argumentation, persuasion, discussion, debate, parliamentary deliberations, and forensic activities." Although of particular significance for the study of rhetoric, the journal's four to six well-documented articles per issue cover all areas of communication, including journalism and mass communication, language and linguistics, and interpersonal and organizational communication. Typical recent features include "The Planet of the Apes: The Fable of the Hundredth Monkey in Anti-Nuclear Discourse" and "Narrative *Montage*: Press Coverage of the Jean Harris Trial." Historical discussions and textual studies are also published. Occasional special issues are devoted to specific topics, such as "Narrative Studies of Argument" and "The State of the Counterplan." The journal usually includes a selection of four to six book reviews. *Argumentation and Advocacy* is indexed in *CIJE* (entry 165).

An alternative title, *Speaker and Gavel* (Huntington, WV: Marshall University, Department of Speech Communication, 1964-), a quarterly official publication of Delta Sigma Rho-Tau Kappa Alpha National Honorary Forensic Society, publishes brief features on topics related to debate and forensics.

337. **ASQ: Administrative Science Quarterly**. Ithaca, NY: Cornell University, Samuel Curtis Johnson Graduate School of Management, 1956- . Quarterly. ISSN 0001-8392.

A major interdisciplinary journal of the social sciences, *ASQ* is useful as a source of research articles in the area of organizational theory and communication. The journal is "dedicated to advancing the understanding of administration through empirical investigation and theoretical analysis"; recent issues have featured studies of leadership and power in organizations, auditor-client relationships, decision making, motivation and loyalty, corporate rhetoric, feedback and performance, group dynamics and influence, networking, and organizational structure. "News and Notes" announces calls for papers and upcoming conferences. In addition, *ASQ* includes selections of 12 or more book reviews as well as a list of publications received. *ASQ* is indexed in *AH&L* (entry 153), *BPI* (entry 160), *CA* (entry 163), *CC* (entry 164), *PA* (entry 183), *PAIS* (entry 181), *SSCI* (entry 185), and *SSI* (entry 186). Full-text searching of *ASQ* is available online on DIALOG.

Another important interdisciplinary journal of the social sciences with interests similar to those of *ASQ, Social Science Quarterly* (Austin, TX: Published for the Southwestern Social Science Association by the University of Texas Press, 1920-), a quarterly, has published numerous articles related to the roles of gender, race, and ethnicity in society; leadership and decision making in organizations; and attitudes and public opinion.

338. **Broadcasting**. Washington, DC: Broadcasting Publications, 1931- . Weekly. ISSN 0007-2028.

Broadcasting offers the most generally useful coverage of current news and concerns (legal, economic, technological, and demographic) of the television, radio, cable, satellite, and home video industries and markets. Brief, to-the-point features and columns on federal and local legislation, FCC decisions and administrative regulations, corporate mergers, buy-outs, power struggles, and advertising strategies, as well as job listings for broadcast communications professions, make *Broadcasting* indispensable. It is among the most frequently cited journals on mass media. *Broadcasting* is indexed in *BPI* (entry 160) and *BioI* (entry 157). Full-text searching of *Broadcasting* is available online on DIALOG.

339. **Cardozo Arts & Entertainment Law Journal**. New York: Yeshiva University, Benjamin N. Cardozo School of Law, 1981- . Semiannual. ISSN 0736-7694.

Cardozo Arts & Entertainment Law Journal features scholarly discussions of the broad range of issues related to the law, ethics, policy, and regulation of communication and media. Recent issues include one to four substantial articles as well as occasional notes, essays, and comments. Typical features have examined topics such as the rights of visual artists, obscenity, author-publisher contracts, policy making of the FCC, telecommunication industry competitiveness, intellectual property and fair access through photocopying, radio and television regulation, election-day projections and the First Amendment, the U.S. Information Agency, pornography and censorship, and video media. While most features have focused on issues of American interest, several have discussed more international topics. Two recent articles treated copyright protection in the People's Republic of China. In addition, issues include one to six book reviews. Issues also provide useful separate indexes of the cases and statutes cited as well as a title index. *Cardozo Arts & Entertainment Law Journal* is indexed in *CA* (entry 163) and *ILP* (entry 172).

340. **Channels: The Business of Communications**. New York: C. C. Publishing, 1986- . 11/year. ISSN 0895-643x.

Formerly *Channels of Communication* (1981-1986), *Channels* — like *Broadcasting* (entry 338) — provides primary documentation on economic, legal, and technological developments, events, and similar issues of practical concern to television industry and electronic communications professionals. It is one of the places to start for current news on the electronic media. Brief articles on current legislation and FCC actions; cable, radio, and other media industry trends; corporate mergers and personnel changes; and the like are staples. Cover stories in recent issues have focused on Price Communications, ESPN, Viacom, MTV, and TCI (Tele-Communications, Inc.). Another recent issue included a survey of the top 100 media corporations. Regular features, like "Technology Management," offer insights and predictions about new communication technologies such as high-definition television and fiber optics. *Channels* is indexed in *RG* (entry 184).

Wider in scope than *Channels, Electronic Media* (Chicago, IL: Crain Communications, 1982-), weekly, ISSN 0745-0311, is another useful source for current news and events on just about everything that is mass communication — television, radio, telecommunications, cable, film, advertising, and public relations.

341. **Child Development**. Chicago, IL: University of Chicago Press, 1930- . 6/year. ISSN 0009-3920.

Sponsored by the Society for Research in Child Development, *Child Development* is historically important in the history of communication research. It has featured several early seminal studies that have influenced current research. Among these are M. Sherman's "Theories and Measurements of Attitudes" (3 [1932]: 15-28) and H. C. Dawes's "An Analysis of Two Hundred Quarrels of Pre-School Children" (5 [1934]: 139-57). Today the journal remains a source of basic experimental research on children's communicative behavior, both verbal and nonverbal, as well as cognitive development, information processing, and language acquisition. Substantial attention has been given to mother-infant and mother-child interaction in intra- and intercultural settings. Other articles have discussed speech-act comprehension in mentally retarded individuals, nonverbal communication skills in children with Downs syndrome, children and lying, and establishing word-object relations, among other topics. *Child Development* is indexed in *CA* (entry 163), *CC* (entry 164), *LLBA* (entry 175), *MLA* (entry 178), *PA* (entry 183), *SSCI* (entry 185), and *SSI* (entry 186).

342. **Columbia Journalism Review**. New York: Columbia University, Graduate School of Journalism, 1962- . Bimonthly. ISSN 0010-194x.

Every issue of *Columbia Journalism Review* includes the following statement from its 1962 founding editorial: "To assess the performance of journalism in all its forms, to call attention to its shortcomings and strengths, and to help define—and redefine—standards of honest, responsible service ... to help stimulate continuing improvement in the profession and to speak out for what is right, fair, and decent." Its "Darts & Laurels" department is noteworthy for speaking out on the shortcomings as well as for applauding the strengths of "journalism in all its forms." The four or five articles in each issue typically reflect current and common topics and concerns and their treatment in the media. *Columbia Journalism Review* is indexed in *BRI* (entry 159), *CC* (entry 164), *HI* (entry 171), *ILP* (entry 172), *PAIS* (entry 181), and *SSCI* (entry 185).

Similar to *Columbia Journalism Review* in purpose and scope, *WJR: Washington Journalism Review* (Washington, DC: Washington Communications Corporation, 1977-), monthly, and *St. Louis Journalism Review* (St. Louis, MO: St. Louis Journalism Review, 1970-), monthly, feature critical commentaries on current issues in journalism. The major research journal on newspaper journalism, *Newspaper Research Journal* (Athens, OH: Ohio University, E. W. Scripps School of Journalism, 1979-), quarterly, sponsored by the Newspaper Division of the AEJMC (entry 460), publishes studies of practical significance to the business operations of newspapers as well as articles on broader topical interest that are intended to assist working journalists.

343. **Comm/Ent: A Journal of Communication and Entertainment Law**. San Francisco, CA: University of California, Hastings College of the Law, 1977- . Quarterly. ISSN 0193-8398.

Aimed at the "legal community," *Comm/Ent* publishes scholarly articles on legal issues and topics of current interest in all areas of communication. Significant attention has focused on AT&T, deregulation, and the FCC. Other articles have covered colorization of original black-and-white films, freedom of speech, legislative and regulatory control of "dial-a-porn" and rock music, legal issues in news gathering, televised sports, cable franchising, defamation, libel, workplace wiretapping, telecommunication regulation, cameras in the courtroom, and copyrighting computer programs. Articles of general historical interest are also published. In addition, *Comm/Ent* regularly publishes substantial annotated bibliographies and other research guides on such topics as visual arts and the law, the right of publicity, and nonbroadcast video. Occasional special issues devoted to specific themes are published. *Comm/Ent* also regularly features brief notes and case commentaries as well as abstracts of recent legal articles on communication topics. Issues include useful subject and cited case indexes. *Comm/Ent* is indexed in *CA* (entry 163) and *ILP* (entry 172).

344. Communication Booknotes: Recent Titles in Telecommunication, Information and Media. Columbus, OH: Ohio State University, Center for Advanced Study in Telecommunications, 1969- . Monthly. ISSN 0748-657x.

Founded and edited by mass communication scholar Christopher H. Sterling, *Communication Booknotes*, formerly *Mass Media Booknotes* (1969-1982), features concise descriptive reviews (typically one to two paragraphs) of selected new monographic publications in the areas of telecommunication, broadcasting and mass communication, media law, new communication technology, and the like. International co-editors provide brief data on selected new publications from around the world, with emphasis on European imprints, in regular and "round-up" features. Coverage of publications of U.S. and foreign governments as well as national and international media organizations is notable. Special issues focus on specific topics. Along with *CA* (entry 163), *Communication Booknotes* is one of the few dependable sources for critical reviews of new book-length publications in the field. The journal's new publisher has expressed interest in publishing *Communication Booknotes*, with cumulated retrospective volumes, in CD ROM format.

345. Communication Education. Annandale, VA: Speech Communication Association, 1952- . Quarterly. ISSN 0363-4523.

This is the major important pedagogical journal in communication, offering discussions of theories and methods of teaching subjects in the field. *Communication Education* can be counted on to offer selections of six to eight features aimed at improving communication in the classroom. Any topic related to "communication in instructional settings" is considered. Past issues have featured bibliographic reviews and historical and textual studies. Recent issues (1988 to the present), however, have reflected a social scientific research bias. "The Status of Instruction in Introducing Undergraduate Communication Research Methods" and "An Analysis of Teachers' Verbal Communication within the College Classroom: Use of Humor, Self-Disclosure, and Narratives" are two typical features. Other features have discussed memory and listening, use of dramatic style in teaching, anxiety in public speaking, language patterns and gender, educational television, and ratings of Ph.D. and master's programs in communication. As might be expected, a significant number of features have focused on evaluation of teacher-student interactions. Issues usually include 6 to 12 scholarly reviews of new publications. *Communication Education* is indexed in *CA* (entry 163), *CC* (entry 164), *CIJE* (entry 165), Matlon (entry 177), *MLA* (entry 178), and *SSCI* (entry 185).

Among other important pedagogical journals, *Journalism Educator* (Columbia, SC: Association for Education in Journalism and Mass Communication, 1945-), quarterly, is intended to document and illustrate teaching methods and issues relevant to journalism education as well as address issues of professional interest in the areas of advertising, public relations, and the mass media. *Feedback* (Washington, DC: Broadcast Education Association, 1977-), quarterly, reports on teaching methods and professional issues in broadcasting.

346. Communication Monographs. Annandale, VA: Speech Communication Association, 1934- . Quarterly. ISSN 0363-7751.

One of the major general scholarly journals in the field, *Communication Monographs* features substantial contributions on all aspects, theories, and research methodologies regarding "human communication processes." Its predecessor, *Speech Monographs*

(1934-1975), also sponsored by the Speech Communication Association (entry 482), published numerous seminal studies that continue to influence communication research, such as W. M. Timmons's "Sex Differences in Discussion" (8 [1941], 68-75); R. D. Brooks and T. M. Scheidel's "Speech as Process: A Case Study" (35 [1968], 1-7); and D. H. Smith's "Communication Research and the Idea of Process" (39 [1972], 174-82). Current issues usually include five studies that range widely in the areas of speech and linguistics and mass, interpersonal, and organizational communication. Recent articles like "Empathy, Communication, and Prosocial Behavior" and "Edmund Burke's *Letter to a Noble Lord:* A Textual Study in Political Philosophy and Rhetorical Action" indicate the journal's variety. Studies of communication between physicians and patients; marital communication and violence; the roles of emotions, anxiety, gender, and culture in communication; television news; silence; nonverbal communication; and political rhetoric, among other topics, all appear in *Communication Monographs*. Historical, rhetorical, and literary analyses of works by the likes of Aristotle, David Lloyd George, and Samuel Beckett are also common. The journal does not publish reviews. *Communication Monographs* is indexed in *AH&L* (entry 153), *CA* (entry 163), *CIJE* (entry 165), *LLBA* (entry 175), Matlon (entry 177), *MLA* (entry 178), *PA* (entry 183), and *SSCI* (entry 185).

347. **Communication Quarterly**. Upper Montclair, NJ: Eastern Communication Association, 1953- . Quarterly. ISSN 0146-3373.

Like other major general scholarly journals in the field, *Communication Quarterly* is wide-ranging in scope, publishing both theoretical and experimental studies (five to six articles per issue) on the role of communication in all disciplines and historical periods. It has published numerous historically important studies. Articles have included discussions of subjects ranging from oratory after the Boston Massacre and the "rhetoric of silence" in Quaker worship services to the rhetoric of anti-Vietnam War protests and the Reagan-Carter presidential debates. Topics in interpersonal and nonverbal communication are given significant attention, usually from a behavioral science research orientation. Studies of the communication theories and strategies of the like of Kenneth Burke and Reverend Jerry Falwell also appear. In addition, *Communication Quarterly* includes four to six extended book reviews. *Communication Quarterly* is indexed in *CA* (entry 163), *CIJE* (entry 165), *HI* (entry 171), *LLBA* (entry 175), Matlon (entry 177), and *SA* (entry 187).

Other less prominent (but frequently cited) journals that publish a similar range of historical theoretical, and experimental studies in all areas of communication include *Canadian Journal of Communication* (Saskatoon, Canada: St. Thomas More College, 1974-), quarterly, the official journal of the Canadian Communication Association, and *Communication* (London: Gordon and Breach, 1975-), quarterly. Both are indexed by *CA* (entry 163).

348. **Communication Research: An International Quarterly**. Beverly Hills, CA: Sage, 1974- . Quarterly. ISSN 0093-6502.

Communication Research is among the major general scholarly journals in the field, publishing articles on all areas in communication. Features focus on the "processes, antecedents, and consequents" of communication in "international, organizational, political, legal, and health systems" as well as on "the role of traditional mass media and the new information technologies." Significant attention has focused on analyses of the effects of television viewing, examining topics like student soap-opera watching, recall and recognition of election information, children's representations of television and real-life stories, ego involvement in television news, and the like. Other topics studied have included public opinion, VCRs, viewing motivation, advertising and children, gender and interpersonal conflict management, press ideology and control in Hong Kong, and methods of media content analysis. Occasional historical articles also appear. Special issues have focused on specific themes such as "Social Cognition and Communication" and "Innovative Research on Innovations and Organizations." Instead of reviews of new books in communication, *Communication Research* typically includes several review essays that place new and old publications in their historical research contexts. In addition, a regular feature, "Far Afield," provides reviews of new books "not primarily" addressed to the field of communication. *Communication Research* is indexed in *CA* (entry 163), *CC* (entry 164), *CIJE* (entry 165), *PA* (entry 183), and *SSCI* (entry 185).

349. Communication Studies. West Lafayette, IN: Purdue University, Department of Communication, 1989- . Quarterly. ISSN 0008-9575.

Sponsored by the Central States Speech Communication Association and formerly named *Central States Speech Journal* (1949-1989), *Communication Studies* features strong scholarly articles representing the "broad field of communication studies" — "communication theory, interpersonal communication, communication education, organizational communication, forensics, history of public address, interpretation of literature, theater, radio-TV-film, rhetorical theory and criticism, and public relations." Typical articles such as "Rhetorical Sensitivity in Three Cultures: France, Japan, and the United States," "Listening to Monotony: All-News Radio," and "Multivariate Communication Networks" indicate the journal's wide scope. Other recent articles have discussed the effects of "laugh tracks" on audiences, nonverbal communication, television quiz shows, story telling, interviewing, conversation, and advertising. Historical and biographically oriented features are notable. These have discussed medieval poetics, the Nixon-Kennedy debates, Abraham Lincoln, and John Lennon. Bibliographies and review essays are also published. Occasional special issues are devoted to specific themes. An issue on public relations included seven articles on historical, professional, and pedagogical topics. No reviews are included. *Central States Speech Journal* was indexed by *CA* (entry 163), *CC* (entry 164), *CIJE* (entry 165), *LLBA* (entry 175), Matlon (entry 177), and *SSCI* (entry 185). Doubtless, *Communication Studies* also will be widely indexed.

350. Communications and the Law: A Quarterly Review. Westport CT: Meckler, 1979- . Quarterly. ISSN 0162-9093.

"Expanding technologies, aggressive use of the media by business, censorship, public opinion formation by government: these and scores of communication issues have daily impact upon legislation, legal, and judicial affairs. *Communication and the Law* is devoted to the study and discussion of such issues." As a source of research on communication from legal perspectives, *Communications and the Law* is second in importance only to *Federal Communications Law Journal* (entry 355). Feature articles cover all areas of communication, although topics in mass communication are emphasized. Topics of current professional interest as well as historical and biographical topics are included. Articles have covered Warren Burger, editorial cartooning, defamation in the workplace, "CBS News," "dial-a-porn," children's programming, cable television and newspaper cross-ownership, political broadcasting in the United States and Britain, cameras in courtrooms, direct broadcasting, satellites and piracy, First Amendment defense of negligent misstatement, pay television, and alcoholic beverage and tobacco advertising. Occasional features have discussed the image rather than the letter and interpretation of the law, such as news media portrayal of the U.S. Supreme Court. Occasional special issues on specific themes also appear. In addition, issues include selections of one to three book reviews. *Communications and the Law* is indexed in *CA* (entry 163) and *ILP* (entry 172).

Of the numerous general law journals that publish research and comments on issues in communication, several merit additional note. *Computer/Law Journal* (Manhattan Beach, CA: Center for Computer/Law, 1978-), quarterly, addresses the legal aspects of new information technology in society, with particular attention centering on issues involving software and information property rights. *Harvard Journal of Law & Public Policy* (Cambridge, MA: Harvard Society for Law & Public Policy, Harvard Law School, 1978-), 3/year, has recently published a significant number of studies about government control of information and national security. *High Technology Law Journal* (Berkeley and Los Angeles, CA: University of California Press, 1986-), 2/year, is particularly attentive to topics related to telecommunication deregulation as well as to issues in space policy, copyrighting software, information property rights, and industrial and organizational innovation. In addition, the journal regularly features a "Legislative Update" that surveys and summarizes recent federal and state legislation in areas of high technology. Similarly, *Yale Journal on Regulation* (New Haven, CT: Yale Law School, 1983-), 2/year, features scholarly articles on "issues of regulatory policy," including regulation and control of the media. Substantial attention has been devoted to deregulation, the break-up of AT&T, and the implications for the telecommunication industry.

351. **Critical Studies in Mass Communication**. Annandale, VA: Speech Communication Association, 1984- . Quarterly. ISSN 0739-3180.

Critical Studies in Mass Communication attempts to serve as a forum for crossdisciplinary research. Scholarly features focus on the "evolution, organization, control, economics, administration, and technological innovations of mass communication systems," including television, radio, newspapers, and film; "the form and structure of mass media content; the relationship between culture and mass communication; and the analysis or illustration of mass media criticism." Articles such as "Television as an Aesthetic Medium," "The Mythos of the Electronic Church," and "Media Consumption and Girls Who Want to Have Fun" are typical. Other articles have examined such topics as freedom of the press, feminist theories, cable television, pornography, news coverage in Latin America and the Soviet Union, the program "60 Minutes," the break up of AT&T, and the penny press. *Critical Studies in Mass Communication* is particularly valuable for criticism of television broadcasting, especially from an international perspective. A significant number of features are historically oriented. The regular "Review and Criticism" section includes discussions and comments by several critics and scholars on a wide range of mass communication subjects, including news research, political broadcasting, and the music industry. "*CSMC* Booknotes" provides brief critical notices of new publications on mass communication. *Critical Studies in Mass Communication* is indexed in *CA* (entry 163), *CIJE* (entry 165), and Matlon (entry 172).

352. **Discourse Processes: A Multidisciplinary Journal**. Norwood, NJ: Ablex, 1978- . Quarterly. ISSN 0163-853x.

Well-documented experimental and theoretical discussions of topics like "prose comprehension and recall, dialogue analysis, text grammar construction, computer simulation of natural language, [and] cross-cultural comparisons of communicative competence" make *Discourse Processes* valuable for research in speech and language that is most applicable to interpersonal and intercultural communication. Particular attention has focused on analysis of conversation among adult and juvenile peers as well as between parents and children. Studies have examined such topics as children's telephone conversations, discourse in courtrooms, comprehension of narratives, surprise-ending stories, language and literacy, and the role of silence in conversation. In addition, *Discourse Processes* publishes occasional special issues devoted to specific themes. "Discourse as Organizational

Process" included 10 features discussing discourse in the media, classroom, and health care. The journal does not publish book reviews. *Discourse Processes* is indexed in *CA* (entry 163), *CC* (entry 164), *CIJE* (entry 165), *LLBA* (entry 175), *MLA* (entry 178), *PA* (entry 183), *SA* (entry 187), and *SSCI* (entry 185).

353. **EC&TJ: Educational Communication and Technology Journal: A Journal of Theory, Research, and Development**. Washington, DC: Association for Educational Communications and Technology, 1953- . Quarterly. ISSN 0148-5806.

EC&TJ publishes features that discuss "theory, development, and research related to technological processes in education." It is useful for identifying novel and practical uses of communication technologies. Issues usually include four to six articles that emphasize practical applications for educational technologies and evaluations of these uses. Articles have discussed such topics as computer-based and computer-assisted instruction, "Sesame Street," "Square One TV," the relationship of pictures and symbols and recall, and the use of the telephone in tutoring. Reviews of research, conference papers, and other reports from abroad are presented in the column "International Review." ERIC documents related to educational technologies are identified and abstracted in "Research Abstracts." *EC&TJ* is indexed in *CA* (entry 163), *CC* (entry 164), *CIJE* (entry 165), *LLBA* (entry 175), *PA* (entry 183), and *SSCI* (entry 185).

Another useful source for research on educational television is the *Journal of Educational Television: Journal of the Educational Television Association* (Humberside, England: Educational Television Association, 1975-), 3/year, the "official journal of the Educational Television Association." The journal provides an "international forum for discussions and reports on developments in the increasingly important and rapidly expanding field of the use of television and related media in teaching, learning, and training." Articles and reports in each issue focus on producing, using, and evaluating educational television and other media.

354. **European Journal of Communication**. London: Sage, 1986- . Quarterly. ISSN 0267-3231.

The primary interest here is comparative national and international mass communication, with particular attention to "policy dilemmas" resulting from new communication technologies. Nation-specific and crossnational studies are published. "What Is Learnt Early Is Learnt Well? A Study of the Influence of Tobacco Advertising on Adolescents" (in Belgium); "Intruders Welcome? The Beginnings of Satellite Television in Hungary"; and "Audiences for International Radio Broadcasts" (about government-sponsored broadcasting) are typical features. Other articles have examined public opinion formation, the media and voter behavior, women in the news, agenda-setting by the media, sex bias in crime reporting, regulation of direct satellite broadcasting, soap opera viewing in Britain, the Spanish newspaper industry, the West German cable industry, and Polish broadcasting. Occasional historical articles also appear. Review articles have surveyed research on new communication technologies and the relationship of television viewing and reading, among other subjects. Special issues devoted to specific themes also appear. Selections of five to eight reviews of new publications are also published in each issue. *European Journal of Communication* apparently is unindexed at this date.

355. **Federal Communications Law Journal**. Los Angeles, CA: University of California, School of Law, and the Federal Communications Bar Association, 1977- . 3/year. ISSN 0163-7606.

This is the most important scholarly journal for research on communication and the law. Every article that appears in this journal is valuable to the communication researcher.

Formerly *Federal Communications Bar Journal* (1937-1976) and sponsored by the Federal Communications Bar Association (entry 462), the journal focuses on "topics of interest to the communications bar"—problems and issues related to the regulation and control of communication, the media, and their products. All areas of communication are covered, including freedom of speech, journalism, telephones, broadcasting, telecommunication, advertising, and public relations. Articles, essays, and commentaries discuss such topics as cable television, remote sensing, computer privacy, indecency in broadcasting, the fairness doctrine, the break up of AT&T, Radio Marti, and telecommunications policy. "The Proliferation of Private Networks and Its Implications for Regulatory Reform," "Copyright Fair Use, the First Amendment, and New Communication Technologies: The Impact of Betamax," and "The Constitutional Right to Puffery: Commercial Speech and the Cigarette Broadcast Advertising Ban" are typical features. In addition, *Federal Communications Law Journal* provides a very convenient "Articles Digest" section, containing 10 or more 1- to 2-page summaries of relevant articles published in other law journals. Selections of reviews of new books also appear. The last quarterly issue contains an index of each volume's contents. Volume 41.4 (1989) includes a "Topical Index for the Eighties," a cumulative index for volumes 32-41 (1980-1989)—a feature that makes *Federal Communications Law Journal* perhaps the most important bibliographic resource for critical scholarship on recent legal issues in mass communication. Extensive, made-to-order listings (a veritable "sweeps" of legal research) are readily available here for such topics as broadcast regulation, cable television, common carrier regulation, copyright, the divestiture of AT&T, the FCC, the First Amendment, the history of telecommunication law, computers, satellites, electronic publishing, and other technologies. *Federal Communications Law Journal* is indexed in *CA* (entry 163) and *ILP* (entry 172).

356. Gazette: International Journal for Mass Communication Studies: Press, Radio, Television, Propaganda, Public Opinion, Advertising, Public Relations. Dordrecht, The Netherlands: Kluwer Academic Publishing Group, 1955- . Bimonthly. ISSN 0016-5492.

Offering "a forum for scientific discussions that include the international exchange and comparison of ideas for editors, politics, government information services, economics, and advertising," *Gazette* is the most important journal for the study of international communication. It is a particularly significant resource for studies of the role of the printed and electronic media and communication technologies in economic, political, and social development. A secondary, more practical interest of the journal is the development of the media professions in developing nations. Attention largely focuses on North-South, information rich-information poor interrelations. Media and cultural imperialism and press freedom are recurrent themes. Articles have focused on news coverage of terrorism; the ethnic press in the United States; the soap opera and film industries in India; the role of media organizations in the training of media professionals; comparisons of press coverage in the United States, Japan, and France; freedom of the press in South Korea, South Africa, China, and Hong Kong; and the evolving Soviet concept of news. Through 1987 issues of *Gazette* published selections of book reviews. *Gazette* is indexed in *AH&L* (entry 153), *CA* (entry 163), and *PAIS Bulletin* (entry 181).

Other important journals that feature scholarly research and critical commentary on issues in international mass communication include *Intermedia* (London: International Institute of Communications, 1973-), bimonthly; *Combroad* (London: Commonwealth Broadcasting Association, 1967-), quarterly; *EBU Review* (Geneva: European Broadcasting Union, 1958-), bimonthly; *Media Information Australia* (North Ryde, N.S.W., Australia: Australian Film and Television School, 1976-), quarterly; and *The Nordicom Review of Nordic Mass Communication Research* (Goteborg, Sweden: Nordic Documentation Center for Mass Communication Research, 1981-), biennial.

357. **Historical Journal of Film, Radio, and Television**. Oxfordshire, England: Carfax Publishing, 1981- . 3/year. ISSN 0143-9685.

Sponsored by the International Association for Audio-Visual Media in Historical Research and Education, this is among the most scholarly and bibliographically useful journals in the area of the mass media. *Historical Journal of Film, Radio, and Television* is an "interdisciplinary journal concerned with the evidence produced by the mass media for historians and social scientists, and with the impact of mass communications on the political and social history of the 20th century." Articles deal with historical topics as well as with historiography. Recent features have discussed internal government propaganda in Nazi Germany, the influence of television's coverage of the Vietnam War on American historiography, the FCC's early allocation of television frequencies, BBC coverage of the Korean War, the use of radio in American presidential campaigns, the use of newsfilm in historical research, and the development of the broadcasting and film industries in Spain, Belgium, Australia, and Japan. Biographical features have discussed the contributions of Billy Wilder, Darryl Zanuck, Leni Riefenstahl, Boris Shumyatsky, and Sergei Eisenstein. Several recent contributions are of bibliographical significance, like David Culbert's "Radio News in Thirties America: The Photographic Archives of the Broadcast Pioneers Library" (8.2 [1988]: 139-51) and William Uricchio's "German University Dissertations with Motion Picture Related Topics: 1910-1945" (7.2 [1987]: 175-90). In addition, the journal includes regular departments that are valuable to communication researchers. "Comments/News/Notices" provides brief announcements and descriptions of upcoming conferences, research in progress, projects in publication, new programs in media studies, new and established special collections and archives, and the like. "American Doctoral and Masters Dissertations on Cinema, Radio, and Television" is a useful and timely supplement to listings in *Journalism Abstracts* (entry 174) and *Dissertation Abstracts International* (entry 166). Likewise, "Recently Published Articles" complements broader indexing services. Issues include selections of six or more reviews of new international publications. *Historical Journal of Film, Radio, and Television* is indexed in *A&HCI* (entry 155), *AH&L* (entry 153), and *CC* (entry 164).

358. **Human Communication Research**. Austin, TX: International Communication Association, 1974- . Quarterly. ISSN 0360-3989.

Sponsored by the International Communication Association (entry 468) and distributed by Sage, *Human Communication Research* publishes 5 to 15 articles per issue that offer research on all "human symbolic activities." Communication in all its possible variations—mass media and interpersonal, verbal and nonverbal—is studied from scientific, social scientific, philosophical, and theoretical perspectives. Similarly, as in other major general scholarly journals in the field, the subjects explored are heavily interdisciplinary. Such topics as communication in businesses and families and between physicians and patients as well as political campaign communication have been discussed. Typical articles have examined audience involvement in soap operas, gender differences in question-asking and interpersonal interactions, and group communication and decision making. These articles also suggest the journal's strong behavioral and experimental research orientation. *Human Communication Research* is indexed in *CA* (entry 163), *CIJE* (entry 165), *LLBA* (entry 175), *PA* (entry 183), and *SSCI* (entry 185).

Another journal sponsored by ICA, *Communication Theory* (Boulder, CO: University of Colorado, 1990-), intends to provide "an international, interdisciplinary forum for theory and theoretically oriented research on all aspects of communication."

359. **Human Relations**. New York: Plenum, 1947- . Monthly. ISSN 0018-7267.

"A journal of studies toward the integration of the social sciences," *Human Relations* is most valuable as a resource of research in the areas of intercultural communication in interpersonal, small group, and organizational relationships. Studies of topics related to effectiveness and performance in the workplace predominate. The influences of gender and ethnicity on communication and performance; attitudes, stress, burnout, and performance; conflict mediation; mentoring, evaluating, and feedback; leadership, decision making, and organizational structure and dynamics; networking, and organizational secrecy and information access are among the topics examined. No book reviews are included. *Human Relations* is indexed in *CA* (entry 163), *CC* (entry 164), *LLBA* (entry 175), *PA* (entry 183), *PAIS Bulletin* (entry 181), *SSCI* (entry 185), and *SSI* (entry 186).

360. **IEEE Communications Magazine**. New York: Institute of Electrical and Electronics Engineers, 1953- . Monthly. ISSN 0163-6804.

IEEE Communications Magazine is an official publication of the IEEE Communications Society (entry 463). The journal is aimed at the communications professional. Clearly one of the journal's main objectives is selling telecommunications and new communication technology. Consumer and industrial applications of LANs, telefacsimile, cellular radio, fiber optics, hardware standardization, and other new communication technologies are typical among the subjects examined. Articles of broader interest have reviewed telecommunication research in Brazil and elsewhere as well as trends in U.S. telecommunication policy. Occasional historical features have described early telegraphy and telecommunication. Special issues on lightwave components and neural networks have recently appeared. In addition, the journal includes several valuable departments. Selections of three to five book reviews are provided. "Scanning the Literature" offers abstracts of significant research articles; "New Products" profiles the latest technology. Particular emphasis is also on professional activities. A calendar of upcoming conferences, announcements for specific conferences, calls for papers, reports on meetings, and extensive job listings in academics and industry are included. *IEEE Communications Magazine* is indexed in *EI* (entry 167).

IEEE publishes two other journals that routinely offer features on telecommunication and new communication technologies that are of professional and scholarly interest. *IEEE Spectrum* (New York: Institute of Electrical and Electronics Engineers, 1964-), the flagship journal of the IEEE, includes news and articles on current technological developments in electronics. *IEEE Technology and Society Magazine* (New York: Institute of Electrical and Electronics Engineers, 1982-), sponsored by the IEEE's Society on Social Implications of Technology, publishes well-documented articles that address the social issues of electrotechnology, information technology, and telecommunication, including topics in public policy, economics, and education.

361. **Information Age**. Guildford, England: Butterworth Scientific, 1978- . Quarterly. ISSN 0261-4103.

Formerly *Information Privacy* (1978-1982), *Information Age* is particularly important for research on telecommunication and new communication technologies. Significant attention remains focused on issues of transborder data flow and data security. Topics related to security, such as computer fraud and computer viruses, have been approached from legal, pedagogical, and practical perspectives. Other articles have discussed such topics as artificial intelligence, MIS services via microcomputers, the information industry in the United Kingdom, telecommunications policy, direct and indirect FCC regulation of computing devices, and global cooperation and transborder data flow. In addition, *Information Age* provides other services that are valuable to information professionals. "News" recounts significant technical and policy activities. A calendar of upcoming meetings is also featured. "Book Reviews" includes a selection of two to five reviews of new publications. *Information Age* is indexed in *CA* (entry 163), *CC* (entry 164), *MC* (entry 176), and *SSCI* (entry 185).

Another important journal in this area, *Transnational Data and Communications Report* (Washington, DC: Transnational Data Reporting Service, 1978-), irregular, formerly *Transnational Data Report: TDR* (1978-1985), examines issues related to the multinational and international implications of data transmission systems, such as data security and national sovereignty, rights to privacy, deregulation and government control of information, government uses of information, and international information cooperation.

362. **Information Economics and Policy.** Amsterdam, The Netherlands: Elsevier Science Publishers, 1983- . Quarterly. ISSN 0167-6245.

Aimed at researchers and professionals ("expert consultants and policy-makers"), this journal publishes highly theoretical and sophisticated scholarly articles that balance "information and (tele)communications media" in relation to economics and policies. Emphasis here is on the value of information; *supply* and *demand* are buzzwords. Issues feature three to four articles on subjects like the role of telecommunications in economic development, copyright, intellectual property, and public access through photocopying; information's effects on productivity in the workplace; new communication technology's influence on employment; the costs of evolving telecommunication technologies; the effect of intra-brand advertising competition on product pricing; and incentives for media regulation. Many features are based on case studies of specific problems — equipment costs for Bell Canada, the impact of economic cycles on Australian telecommunications, and the information economies of Japan and Korea. In addition, issues include three to six reviews of new publications in the areas of information policy and telecommunications. *Information Economics and Policy* is indexed in *CA* (entry 163).

363. **Information Society.** London: Taylor & Francis, 1981- . Quarterly. ISSN 0197-2243.

Intended to answer "questions about the Information Age," this is a major journal for research on communication theory as well as mass communication, telecommunication, and new communication technologies. Topics in the areas of transborder data flow, government regulation of the communication industry and control of information, the impact of information and information industry development on society, and information and economic development are regularly discussed. These topics are addressed from international perspectives. A representative feature is "Appropriate High Tech: Scientific Communication Options for Small Third World Countries." Electronic mail, technology transfer, information's impact on religious belief, and the Japanese computer industry have also been discussed. *Information Society* is indexed by *CA* (entry 163) and *PAIS Bulletin* (entry 181).

364. **International Journal of Advertising: The Quarterly Review of Marketing Communications.** London: Cassell Educational, 1982- . Quarterly. ISSN 0265-0487.

Sponsored by the Advertising Association, this journal features research and other studies on "all aspects of marketing communications from academic, practitioner, and public policy perspectives." Topics within the journal's scope include "consumer advertising, marketing research, public relations, industrial marketing and advertising, consumerism, role of the media, business and economic environment, relevant legislation and regulation, international marketing, research and behavioral studies, product management, sales promotion, media research techniques and developments, communication practice and ethics in marketing." Typical articles have examined the use of the "made in" concept in advertising slogans, tobacco advertising and children, and the use of music in advertisements for "unmentionable" products. Significant recent attention has focused on advertising in the medical and legal professions. Topics have been addressed from ethical, economic, and legal perspectives. Features on advertising in China, France, the Soviet Union, and Hong Kong attest to the journal's international interest. Other articles have discussed misleading advertising, industry self-regulation, the effectiveness of brand names, coverage of sports as news (as opposed to sports), and content analysis of magazine advertisements. Occasional historical articles also appear. One traced the role of Thomas Barratt, of Pear's soap fame, in the development of British advertising. Occasional bibliographic essays and literature reviews as well as book reviews are also published. *International Journal of Advertising* is indexed in *CA* (entry 163), *LLBA* (entry 175), *PAIS Bulletin* (entry 181), and *SSCI* (entry 185).

365. **JMIS: Journal of Management Information Systems**. Armonk, NY: M. E. Sharpe, 1984- . Quarterly. ISSN 0742-1222.

JMIS publishes five to eight articles per issue that address theoretical and practical issues related to the field of MIS, or management information systems—where organizational communication interfaces with new communication technologies. Articles address "all aspects of the structure, development, and utilization of management information systems; pragmatic designs and applications; systems development methodologies and other techniques of software engineering; [and] analyses of informational policy making." Recent features have focused on such topics as the relationship of display format on system design, factors influencing information system use, and dissemination of information across management levels. A recent special issue was devoted to the theme "Decision Support and Knowledge-Based Systems." *JMIS* apparently is unindexed at this time.

Another useful journal in the MIS field, *Information & Management: The International Journal of Information Systems Applications: Systems, Objectives, Solutions (SOS)* (Amsterdam, The Netherlands: Elsevier Science Publishers, 1978-), 10/year, features research results and findings that are intended to give organizations competitive advantages through enhanced access and control of information.

366. **JMR: Journal of Marketing Research**. Chicago, IL: American Marketing Association, 1964- . Quarterly. ISSN 0022-2437.

Issues feature 10 or more articles, research notes, and other communications in the areas of advertising and marketing. Effective interpersonal and organizational communication in advertising and marketing are also emphasized. Studies focus on consumers, consumer decision making, and consumer behavior; ethics in marketing and advertising; the effective uses of electronic and print media; and selling, managing, and negotiating. Particular attention has been paid to the effectiveness of music, graphics, and repetition in commercials. Issues include selections of 6 to 10 reviews of new books. *JMR* is indexed in *BPI* (entry 160), *CA* (entry 163), *CC* (entry 164), *PA* (entry 183), *PAIS Bulletin* (entry 181), and *SSCI* (entry 185).

367. **Journal of Advertising**. Athens, GA: University of Georgia, School of Journalism, 1972- . Quarterly. ISSN 0091-3367.

Sponsored by the American Academy of Advertising, *Journal of Advertising* publishes the results of research that support the "development of advertising theory and its relationship to advertising practices and processes." All areas of advertising are included, from electronic media to labels on cigarette packages. Recent articles emphasize academic theory more than professional practice. A significant portion of the feature articles analyze and evaluate the content of advertisements. Articles like "How Does an Ad Mean?: Language in Services Advertising" and "An Evaluation of Subliminally Embedded Sexual Stimuli in Graphics" are typical. Similarly, features have discussed the variables of characterization and imagery; race, gender, and age; and language, verbal content, visuals, and sound. Other articles assess trends and developments in the advertising business or the segmentation of the audience and marketplace. Topics recently discussed include the effectiveness of one-sided and two-sided celebrity endorsements; self-regulation in advertising; advertising and programming scheduling; humor in American and British commercials; political advertising; and the legal, economic, and ethical issues of professional advertising, especially in medicine. Some features are quite topical, like a study of the relationship of AIDS-related anxiety and condom advertisements. Articles of historical interest also appear. In addition, issues usually include three to six book reviews. *Journal of Advertising* is indexed in *BPI* (entry 160), *CA* (entry 163), *PA* (entry 183), *PAIS Bulletin* (entry 181), and *SA* (entry 187).

368. **Journal of Advertising Research**. New York: Advertising Research Foundation, 1960- . Bimonthly. ISSN 0021-8499.

Journal of Advertising Research reports research results that are aimed at researchers and other professionals in the field of advertising, marketing, and public relations. Contributors include a healthy mixture of academics and advertising and other professionals. Significant attention (reflecting real practical concerns) has been focused on the VCR and its effect on advertising. "VCR Viewing Patterns: An Electronic and Passive Investigation" is typical. Another topic of perennial interest is that of audience segmentation. Articles have described research on advertising and Hispanics, the elderly, and women. Other articles have focused on the types of commercials in prime time, brand advertising, attention to advertising, transnational advertising practices, video music and recall, celebrity advertising, country affiliation (the "made in" concept) and product credibility, advertiser and agency uses of satellite and cable television, newspaper advertising, and the effectiveness of rebates. *Journal of Advertising Research* irregularly features "Research Contents," which includes "current comments and opinion on research"—specifically, the state of research and specific research methodologies—by two or three professionals or academics. In addition, *Journal of Advertising Research* regularly publishes special issues devoted to specific themes. Recent special issues have focused on advertising management and values in advertising. No book reviews are published. *Journal of Advertising Research* is indexed in *BPI* (entry 160), *CA* (entry 163), *CC* (entry 164), *LLBA* (entry 175), *PA* (entry 183), and *SSCI* (entry 185).

Several other journals are significant sources of advertising research. Articles in *European Journal of Marketing* (West Yorkshire, England: MCB University Press, 1967-), 10/year, emphasize market analysis and marketing strategy. In addition, through volume 22.8 (1988), the journal concurrently published issues with *Journal of Advertising History* (London: History of Advertising Trust, 1977-). The prestigious *Journal of Business* (Chicago, IL: University of Chicago Press, 1928-), quarterly, has focused particular attention on theoretical and empirical studies of advertising and public relations. *Journal of Consumer Affairs* (Madison, WI: University of Wisconsin Press, 1967-), semiannual, the official publication of the American Council on Consumer Interests, has focused special attention on such topics as the influence of children's behavior on the family's consumer habits; the uses, benefits, and economics of information provided to consumers regarding goods and services (especially professional health care services); and the role of consumer researchers in policy making. *Journal of Economic Psychology* (Amsterdam, The Netherlands: Elsevier Science Publishers, 1981-), quarterly, publishes research on the uses of psychological knowledge in business or, more specifically, on the uses of psychology to obtain a competitive edge in business. The journal is most valuable as a source of research relevant to advertising and, more subtly, the elemental theories of mass communication. Similarly, *Psychology & Marketing* (New York: John Wiley & Sons, 1984-), quarterly, has featured significant studies on the emotional and cognitive responses to advertising as well as the uses of sex and sex roles in advertising.

369. **Journal of Applied Communication Research**. Tampa, FL: University of South Florida, Department of Communication, 1973- . 2/year. ISSN 0090-9882.

Emphasis in *Journal of Applied Communication Research* (which refers to itself as *JACR*) is on the real, the practical, and the pragmatic — "questions and problems regarding pragmatic social phenomena addressed through the analysis of human communication." Issues feature 3 to 6 articles (a recent double issue included 10) that cover all areas of the field, including mass, organizational, and interpersonal communication, as well as language and linguistics. Recent articles have focused on communicating the dangers of smoking to adolescents, the use of animation in advertising, the effectiveness of organizational mission statements, the rhetoric of the "Made in the U.S.A." label, nurse-physician communication, public relations, political advertising, marital communication, and communication of corporate administrators and organizations, as well as studies of the roles of gender, culture, and age in communication. Book reviews are occasionally included. *Journal of Applied Communication Research* is indexed in *CA* (entry 163), *CIJE* (entry 165), *LLBA* (entry 175), and *SA* (entry 187).

370. **Journal of Broadcasting & Electronic Media**. Washington, DC: Broadcast Education Association, 1957- . Quarterly. ISSN 0883-8151.

Journal of Broadcasting & Electronic Media, formerly *Journal of Broadcasting* (1957-1984), publishes substantive research articles on the role of electronic media in a global society. Coverage of radio, television, and telecommunications is international. The journal's importance cannot be overemphasized. Every feature article focuses on a mainstream concern in all areas of the broad field of communication, including advertising, public relations, journalism, speech, language, rhetoric, and organizational and interpersonal communication, as related to electronic media. Issues usually include five to seven feature articles and two to three briefer notes and reports in "Research in Brief." Typical articles emphasize the interactions and influences of media content and technology on the audience — and vice versa. A significant number of articles have focused on children and television, VCR technology, cable television, and the role of television in the development of national and cultural identities. The topics covered range from learning from television news to using television to manage moods during pregnancy. Typical features include "Children's Perceptions of Television Reality," "Appeals and Strategies of Negative Political Advertising," and "Impact of the Television Marketplace on the Structure of Major League Baseball." In addition, the journal has published a number of historical features on such subjects as military broadcasting in postwar Germany, political broadcasting in the presidential campaigns of 1924 and 1948, and the development of the electronic church. Special issues have focused on specific themes in mass communication. *Journal of Broadcasting & Electronic Media* also offers several regular departments. These include "Books in Brief," which summarizes new publications, and editorial introductions for the features and the book reviews. *Journal of Broadcasting & Electronic Media* is indexed in *CA* (entry 163), *CIJE* (entry 165), *HI* (entry 171), *ILP* (entry 172), Matlon (entry 177), *PA* (entry 183), *PAIS Bulletin* (entry 181), and *SSCI* (entry 185).

371. **Journal of Business and Technical Communication**. Ames, IA: Iowa State University, Department of English, 1987- . 2/year. ISSN 0892-572x.

Formerly *Iowa State Journal of Business and Technical Communication* (1987-1988) and now calling itself *JBTC*, this journal offers a "forum for discussion of communication practices, problems, and trends in business, professional, scientific, and governmental fields." This emphasis makes the journal most relevant to research in organizational communication. Articles address topics related to "state-of-the-art communication technologies; innovative instruction; qualitative and quantitative research in governmental, industrial, or academic settings; and theoretical approaches to business and technical communication." Typical articles have focused on narration in technical communication, the role of technical communication in organizations, and online documentation. In addition, *JBTC* regularly features discussions of pedagogical and pragmatic issues and topics, such as the effective use of employee newsletters and the use of U.S. government documents in technical writing classes. A section of book reviews typically completes each issue. *Journal of Business and Technical Communication* apparently is unindexed at this time.

372. **Journal of Business Communication: JBC.** Urbana, IL: Association for Business Communication, 1963- . Quarterly. ISSN 0021-9436.

JBC publishes both research and practical articles on written, graphic, and verbal communication in business, managerial, and organizational contexts. Significant attention is given to technical writing in its many possible manifestations — in resumes, annual reports, newsletters, written evaluations, and the like. Other articles have focused on such topics as the use of graphics in teleconferences, the use of videotaping in developing interpersonal communication skills, interviewing, the use of microcomputers in writing, electronic mail, corporate communication policies, communication and work stress, and the effects of style and organization on reader perception of text. A significant number of features have examined gender issues in organizational communication. The section "News and Notes" announces competitions, calls for papers, and conferences. The journal also includes review essays and selections of reviews of new books. *JBC* is indexed in *BPI* (entry 160), *CA* (entry 163), *CIJE* (entry 165), and *MC* (entry 176).

Another journal that publishes significant research on technical communication, *Journal of Technical Writing and Communication* (Amityville, NY: Baywood, 1971-), quarterly, includes theoretical and practical articles on a wide range of topics related to "professional writing."

373. **Journal of Child Language.** Cambridge: Cambridge University Press, 1974- . 3/year. ISSN 0305-0009.

Journal of Child Language is interested in "all aspects of the scientific study of language behavior in children and the principles which underlie it." Topics covered include "sounds, grammar, lexicon, semantics, pragmatics, sociolinguistics, [and] bilingualism," among others. Both theoretical and experimental articles appear. A significant number of articles have focused on "motherese" and mother-prelingual child interactions in comparative cultural settings (France, Japan, United States, Israel). Most studies examine aspects and problems related to children's language acquisition. Subjects of articles have included acquisition of idioms, understanding of the speech act of "promising," the role of nursery rhymes and the development of phonological skills, babbling, and agentivity and control. *Journal of Child Language* is indexed in *CA* (entry 163), *CC* (entry 164), *CDA* (entry 161), *CIJE* (entry 165), *LLBA* (entry 175), *MLA* (entry 178), *PA* (entry 183), *SA* (entry 187), and *SSCI* (entry 185).

Another journal that is an important source of research on children's acquisition of language is *American Educational Research Journal* (Washington, DC: American Educational Research Association, 1964-), quarterly. In addition, *Developmental Psychology* (Arlington, VA: American Psychological Association, 1969-), bimonthly, has given special attention to maternal- and paternal-infant communication. Similarly, *Merrill-Palmer Quarterly: Journal of Developmental Psychology* (Detroit, MI: Wayne State University Press, 1954-), quarterly, has focused on mother-child, child-peer, child-teacher, and child-environment interaction.

374. **Journal of Communication**. New York: Oxford University Press, 1951- . Quarterly. ISSN 0021-9916.

Journal of Communication is among the most prominent journals in the field. It has published numerous articles, such as G. R. Miller's "On Defining Communication: Another Stab" (16 [1966]: 88-98), that continue to influence research. The general scholarly journal publishes five to six articles per issue on the broadest possible range of topics related to "communication theory, research, practice, and policy." Studies have focused on subjects of significant recent topical or political interest, like the reporting in the Soviet media on the war in Afghanistan, media coverage of new religious movements, and the effects of deregulation on telephone service, as well as others of a more descriptive behavioral nature, like an analysis of the use of clichés by sports announcers. Articles on subjects like media imperialism and propaganda, the use of videotext, and the advent of new information technologies also appear. Review essays on the contributions to the field by important communication theorists and scholars like Wilbur Schramm and Raymond Williams are common. In addition, issues of *Journal of Communication* feature an important news announcement department: "Intercomm" briefly announces current and future activities of international communication organizations, centers, and associations, including seminars and conferences and calls for papers. Collection development librarians should note that this feature also regularly announces publications of new journals and major bibliographies and reference works. Issues of *Journal of Communication* also include about 15 extended book reviews as well as others "briefly noted." *Journal of Communication* is indexed by *AH&L* (entry 153), *BRI* (entry 159), *CA* (entry 163), *CC* (entry 164), *CIJE* (entry 165), *HI* (entry 171), *LLBA* (entry 175), Matlon (entry 177), *MLA* (entry 178), *PA* (entry 183), *SSCI* (entry 185), and *SSI* (entry 186).

375. **Journal of Communication Disorders**. New York: Elsevier, 1968- . Bimonthly. ISSN 0021-9924.

Journal of Communication Disorders focuses on problems in speech communication at its most basic levels — "the biological foundations of communicative processes related to disorders of communication, as well as psychopathological, psychodynamic, diagnostic, and therapeutic aspects of communication disorders." Articles include reports of experimental results, case studies, and theoretical discussions. The journal's research orientation is international. "How Do Aphasic and Normal Speaking Subjects Restate a Message in Response to Feedback" and "Selective Characteristics of Narrative Discourse in Head-Injured and Normal Adults" are typical features. Other studies of language production, hearing impairments, and the uses of technology in speech and hearing have appeared. Significant attention is devoted to speech development in children. *Journal of Communication Disorders* is indexed in *CC* (entry 164), *CIJE* (entry 165), *LLBA* (entry 175), *PA* (entry 183), and *SA* (entry 187).

376. **Journal of Communication Inquiry**. Iowa City, IA: University of Iowa, Iowa Center for Communication Study, 1974- . 2/year. ISSN 0196-8599.

"Interdisciplinary inquiry into communication and mass communication phenomena with cultural and historical perspectives" is the focus of this important scholarly critical journal. It attempts to offer a forum for well-documented articles that "emphasize philosophical, evaluative, empirical, legal, historical, and/or critical inquiry into relationships between mass communication and society across time and culture." Special issues devoted to specific themes are the rule rather than the exception. Recent issues have focused on music television; advertising, ideology, and consumer culture; and cultural studies in South Africa. The special issue "History, Historiography, and Communication" offered eight features on topics ranging from the presentation of science in the media to the influence of working-class newspapers in the United States. "The Feminist Issue" included articles dealing with topics in mass, political, and organizational communication. Regular (that is, nonfocused) issues cover the broad range of topics in mass communication, including newspapers, electronic media, and book publishing. The journal does not publish book reviews. *Journal of Communication Inquiry* is indexed in *CA* (entry 163) and *SA* (entry 187).

377. **Journal of Consumer Research**. Gainesville, FL: University of Florida, College of Business Administration, 1974- . Quarterly. ISSN 0093-5301.

This journal is most valuable as a source of theoretical, historical, and empirical research relevant to advertising and marketing. Most studies are highly sophisticated, focusing on analysis of consumers and consumer behavior. Articles on such topics as the influences of brand-name length on consumer memory and of a product's country of origin on consumers' perception of quality are representative features. No reviews are included. *Journal of Consumer Research* is indexed in *BPI* (entry 160), *CA* (entry 163), *CC* (entry 164), *LLBA* (entry 175), *MC* (entry 176), *PA* (entry 183), *SA* (entry 187), and *SSCI* (entry 185).

378. **Journal of Cross-Cultural Psychology**. Newbury Park, CA: Sage, 1970- . Quarterly. ISSN 0022-0221.

Sponsored by the Center for Cross-Cultural Research in affiliation with the International Association for Cross-Cultural Psychology, *Journal of Cross-Cultural Psychology* is devoted to research that examines variations in responses of individuals and groups from different cultures or environments to similar stimuli or situations. Features relevant to interpersonal, small group, and intercultural communication are published. "First Conversations; Verbal Content of Mother-Newborn Interaction," "Communication and Sense of Community among the Members of an Immigrant Group," and "Communication Patterns of Adult-Infant Interactions in Western and Non-Western Cultures" are typical contributions. The journal occasionally publishes special issues devoted to specific themes as well as selections of reviews of new publications. *Journal of Cross-Cultural Psychology* is indexed in *CA* (entry 163), *CC* (entry 164), *CDA* (entry 161), *CIJE* (entry 165), *LLBA* (entry 175), *PA* (entry 183), and *SSCI* (entry 185).

Among several other journals that address topics in intercultural and crosscultural communication, *Journal of Community Psychology* (Brandon, VT: Clinical Psychology Publishing, 1973-), quarterly, features studies particularly related to social networking and support groups. *Gerontologist* (Washington, DC: Gerontological Society of America, 1961-), bimonthly, a professional journal, has focused substantial attention on developing social networks for the aging and the applications of communication technologies in the care of the aging as well as the images of the elderly in the media. *Phylon: A Review of Race and Culture* (Atlanta, GA: Atlanta University, 1940-), quarterly, features research on the Afro-American experience and its manifestations in literature, the media, culture, and society. Approaches are generally critical, historical, biographical, political, or sociological. *Sex Roles* (New York: Plenum, 1975-), monthly, has published significant studies on attitudes about gender and sex-role stereotyping and their economic, political, educational, and social implications.

379. **Journal of Educational Psychology**. Arlington, VA: American Psychological Association, 1910- . Quarterly. ISSN 0022-0663.

A journal of applied communication, *Journal of Educational Psychology* is significant in the history of communication research for features such as A. Kroll's "The Teacher's Influence upon the Social Attitudes of Boys in the Twelfth Grade" (25 [1934],

274-80). Today *Journal of Educational Psychology* continues to publish numerous articles that report the results of research on fundamental issues and problems in communication in educational settings—research largely pertinent to the areas of interpersonal and small group communication. Studies have focused on cognition and comprehension, motivation and achievement, teacher attitudes and effectiveness, learning strategies, individual differences in competence and confidence, and helplessness and help seeking, among other topics. Significant attention is paid to classroom interactions. The effects of praise and blame on behavior; age, gender, and cultural influences on performance; and stereotyping of teachers and students have been studied. A major scholarly journal in the fields of education and psychology, the journal also publishes professional announcements and calls for papers. No reviews are published. *Journal of Educational Psychology* is indexed in *CA* (entry 163), *CDA* (entry 161), *CIJE* (entry 165), *PA* (entry 183), and *SSCI* (entry 185).

380. **Journal of Marketing**. Chicago, IL: American Marketing Association, 1934- . Quarterly. ISSN 0022-2429.

Journal of Marketing provides a wide range of information that is valuable to research on advertising and consumer and audience behavior. The journal nicely complements *Journal of Advertising* (entry 367), which attends largely to the analysis of advertising content. *Journal of Marketing*, in contrast, publishes analyses of audiences and the segmented marketplace; its emphasis is on the receiver. Studies focus on buyers' perceptions of price, complexity, innovation, quality, value, and the like. A few advertising content analyses have also appeared, treating subjects like sex roles in advertising and comparisons of information content in American and British television advertising. In addition, *Journal of Marketing* provides two significant bibliographic services. "Legal Developments in Marketing" offers abstracts of current regulations, legislation, and decisions related to the marketing environment. The topical arrangement includes "Advertising" and "Nonadvertising Promotional Methods" in section 5, "Regulation of Unfair Competition." Similarly, "Marketing Literature Review" is a classified bibliography that includes briefly annotated entries for recent articles in the field. The category "Marketing Functions" includes listing 2.9, "Advertising." Issues usually include a selection of three to six book reviews. *Journal of Marketing* is indexed in *BPI* (entry 160), *CA* (entry 163), *CC* (entry 164), *MC* (entry 176), *PA* (entry 183), *PAIS Bulletin* (entry 181), and *SSCI* (entry 185).

381. **Journal of Marriage & the Family**. St. Paul, MN: National Council on Family Relations, 1939- . Quarterly. ISSN 0022-2445.

A basic journal for research in interpersonal, small group, and intercultural communication, issues of *Journal of Marriage & the Family* publish 20 or more articles and review essays. Marital and familial communication are a central focus. Articles have addressed the communication of attitudes and perceptions within the family, stereotyping and behavior, and sexual communication. Particular attention has focused on the family as a social network of support and education as well as the interrelations of the individual and the family. "Looking for Mr. or Ms. Right: Self-Presentation in Videotaping," "Informal Helping in Partner and Stranger Dyads," and "Family Stories: Events (Temporarily) Remembered" are typical articles. Other articles have examined the transmission of religious beliefs and practices from parents to children, the role of children in the family's social support network, and the communication of stress in the family. Issues include selections of three or more reviews of new publications. *Journal of Marriage & the Family* is indexed in *BRI* (entry 159), *CA* (entry 163), *CC* (entry 164), *CDA* (entry 161), *CIJE* (entry 165), *HI* (entry 171), *LLBA* (entry 175), *PA* (entry 183), *SSCI* (entry 185), and *SSI* (entry 186).

Other journals that are significant sources of research on marital and familial communication include *The American Journal of Family Therapy* (New York: Brunner/Mazel, Inc., 1973-), quarterly, a professional journal that examines topics such as effective interviewing, mediating, counseling, and therapeutic communication in difficult familial situations. The interpretation of verbal and nonverbal communication of emotions and states of intimacy, stress, and aggression is emphasized. Similarly, *Family Process* (New York: Family Process, 1962-), quarterly, has addressed such topics as the perceptions of power, helplessness, and loneliness within families; decision making and behavior; the expression of emotions and attitudes; and family relations in difficult situations. *Journal of Applied Developmental Psychology* (Norwood, NJ: Ablex, 1980-), quarterly, publishes research on developmental relationships between children and parents, the family, peers, and society.

382.   **Journal of Mass Media Ethics**. Provo, UT: Brigham Young University, Department of Communications, 1985- . Semiannual. ISSN 0890-0523.

"Devoted to issues in mass media ethics," each issue of this new journal features eight articles on ethics in print and broadcast journalism and mass communication. Features have discussed the ethical, legal, and moral responsibilities of media professionals in providing news about AIDS victims and covering judicial proceedings. "Ethical Implications of Electronic Still Cameras and Computer Digital Imaging in the Print Media" is a representative feature. Special issues devoted to specific themes have focused on topics such as ethics in photojournalism. *Journal of Mass Media Ethics* is unindexed at this time.

383.   **Journal of Nonverbal Behavior**. New York: Human Sciences Press, 1976- . Quarterly. ISSN 0191-5886.

"Nonverbal behavior in social interaction, communication, and emotional expressions" is the focus of this journal. Areas of interest include "interpersonal distance, gaze, facial expressiveness, kinesics, paralanguage, posture, gestures," and other related behaviors. Articles have addressed communication apprehension, seating distance as indicative of degree of intimacy, same- and opposite-sex touch avoidance, laughter as communication, physician-patient communication, familial interactions, and nonverbal responses to the handicapped, aged, and victims of diseases. Typical articles are "Verbal and Nonverbal Cues as Mediators of Deception Ability" and "The Identification of Emotions from Gait Information." Special issues devoted to specific themes have focused on deception and touch, among other topics. No reviews are published. *Journal of Nonverbal Behavior* is indexed in *CA* (entry 163), *CDA* (entry 161), *CIJE* (entry 165), *MLA* (entry 178), *PA* (entry 183), and *SSCI* (entry 185).

384.   **Journal of Personality and Social Psychology**. Arlington, VA: American Psychological Association, 1965- . Monthly. ISSN 0022-3514.

Journal of Personality and Social Psychology is the most significant of several major journals in psychology that publish substantial numbers of studies relevant to communication. Arranged in the sections "Attitudes and Social Cognition," "Interpersonal Relations and Group Processes," and "Personality Processes and Individual Differences," articles reflect current experimental research. In recent issues, articles relevant to areas of interpersonal and small group communication, mass communication effects, advertising, and public relations have appeared in all three sections. Articles have discussed gender differences in communicative styles, persuasion in the courtroom, the influence of speaker status on memory of conversation, long-term effects of media violence and sex-role stereotyping, group participation, shyness and help-seeking behavior, communication anxiety and apprehension, self-awareness and disclosure, nonverbal communication, the uses of cues in communication, the roles of expertise and attractiveness in persuasion, and attitude formation. Issues include about 20 features, with the third section consistently including the most. The journal does not publish reviews. *Journal of Personality and Social Psychology* is indexed in *CA* (entry 163), *CC* (entry 164), *MLA* (entry 178), *PA* (entry 183), *SSCI* (entry 185), and *SSI* (entry 186).

385. **Journal of Popular Culture**. Bowling Green, OH: Popular Press, Bowling Green State University, Department of Popular Culture, 1967- . Quarterly. ISSN 0022-3840.

The official joint publication of the Popular Culture Association, the Popular Literature Section of the Modern Language Association of America, and the Popular Culture Section of the Midwest Modern Language Association, *Journal of Popular Culture* is a treasure trove of articles relevant to communication research. Indeed, the journal publishes studies of interest to researchers in organizational, interpersonal, small group, intercultural, and mass communication; advertising; rhetoric; speech; and language. The images of black families and same-gender friendships on television, vitamin advertising, religious broadcasting and the electronic church, tee-shirts and bumper stickers as communication, the western and the romance novel, magazine publishing, video games, newspaper propaganda, sports on television, MTV, political cartoons, public opinion, CB radio, and Woody Allen are among subjects that have been examined. Numerous historical studies appear. No reviews are published. *Journal of Popular Culture* is indexed in *AH&L* (entry 153), *A&HCI* (entry 155), *CA* (entry 163), *CC* (entry 164), *HI* (entry 171), *MLA* (entry 178), and *SSCI* (entry 185).

386. **Journal of Psycholinguistic Research**. New York: Plenum, 1971- . Bimonthly. ISSN 0090-6905.

Basic theoretical, experimental, and critical research on how people solve or negotiate problems in human communication and information processing is the central focus of *Journal of Psycholinguistic Research*. The journal explores "the social and anthropological bases of communication; development of speech and language; semantics (problems in linguistic meaning); biological foundations; psychopathological aspects; educational psycholinguistics"; and other interdisciplinary areas. International contributors are largely from the fields of linguistics and psychology. Articles have examined the occurrence and duration of pauses in speech, the influence of age and gender on preschoolers' use of eye contact while speaking, ability to memorize lists, aphasia, self-awareness of language use, language acquisition, linguistic intuition, conversational structure, baby talk and mother-child communication, vocal rhythm, and idiom comprehension. Special issues devoted to specific topics are also published. A recent special issue focused on sentence processing. No reviews are published. *Journal of Psycholinguistic Research* is indexed in *CA* (entry 163), *CDA* (entry 161), *LLBA* (entry 175), *MLA* (entry 178), *PA* (entry 183), *SA* (entry 187), and *SSCI* (entry 185).

Several other journals are useful sources of research on human information processing and communication. The prestigious *American Journal of Psychology* (Champaign, IL: University of Illinois, 1887-), quarterly, ISSN 0002-9556, has published numerous historically significant studies of cognition and communication and continues to focus significant attention on encoding and its effects on information processing. Similarly, *Memory & Cognition* (Austin, TX: Psychonomic Society, 1973-), bimonthly, features numerous articles that examine and measure the effectiveness of verbal (written and oral) and visual message transmission and comprehension, with emphasis on text recognition and recall. *Journal of General Psychology: Experimental, Physiological, and Comparative Psychology* (Washington, DC: Heldref, 1927-), quarterly, which has featured numerous historically important articles in communication research, has more recently published research on the influence of information/misinformation contained in pictorial and auditory messages, cues, and feedback on task performance.

387. **Journal of Social Psychology**. Washington, DC: Heldref, 1929- . Bimonthly. ISSN 0022-4545.

Founded in 1929 by John Dewey and Carl Murchison, *Journal of Social Psychology* is prominent among the several journals from outside the field that have featured historically important studies that continue to influence the content and orientation of communication research. Among these articles are L. L. Thurstone's "Influence of Motion Pictures on Children's Attitudes" (2 [1931], 291-305); M. H. Landis and J. W. H. Ross's "Humor and Its Relation to Other Personality Traits" (4 [1933], 156-75); K. Lewin, R. Lippitt, and R. White's "Patterns of Aggressive Behavior in Experimentally Created 'Social Climates' " (10 [1939], 271-99); and R. M. Bateman and H. H. Remmer's "A Study of the Shifting Attitudes of High School Students When Subjected to Favorable and Unfavorable Propaganda" (13 [1941], 395-406). Today the journal publishes "experimental, empirical, and especially field studies of groups, cultural effects, cross-national problems, language, and ethnicity." Extended articles and brief notes are most relevant to interpersonal, organizational, and intercultural communication. Topics in nonverbal behavior, like the reciprocation of smiling, eye contact perceived as threatening behavior, touching, and physical attraction and attractiveness, have been examined. Self-esteem and self-perception; stereotyping in relation to age, race, gender, and social class; the influence of gender on management decision making; subliminal messages and persuasion; audience influence on performance; attitude and public opinion formation and change; help-seeking behavior; group and individual decision making; leadership styles; and cooperation and conflict resolution in the workplace have also been discussed. No reviews are included. *Journal of Social Psychology* is indexed in *CA* (entry 163), *CDA* (entry 161), *CIJE* (entry 165), *LLBA* (entry 175), and *PA* (entry 183).

388. **Journalism History**. Northridge, CA: California State University, Department of Journalism, 1974- . Quarterly. ISSN 0094-7679.

Jointly sponsored by the History Division of AEJMC (entry 460) and the California State University at Northridge Department of Journalism of the School of Communication and Professional Studies, *Journalism History* publishes articles on the "full scope of mass communication history." Substantial attention has focused on printed media. Articles have treated political cartooning, the suppression of the anarchist press in the United States in 1901-1914, journalism in Japanese-American internment camps during World War II, women and blacks in journalism, and the press coverage of the Vietnam War. Other features have examined abortion advertising in the nineteenth century and innovation in early network television news. Biographical studies have surveyed the contributions of James Gordon Bennett, Edwina Drumm, and H. V. Kaltenborn. Other articles have discussed journalism historiography. Occasional special issues devoted to specific themes or topics are also published. A recent special issue focused on the Constitution and included features on freedom of speech and freedom of the press. *Journalism History* also contains a useful bibliography of historical scholarship in journalism. "Communication History Abstracts" annotates books, parts of books, and articles in the field. The journal publishes selections of 12 or more reviews of new publications. *Journalism History* is indexed in *AH&L* (entry 153), *CA* (entry 163), and *HI* (entry 171).

389. **Journalism Monographs**. Columbia, SC: Association for Education in Journalism and Mass Communication, 1966- . Quarterly. ISSN 0022-5525.

Each numbered issue presents a single, extended, 30- to 40-page article on a specific topic in communication. Many of the studies have been historically oriented, examining topics such as early advertising, the development of professional public relations, the history of the AEJMC (entry 460), sports reporting, news coverage of President John F. Kennedy's assassination, and Edward R. Murrow's role in broadcasting. Particular attention has addressed printed and electronic media coverage of domestic, foreign, and global political and military activities (that is, elections and wars), as well as international media development and media imperialism. Other articles have employed social scientific methodologies to study topics in organizational communication, mass media uses and effects, and mass communication theory. Contributors have included prominent scholars in the field, such as James E. Grunig, Steven H. Chaffee, George Gerbner, Guido H. Stempel III, and Edwin Emery. No reviews are featured. *Journalism Monographs* is indexed in *AH&L* (entry 153), *CA* (entry 163), and *CIJE* (entry 165).

390. **JQ: Journalism Quarterly**. Columbia, SC: Association for Education in Journalism and Mass Communication, 1924- . Quarterly. ISSN 0196-3031.

"Devoted to research in journalism and mass communication," *JQ* is one of the most historically and currently important journals in communication. Along with the articles that have appeared in *Public Opinion Quarterly* (entry 404) and *Quarterly Journal of Speech* (entry 407), *JQ*'s contributions have shaped and influenced current communication research and the profession more than those in other scholarly journals. Among the historically influential features are G. Gallup's "A Scientific Method for Determining Reader-Interest" (7 [1930], 1-13); A. Geller, D. Kaplan, and H. D. Lasswell's "An Experimental Comparision of Four Ways of Coding Editorial Comment" (19 [1942], 362-71); D. M. White's "The 'Gate-Keeper': A Case Study in the Selection of News" (27 [1950], 383-90); and W. Geiber's "Across the Desk: A Study of 16 Telegraph Editors" (27 [1956], 383-90). Issues of *JQ* today include 24 or more articles (some necessarily quite brief) in a wide range of areas, including mass communication effects and uses, international and intercultural communication, information and communication theory, advertising, public relations, and public opinion. Articles have focused on topics such as government and the media, measuring newspaper and media audiences, cartoons and political satire, the FCC, advertising and children's programming, the high school press, censorship in South Africa, media imperialism in Latin America, media development, MTV, the use of satellites in news broadcasting, images of gender and race in television programming, photojournalism, and international terrorism and the media, as well as topics specific to regional, state, and local media. A significant number of features are biographical and historical. In addition, *JQ* regularly publishes features on pedagogical and professional issues, such as gender and pay in relation to faculty job satisfaction and research productivity of mass communication faculty. *JQ* also includes a number of bibliographically important features. "Articles on Mass Communication in U.S. and Foreign Journals: A Selected Annotated Bibliography" is a classified listing of briefly annotated entries for articles on advertising, broadcasting, communication theory, community journalism, courts and laws, criticism and defense of the media, education, government and media, history and biography, international communication, magazines, management, minorities, public opinion, public relations, research methods, technology, visual communication, and women and media. *JQ* also provides an extensive book review section, usually including as many as 50 page-long reviews of current publications in addition to brief notices for others. *JQ* is indexed in *AH&L* (entry 153), *CA* (entry 163), *CC* (entry 164), *CIJE* (entry 165), *HI* (entry 171), *LLBA* (entry 175), *MLA* (entry 178), *PA* (entry 183), *PAIS Bulletin* (entry 181), and *SSCI* (entry 185).

391.   **Knowledge: Creation, Diffusion, Utilization.** Newbury Park, CA: Sage, 1979- .
Quarterly. ISSN 0164-0259.

Knowledge is a basic journal for research on theoretical and practical issues related to
the influence of information on behavior. A subtle twisting of this rather generic
description of the journal's focus is perhaps more accurate: *Knowledge* focuses on
behavior with information. Although a relatively new publication, the journal has
published several influential articles, such as J. S. Coleman's "The Structure of Society and
the Nature of Social Research" (1 [1980], 333-50). Recent attention to topics in business
and public policy suggests the larger ethical considerations inherent to the possession of
information. Features are most relevant to organizational decision making. The uses of
recommendations and expert witness testimony and the effects of time on the use of
information are topics of recent studies. Occasional special issues on specific themes, like
"Managing Knowledge in Policymaking," include numerous articles that underscore the
importance of information's role in society. *Knowledge* is indexed in *CA* (entry 163) and
SSCI (entry 185).

392.   **Language & Communication: An Interdisciplinary Journal.** Elmsford, NY:
Pergamon Press, 1981- . Quarterly. ISSN 0271-5309.

Language & Communication is devoted to "language and its communicational
functions" as these are applied in fields including anthropology, artificial intelligence,
education, ethology, linguistics, philosophy, physiology, psychology, and the social
sciences. Recent emphasis has been on the linguistic analysis of the message in the
communication model, rather than on its sender, transmission, receiver, or medium.
Research methodologies discussed have employed both human and animal subjects,
particularly primates. Significant recent attention has been given to comparative study of
communication processes in contrasting segments of the population, focusing on male-
female and young-old as well as racial communication differences. Analyses of baby talk
and "elder-speak" and "Do Men and Women Talk Differently?" offer insightful
discussions of readily observable situations in modern society. Other articles have
examined topics like the expression of intimacy in personal advertisements and belief in
rumor and rumor transmission. Unfortunately, much of the research reported in *Language
& Communication* is highly technical and of British or Commonwealth origins, making it
somewhat remote for American students. A useful calendar of upcoming conferences and
seminars, including calls for papers, concludes each issue. No book reviews are included.
Language & Communication is indexed in *CA* (entry 163), *LLBA* (entry 175), *MLA* (entry
178), *PA* (entry 183), and *SSCI* (entry 185).

393.   **Language and Speech.** Teddington, England: Kingston Press Service, 1958- .
Quarterly. ISSN 0023-8309.

A highly technical journal, *Language and Speech* typically features four to six articles
(largely experimental) in the areas of "speech perception, speech production, psycholinguistics, sociolinguistics, language learning and development, communication disorders,
and reading." Coverage of topics in the areas of interpersonal, small group, and
comparative and intercultural communication is also significant. The use of proper names
to control conversation, children's comprehension of complex sentences, the perception of
intonation in questions, and comprehension of foreign slang expressions are typical of the
subjects examined. Other articles have focused on stuttering; narrative styles of adults and
children; analyses of Hebrew, Cantonese, French, and Spanish; and the like. A few
extensive book reviews and a list of publications received are also included. *Language and
Speech* is indexed in *CC* (entry 164), *CIJE* (entry 165, *LLBA* (entry 175), *MLA* (entry 178),
PA (entry 183), and *SSCI* (entry 185).

394. **Management Communication Quarterly**. Newbury Park, CA: Sage, 1987- . Quarterly. ISSN 0893-3189.

A journal that has quickly become significant in the field, *Management Communication Quarterly* features articles, research notes, and commentaries on "managerial writing, managerial presentation, interpersonal communication in organizations, organizational communication, and external communication." Each issue contains five to eight articles on topics such as the exhibition of leadership in informal conversations, negotiating in conversations, organizational culture, effective upward and vertical communication, effects of graphs versus tables on decision making, gender and influence in organizations, group decision making, computers and organizational effectiveness, effective letters of recommendation, communication climate and job satisfaction, and auditing communication. Particular attention focuses on writing in the workplace and written communication in general. "Research Results" presents evaluations of different measurement instruments, such as questionnaires and surveys. Special issues on specific themes have included "Communication and Conflict Styles in Organizations." No reviews are published. *Management Communication Quarterly* is indexed in *CA* (entry 163).

Another significant journal in organizational communication, *Columbia Journal of World Business* (New York: Columbia University, Columbia Business School, 1963-), quarterly, gives special attention to the roles of leadership and decision making in international development and organizational structure and design for obtaining and maintaining competitive advantage.

395. **Mass Comm Review**. Columbia, SC: Association for Education in Journalism and Mass Communication, 1973- . 3/year. ISSN 0193-7707.

Sponsored by the Mass Communications and Society Division of AEJMC (entry 460), *Mass Comm Review* publishes research articles on all aspects of mass communication, including advertising, public relations, public opinion, mass media business and industry, mass media uses and effects, and telecommunication and new communication technologies. Particular attention focuses on issues of information policy and regulation. Topics recently discussed include direct broadcasting satellites, images of minorities and women in journalism, journalism ethics, and the impact of VCRs and pay television on movie theater attendance. Other articles have discussed research opportunities in political communication and international mass communication. In addition, special issues devoted to specific themes are published. "Freedom and Equity" included seven articles on topics relevant to broadcasting and print journalism, advertising, and public relations. No reviews are published. *Mass Comm Review* is indexed in *CA* (entry 163).

396. **Media Asia: An Asian Mass Communication Quarterly**. Republic of Singapore: Asian Mass Communication Research and Information Centre, 1974- . Quarterly. ISSN 0129-6612.

Sponsored by the Asian Mass Communication Research and Information Centre, *Media Asia* is an important source of authoritative research and commentaries on all areas and aspects of mass communication in Asian nations. Significant emphasis and attention are given to discussions of the different roles of mass communication in economic, political, and social development. Issues focus on specific themes, such as "Youth Culture and the Media," "Development of the Rural Press in Asia," "Communication Technology and Development," and "Media, Ethnicity and National Unity." Articles have focused on topics in advertising, behavior, mass communication's influences on juvenile behavior, the Indian film industry, the electronic media in post-revolutionary Iran, popular and folk culture, freedom of the press, news flow, magazine and newspaper publishing, appropriate new communication technology and national development, and television broadcasting.

Roundtable commentaries and discussions of topics such as government regulation of telecommunication, the roles and responsibilities of newspaper editors in national political development, and the relations of information-rich and information-poor societies are staples. *Media Asia* also includes several bibliographically useful departments. In addition to selections of a few lengthy book reviews, "Amicinfo" offers short notices of new publications held by the center. "Documentation List" records both published and unpublished government materials. *Media Asia* is indexed in *CA* (entry 163).

397. **Media, Culture & Society**. London: Sage, 1979- . Quarterly. ISSN 0163-4437.

Media, Culture & Society publishes contributions that discuss the "mass media (television, radio, journalism) within their political, cultural, and historical contexts" as well as issues related to the "information society"—"those issues raised by the convergence of the mass media with systems of cultural production and diffusion based upon tele-communications and computing." In addition, topics are drawn from literature, the visual and performing arts, photography, and publishing, among other areas. Issues focusing on specific themes are the rule rather than the occasional exception. Each issue is assembled by a guest editor and includes an introductory editorial, five articles, and a selection of two to five reviews of new publications. The issue "Sociology of Information" included features on topics like *glasnost* and restructuring in the Soviet media and satellite television in Western Europe. The issue "Latin American Perspective" included contributions that discussed research on communication research theory in Latin America as well as U.S. media imperialism and local economic and cultural development. Themes of other recent issues are "Western European Broadcasting," "Broadcasting and the Public Sphere" (about public service broadcasting), and "Radio History." Articles in nonthematic issues cover topics in political communication, news coverage, and commercial television. *Media, Culture & Society* is indexed in *CA* (entry 163), *CC* (entry 164), and *SSCI* (entry 185).

398. **Media Law Reporter**. Washington, DC: Bureau of National Affairs, 1977- . Weekly, with annual cumulations. ISSN 0148-1045.

This reports in either full-text or digest form, with annotations, the decisions of federal and state courts and administrative agencies in areas of the media. *Media Law Reporter* is typically the most convenient source to locate the texts of U.S. Supreme Court decisions on media cases. Significant cases are highlighted on the cover. The texts of all decisions are identified as either full or condensed and are assigned one of four broad subject descriptors—"regulation or media content," "regulation of media distribution," "newsgathering," or "media ownership." Annual cumulations include indexes for topics, tables of cases, and tables of cases by jurisdiction.

Several other sources provide information on court decisions relevant to communication. Printed and online newsletters such as *Communications Daily* (entry 295), *FCC Daily Digest* (entry 302), and *FCC Week* (entry 303), among others, strive for currency. All are quite expensive. Similarly, both *Lexis* (entry 306) and *Westlaw* (entry 321) offer superior coverage of court decisions. Access to them, however, is typically limited. Another significant resource, *Pike & Fischer Radio Regulation* (Bethesda, MD: Pike & Fischer, 1939-), offers subscribing researchers the full-text of FCC opinions, as well as important court decisions, digests, and analyses. The full service costs over $2,000 annually. Researchers interested in media law quickly discover that you get what you pay for.

399. **Organizational Behavior and Human Decision Processes: A Journal of Fundamental Research and Theory in Applied Psychology**. Duluth, MN: Academic Press, 1966- . Bimonthly. ISSN 0749-5978.

Devoted to the study of "human performance theory and organizational psychology," *Organizational Behavior and Human Decision Processes* regularly publishes numerous articles relevant to research in the areas of interpersonal, small group, and organizational communication. Substantial attention is given to the basic interactions of information seeking, processing, and use. Articles like "The Effects of Interviewers' Initial Impressions on Information Gathering" and "Misperceptions of Feedback in Dynamic Decision Making" are typical. Other features have discussed topics like the influence of goal-setting, cues, and feedback on individual and group performance; conflict mediation; the influence of gender on organizational hiring practices; charismatic leadership; and the sense of powerlessness and participation in organizations. No reviews are published. *Organizational Behavior and Human Decision Processes* is indexed in *BPI* (entry 160), *CA* (entry 163), *CC* (entry 164), *PA* (entry 183), and *SSCI* (entry 185).

400. Personality and Social Psychology Bulletin. Newbury Park, CA: Sage, 1975- . Quarterly. ISSN 0146-1672.

Sponsored by the Society for Personality and Social Psychology, the journal focuses on the "interface of personality and social psychology." Issues contain 15 or more articles on such topics as the influences of verbal and nonverbal cues on attitudes, attitudes on behavior, and interpersonal and group interactions and behavior in society. "Perceptions of Social Behavior: Evidence of Differing Expectations for Interpersonal and Intergroup Interaction" and "Women's Vocal Reactions to Intimate and Casual Male Friends" are representative articles. Other articles have discussed gender and persuasion; stereotyping; the physical attributes of a communicator and perceived honesty, persuasiveness, and effectiveness; and television viewing frequency. Particular attention has focused on the influence of self-image (self-esteem and self-handicapping) on social interaction. No reviews are published. *Personality and Social Psychology Bulletin* is indexed in *CA* (entry 163), *CDA* (entry 161), *LLBA* (entry 175), *MLA* (entry 178), *SSCI* (entry 185), and *SSI* (entry 186).

401. Philosophy and Rhetoric. University Park, PA: Pennsylvania State University Press, 1968- . Quarterly. ISSN 0031-8213.

The interest here is on the use and users of language in argumentation in society, past and present. *Philosophy and Rhetoric* publishes scholarly articles on "theoretical issues involving the relationship between philosophy and rhetoric (including the relationship between formal and informal logic and rhetoric), articles on philosophical aspects of argumentation (including argumentation in philosophy itself), studies of philosophical views on the nature of rhetoric of historical figures and during historical periods, philosophical analyses of the relationship to rhetoric of other areas of human culture and thought and psychological and sociological studies of rhetoric with a strong philosophical emphasis." Most studies are historically or biographically oriented. Articles have appeared on Cicero's use of historical examples in moral argument, Thomas Wilson's *Arte of Rhetoric*, and Immanuel Kant's theory of metaphor. Others have focused on Plato, Aristotle, Zeno, Roger Bacon, Rene Descartes, Giovanni Battista Vico, Martin Heidegger, Jean Paul Sartre, Pablo Neruda, Benedetto Croce, James Joyce, Kenneth Burke, and Chaim Perelman. Features of broader current interest have examined rhetoric in relation to new electronic technologies. In addition, the journal usually includes selections of reviews of new books and announcements of conferences, calls for papers, and research in progress. *Philosophy and Rhetoric* is indexed in *A&HCI* (entry 155), *CC* (entry 164), *HI* (entry 171), *LLBA* (entry 175), Matlon (entry 177), *MLA* (entry 178), *PI* (entry 182), and *SSCI* (entry 185).

402. **Political Communication and Persuasion: An International Journal**. New York: Crane Russak, 1980- . Quarterly. ISSN 0195-7473.

This journal offers critical analyses of the role of communication in historical and political events. Issues feature five to seven theoretical or critical articles on subjects that include propaganda, psychological warfare, and political persuasion via both speech and the media. Significant recent attention has been given to the study of terrorism. Issues for 1987 featured a bibliography of studies on terrorism and the news media. Articles have assessed the role of communication in specific terrorist incidents as well as analyzed the broader treatment of terrorism in particular print and broadcast media. Methodologies have included analyses of media content and effects, analyses of speeches, and theoretical discussions. Studies of other equally topical subjects such as acid rain, presidential election campaigns, Ronald Reagan's Strategic Defense Initiative, and the United Nations and its agencies, like Unesco, have also appeared. Special reports have discussed popular culture phenomena like the recent growth of the "skinhead" movement. Early issues included more historically oriented articles (on Dwight Eisenhower's post-World War II image and Adolf Hitler's treatment of Armenia, for example) and also featured book reviews. *Political Communication and Persuasion* is indexed in *CA* (entry 163) and *PAIS Bulletin* (entry 181).

403. **Popular Music and Society**. Bowling Green, OH: Bowling Green State University, Department of Sociology, 1972- . Quarterly. ISSN 0300-7766.

Popular Music and Society features significant research relevant to the study of mass communication. Scholarly discussions of issues relevant to mass communication theory, aesthetics, uses, and effects as well as media industry management, law, and policy predominate. The journal is particularly valuable as a source of research on popular manifestations of political communication, evidenced in articles like "Protest Music as Political Persuasion" and "Calypso, Reggae, and Cultural Imperialism by Reexportation." Historical studies of protest music in Israel, the United States, and other nations have also been published. Other features have discussed research on popular music consumers and consumption; music in the motion picture industry; music-video viewing; gender and management in the music industry; and, of course, sex and violence in music. MTV has been analyzed and re-analyzed. In addition, the journal regularly publishes comprehensive review essays and reviews of records, videos, and books. *Popular Music and Society* is indexed in *A&HCI* (entry 155), *BRI* (entry 159), *CA* (entry 163), and *CC* (entry 164).

404. **Public Opinion Quarterly: Journal of the American Association for Public Opinion Research**. Chicago, IL: University of Chicago Press, 1937- . Quarterly. ISSN 0033-362x.

Public Opinion Quarterly, along with *JQ* (entry 390) and *Quarterly Journal of Speech* (entry 407), is one of the most important journals in communication. Among its numerous historically influential contributions are such articles as P. F. Lazarsfeld and R. Wyant's "Magazines in 90 Cities—Who Reads What?" (1 [1937], 29-41); J. McDiarmid's "Presidential Inaugural Addresses: A Study of Verbal Symbols" (4 [1937], 79-82); R. O. Nafziger's "World War Correspondents and the Censorship of the Belligerents" (14 [1937], 226-43); J. D. Ames's "Editorial Treatments of Lynchings" (2 [1938], 77-84); H. H. Reemers's "Propaganda in the Schools—Do the Effects Last?" (2 [1938], 197-210); H. F. Gosnell and S. DeGrazia's "A Critique of Polling Methods" (6 [1942], 378-90); and Bernard Berelson's "The State of Communication Research" (23 [1959], 1-6). Articles in *Public Opinion Quarterly* today continue to offer assessments, interpretations, and criticisms of public opinion in America as well as analyses of the production and measurement of that public opinion. A significant number of articles have focused on interviewing and questioning methods and processes. Topics have included the training of interviewers, the effects of race on interviewing effectiveness, and the effectiveness of mail and telephone surveys. Other articles have focused on attitudes about wiretapping in Canada, suicide, and the Panama Canal Treaties of 1977. Many other features have explicitly assessed the role of the media in attitude formation. A recent one addressed the influence of investigative reporting on attitudes toward toxic wastes. In addition, the journal includes several other features of interest. "The Polls" includes reviews and reports on survey research and other studies on such topics as women's and men's attitudes about the place and role of women, ideological identification of "liberals" and "conservatives," human rights, nuclear energy, and other topics of current interest. The proceedings of the American Association for Public Opinion Research's annual meetings are reported. A selection of 3 to 10 reviews of new publications is also included. "In Memoriam" features provide biographical sketches of recently deceased individuals in the field of communication and social science research. One for the prominent media scholar Wilbur Schramm appeared in 52 (Fall 1988), 372-73. *Public Opinion Quarterly* is indexed in *CA* (entry 163), *CC* (entry 164), *LLBA* (entry 175), *PAIS Bulletin* (entry 181), *SA* (entry 187), and *SSCI* (entry 185).

405. Public Relations Journal. New York: Public Relations Society of America, 1945- . Monthly. ISSN 0033-3670.

Sponsored and published by the Public Relations Society of America (entry 479), *Public Relations Journal* is the major professional journal of the public relations industry. The glossy issues consist of readable, to-the-point news features and other articles on topics of current professional interest as well as regular departments that chronicle industry developments, products, and services. Cover stories have focused on minorities in the industry and on capitalizing on labor shortages in other industries, as well as on the variety of current problems that present challenges to the public relations professional, such as dealing with federal legislation on toxic chemical disclosure and image problems of professional sports. Classic examples of public relations challenges, such as the rehabilitation of NASA's image after the *Challenger* disaster, also make the journal's cover. Regular departments are full of practical information for better agency management. "Briefings" offers news about relevant legal, business, and technical developments. "Workshops" examines the full range of topics relevant to running a public relations business—like getting the most out of health care packages, displaying at conventions, and composing annual reports. "People" provides biographical information about who is new and who is moving up or out of the field. "Literature Showcase" details new publications. A similar feature, "Technology Update," describes new electronic media. "Executive Forum," providing a global perspective on public relations issues, completes each issue. *Public Relations Journal* is indexed in *BPI* (entry 160), *CA* (entry 163), and *PAIS Bulletin* (entry 181).

406. Public Relations Review: A Journal of Research and Comment. Silver Spring, MD: Communication Research Association, 1975- . Quarterly. ISSN 0363-8111.

Sponsored by the Foundation for Public Relations Research and Education, *Public Relations Review* features research and discussions of broad topics as well as case studies of particular public relations problems and solutions. Typical features are relevant to research in advertising and organizational and mass communication. Articles have addressed such broad topics as organizational response to adverse media reporting and the use of corporate advertising to obtain political influence as well as analyses of public relations associated with specific cases, such as the abortion rights movement, the CIA, the accounting profession, the *Challenger* disaster, and Eastern Airlines' bankruptcy. In addition, *Public Relations Review* has undertaken a significant bibliographic project, "Public Relations Body of Knowledge." This multipart review essay and bibliography, still in progress, has attempted to identify, outline, and describe the literature of public relations. Volume 13 (Winter 1987), pages 11-18, described the rationale for the project. Volume 14 (Spring 1988), pages 3-40, listed an "initial reading" bibliography. Later parts will annotate the field's core literature. *Public Relations Review* also publishes numerous special issues devoted to specific themes. "Women and Public Relations" included articles that analyzed images both in the industry's professional literature as well as in the literature produced by the profession. Another special issue, "Measuring Public Relations Impact," included a bibliography of studies and analyses of public relations programs, attitude, and evaluation research. Issues typically include 5 to 10 reviews of new publications in addition to brief notices for others. *Public Relations Review* is indexed in *BPI* (entry 160), *CA* (entry 163), *PAIS Bulletin* (entry 181), and *SSCI* (entry 185).

407. Quarterly Journal of Speech. Annandale, VA: Speech Communication Association, 1915- . Quarterly. ISSN 0033-5630.

The premier journal for the critical analysis of oratory and speech communication, *Quarterly Journal of Speech* is an official publication of the Speech Communication Association (entry 407). With *JQ* (entry 390) and *Public Opinion Quarterly* (entry 404), *Quarterly Journal of Speech* is historically one of the most important and influential journals in the field. Among its studies that continue to shape research are H. L. Ewbank's "Studies in the Techniques of Radio Speech" (18 [1932], 560-71); G. L. Borcher's "Speech without Work" (21 [1935], 376-78); and "An Approach to the Problem of Oral Style" (22 [1936], 114-17); D. Dusenbury and F. H. Knower's "Exceptional Studies of the Symbolism of Action and Voice—I: A Study of the Specificity of Meaning in Facial Expressions" (24 [1938], 424-26); R. H. Simpson's "The Effect of Discussion on Intra-Group Divergencies of Judgment" (25 [1939], 546-52); P. J. Fay and W. C. Middleton's "Judgment of Introversion from the Transcribed Voice" (28 [1942], 226-28); and D. R. Smith's "The Fallacy of 'Communication Breakdown' " (56 [1970], 343-46). Today *Quarterly Journal of Speech* remains a major source for critical scholarship on all aspects of public communication. Issues generally feature five to eight scholarly articles on the subjects related to the theories of speech and communication as well as on the roles of oratory, rhetoric, and the media in historical and recent political events. Analyses of the rhetorical theories and strategies of figures like Isocrates, Hans-Georg Gadamer, Michel Foucault, and Kenneth Burke are abundant. Similarly, discussions of such topics as the rhetoric of the biblical story of creation, the Abraham Lincoln-Stephen Douglas debates, and Ronald Reagan's "star wars" address regularly appear. A significant number of studies focus on the analyses of the communication skills of prominent historical personalities, including Benjamin Franklin, John Quincy Adams, Salmon P. Chase, Harry S. Truman, Mayor Richard J. Daley of Chicago, John Fitzgerald Kennedy, Bertolt Brecht, and Mahatma Ghandi. Extended review essays, such as the recent "The Renaissance of American Public Address: Text and Context in Rhetorical Criticism" and "Academic Practice of Television Criticism," explore and evaluate the issues and the literature on broad questions and problems of human communication. Similarly, like the major journals in other fields, *Quarterly Journal of Speech* attempts to review a significant portion of new publications in the field. Issues typically feature several dozen extended scholarly reviews of new books on speech and the media. *Quarterly Journal of Speech* is indexed in *A&HCI* (entry 155), *CA* (entry 163), *HI* (entry 171), Matlon (entry 177), and *MLA* (entry 178).

408. Rhetoric Society Quarterly. St. Cloud, MN: St. Cloud State University, 1968- . Quarterly. ISSN 0277-3945.

Sponsored by the Rhetoric Society of America, this journal features four to ten articles per issue that discuss "rhetorical theory, rhetorical criticism, history of rhetoric, rhetorical pedagogy, and rhetoric research." As in other journals that focus on rhetoric, substantial attention is devoted to studies of individual historical personalities. Recent articles have discussed the contributions of Cicero, Adam Smith, Samuel Taylor Coleridge, Anthony Trollope, Martin Luther King, Jr., John D. MacDonald, and I. A. Richards. Other features have examined topics ranging from the rhetoric of the Iran-Contra case to teaching a course in classical rhetoric. In addition, *Rhetoric Society Quarterly* has published several bibliographies and bibliographic reviews. These include a bibliography of studies of argumentation, twentieth-century studies of Richard Whatley, and "George Campbell: Manuscripts in Scottish Archives." Issues of *Rhetoric Society Quarterly* also feature the "Current Bibliography from the *Weekly Record*," a classified bibliography of new book-length publications. A regular section, "Notes," includes announcements of conferences, calls for papers, research in progress, competitions, and scholarships. About six to twelve reviews of new books are also included. An important journal, *Rhetoric Society Quarterly* has outgrown its awkward mimeographed, 8½ by 11-inch, stapled format. *Rhetoric Society Quarterly* is indexed in *MLA* (entry 178).

409. **Rhetorica: A Journal of the History of Rhetoric**. Berkeley and Los Angeles, CA: University of California Press, 1983- . Quarterly. ISSN 0734-8584.
    Sponsored by the International Society for the History of Rhetoric, *Rhetorica* is the most sophisticated and scholarly journal in the area of rhetoric. Its purpose is "to promote the study of both the theory and the practice of rhetoric in all periods and languages and its relationships with poetics, philosophy, politics, religion, law, and other aspects of the cultural context." Its orientation is truly international. Features are published in English, French, German, and Italian. Abstracts are provided in all four languages. Typical articles have focused on Kenneth Burke's *Auscultation* and Marxist dialectic and rhetoric, Cicero's political style in *Letters to Atticus*, magic and rhetoric from antiquity to the Renaissance, and speech in medieval ethical and courtesy literature. Other articles have discussed Aristotle, Isocrates, Pierre de Ronsard, Giovanni Battista Vico, Richard Whatley, and Paul De Man. Bibliographies and bibliographical essays have also been published, including ones on eighteenth- and nineteenth century Spanish rhetorical treatises and "Pre-Modern Jewish Study of Rhetoric." Special issues devoted to specific interests and activities of the society have appeared. These have described conferences and symposia on Cicero's *De Oratore* and the rhetoric of science. Both have featured bibliographies of basic readings. Selections of reviews of new books conclude each issue. *Rhetorica* is indexed in *A&HCI* (entry 155) and *CC* (entry 164).

410. **Small Group Behavior: An International Journal of Therapy, Counseling, and Training**. Newbury Park, CA: Sage, 1970- . Quarterly. ISSN 0090-5526.
    A basic journal for research in the area of interpersonal and small group communication, *Small Group Behavior* publishes articles that analyzed the interactions of individuals in groups and of groups within larger contexts. Significant critical attention has focused on assertiveness training, group leadership, and group processes in decision making. Studies have examined group task performance by age and gender; the functions of humor and joke-telling in the workplace; motivation; leaders and leadership; group structure; verbal and nonverbal cues and feedback; feedback and self-assessment in small group discussions; counseling, interviewing, and training strategies; and group communication within political, educational, and professional environments. Occasional issues include theme sections. For example, the recent "Microprocesses in Small Groups" section included articles analyzing speech acts in small groups as well as social predictors of participation. In addition, occasional special issues devoted to specific themes are published. "Group Process in Teaching and School Settings" included several features on language use in

groups. The journal does not publish reviews. *Small Group Behavior* is indexed in *CA* (entry 163), *CC* (entry 164), *CIJE* (entry 165), *LLBA* (entry 175), and *SSCI* (entry 185).

411. **Southern Communication Journal**. Boone, NC: Appalachian State University, 1935- . Quarterly. ISSN 0361-8269.

This major general scholarly journal is sponsored by the Southern States Communication Association (entry 481) and was formerly known as *Southern Speech Communication Journal* (1935-1971). *Southern Communication Journal* publishes research in all areas of communication, including mass, organizational, and interpersonal communication; public relations; advertising; journalism; language; speech; and rhetoric. Approaches are strongly historical and biographical. Rhetoric in ancient India, the Know-Nothing Party, epideictic speaking in the post-Civil War South, Grace Paley's fiction, Ronald Reagan's economic metaphors, Mario Cuomo, I. A. Richards, Lee Iacocca, and conversation in America from 1776-1928 are among the subjects that have been discussed. Other articles have examined media evangelists; the influence of sports-figure product endorsements on adolescents; employee evaluation; marital and nonverbal communication; conflict; conversation; compliments; the roles of gender, culture, and age; political rhetoric; suicide as protest rhetoric; and pedagogical subjects, like the use of video in classrooms. *Southern Communication Journal* is indexed in *CA* (entry 163) and Matlon (entry 177).

412. **Telecommunication Journal**. Geneva: International Telecommunication Union, 1933- . Monthly. ISSN 0497-137x.

The official journal of the ITU (entry 471), *Telecommunication Journal* is absolutely essential for the study of the legal, technical, economic, and social implications of telecommunication and new communications technologies for global development. Formerly *Journal Telegraphique* (1869-1933), *Telecommunication Journal* is published in English, French, and Spanish editions. In addition to functioning as a primary source of information about the activities of the numerous committees and working groups of the ITU, it also includes international news about developments in the field, calendars for upcoming conferences and meetings sponsored by the ITU and other telecommunication organizations, and announcements of new products. Feature articles in each issue focus on topics of broad interest. Recent articles have treated the use of rural communication satellites in Peru, network management in Australia's national network, and the telecommunications systems of the International Red Cross and the United Nations. Other articles reflect the state of the art. Features do not necessarily express the opinions of the ITU. *Telecommunication Journal* also includes several extremely valuable bibliographic services. "ITU Publications" lists publication and sale information for retrospective, current, and forthcoming international reports and other documents. Similarly, "ITU Film Library" identifies and summarizes new films and videos that document the technological and sociological impacts of telecommunication around the world or that provide educational or instructional introductions to foster telecommunication development. New monograph publications are reviewed in "Books." Finally, *Telecommunication Journal's* "Review of Reviews" section lists the contents of current issues of a wide range of international telecommunication journals, such as the numerous IEEE publications as well as *Annales des Telecommunications, Funk, Mundo Electronico*, and *Transmissione Dati e Telecommunicazioni*. *Telecommunication Journal* is indexed in *AS&TI* (entry 154), *CA* (entry 163), *CC* (entry 164), and *EI* (entry 167).

413. **Telecommunications**. Norwood, MA: Horizon House-Microwave, Inc., 1967- . Monthly. ISSN 0040-2494.

Telecommunications is more important for information on current events and other topics of professional interest than for critical scholarship or technical research. Features endeavor to translate the extremely specialized and technical language of high-technology research and development into one that the average businessman and the popular reading public might find readily comprehensible and attractive. Graphics and other illustrations are abundant. Major objectives, of course, are selling new telecommunication products to corporate America and, perhaps more significantly, convincing American business that telecommunication is a potential solution to its problems. In addition to the ubiquitous reader's service cards for the products advertised here, regular departments feature news and other factual accounts of the latest developments on the industry's business, regulatory, and technological research fronts. Editorials discuss events of timely significance. Likewise, feature articles address current issues, such as ISDN (Integrated Services Digital Network) development in France, computer viruses, facsimile transmission systems, metropolitan area networks (MANs), teleports, and fiber optics. *Telecommunications* features a significant number of interviews and articles by top international telecommunication managers and regulators. A special issue on telecommunication in the 1990s included remarks on the future of the industry by 12 CEOs and other key executives. Accounts of activities of major players and powers in the field, like Philips, AT&T, FCC, and ITU, make *Telecommunications* an important source for corporate intelligence. Students of telecommunications should monitor its contents for current information. *Telecommunications* is indexed in *BPI* (entry 160) and *EI* (entry 167). Full-text searching of *Telecommunications* is available online on DIALOG.

Another useful journal for news and information about current industry developments, *High Technology Business* (Boston, MA: Infotechnology Publishing, 1987-), monthly, formerly *High Technology* (1981-1987), is a *Business Week* of high-tech industries. Cover stories and other features describe new technologies and "Newsletter Digest" excerpts significant information from major communication industry publications, like *Computer Daily, Fiber Optics Weekly Update*, and *Television Digest. High Technology Business* conveniently is indexed in *RG* (entry 184). Full-text searching of *High Technology Business* is available online on Mead Data Central.

414. **Telecommunications Policy**. Guildford, England: Butterworth Scientific, 1977- . Quarterly. ISSN 0308-5961.

The focus here is the economics and politics of international telecommunication. Research articles and comments address "any aspect of the assessment, control, and management of developments in telecommunications and information systems." Most articles indicate the significance of telecommunication in national economic development and the inherent political implications. Articles have discussed telecommunication and new communication technologies in Brazil, France, New Zealand, West Germany, Hong Kong, United Kingdom, and Italy, as well as such topics as ISDN (Integrated Services Digital Network), the role of the ITU in financially supporting development, telecommunication policy in the European Economic Community, scrambling and DBS (Direct Broadcasting Satellite), local measured service, spectrum assignments, technical standards, privatization and world television trade, and presidential leadership in U.S. telecommunication policy. Features on "telecottages" in Scandinavia and mobile satellite services have emphasized the role of telecommunication in local development. Others on U.S.-Caribbean telecommunication have focused on the topic of cultural imperialism and economic development. In addition, the journal occasionally includes literature reviews, such as Marcellus S. Snow's "Telecommunication Literature: A Critical Review of the Economic, Technological, and Public Policy Issues" (12 [1988], 153-83). Issues include lists of new publications (with abstracts), calendars of international meetings, and brief reports on conferences. *Telecommunications Policy* is indexed in *CA* (entry 163), *CC* (entry 164), and *PAIS Bulletin* (entry 181).

Also important for the study of telecommunication policy, *Space Policy* (Guildford, England: Butterworth Scientific, 1985-), quarterly, addresses topics related to the multinational and international politics of the exploration, study, and uses of outer space, such as remote sensing, meteorological satellite networks, telecommunications and national security, and data protection.

415.   Telematics and Informatics: An International Journal. New York: Pergamon Press, 1984- . Quarterly. ISSN 0736-5853.

Telematics and Informatics is particularly important for the study of telecommunication and new communication technologies from legal and economic perspectives. Issues feature four to six documented articles on applied telecommunications and information technology, information resource management, socioeconomic implications, international issues in communication, and information policy and legislation. Topics of recent articles include computer graphics, microelectronics, speech synthesis, voice recognition, digital radio networks, data encryption, satellite television, videotext, ISDNs, earth stations, expert systems, and cable subscriptions. Two to three special issues in each volume are devoted to specific themes, such as "Telecom Policies in the Bush Administration" and "Local Area Networks." Both regular and special issues include several departments. "Legislative and Policy Focus" includes articles on topics like the First Amendment and new communication technologies and "The Regulation of Political Extremism on Cable Access." Useful bibliographic features include the "NTIS Section," which lists and abstracts new government publications, and the "Patsearch Section," which identifies and abstracts selected new U.S. and foreign patents. Book reviews also appear. *Telematics and Informatics* is indexed in *CA* (entry 163) and *CC* (entry 164).

416.   Television/Radio Age. New York: Television Editorial Corporation, 1953- . Biweekly. ISSN 0040-277x.

A professional journal of the broadcast industry, *Television/Radio Age* features news of current interest as well as two to three cover stories on topics of similar currency. Features on such subjects as hit programs, FCC decisions and regulations, corporate trading, advertising, and rating systems technologies are staples. Annual reports on children's programming, "Kid Vid," and regular reports on market shares are also included. Other cover features have profiled particularly successful stations, like Chicago's WGN-TV, as well as broadcasting in the Soviet Union and Eastern Europe. Regular departments, like "Station Report," detail local media business activities, identify personnel, and describe local programming. Other departments review activities in international broadcasting, television network programming, and radio. "Washington Roundup" keeps tabs on actions of the FCC, NTIA (National Telecommunications and Information Administration), and NAB (National Association of Broadcasters). "Feedback" polls the opinions of top media executives on a wide range of perennially troublesome issues, such as advertising and children's programming; advertising and programming containing sex, violence, and controversial content; pretaped versus live primetime coverage; and the conflicting interests of networks and affiliates. Of course, the journal also features want ads and job listings. *Television/Radio Age* is indexed in *BPI* (entry 160).

417.   TV Guide. Radnor, PA: News America Publications, 1953- . Weekly. ISSN 0039-8543.

TV Guide is recognized here as a primary source of information about local programming and, in the larger view of television broadcasting, as a record or chronicle of America's popular tastes and attitudes as reflected in the media. Similarly, the featured cover articles themselves are the "stuff" of research on popular culture in America. They exist to encourage America to tune in or, to put in another way, to indicate what America is tuned into. And if tuning in is impossible, features like "Soap Opera Guide" capsulize what was missed. *TV Guide* is indexed in *RG* (entry 184) and *Topicator* (entry 189). In addition, annual and cumulative retrospective author and subject indexing of *TV Guide* is provided in:

> 417.1. **TV Guide 25 Year Index: By Author and Subject: April 3, 1953-December 31, 1977**. Radnor, PA: Triangle Publications, 1979. 506p. LC 79-67725.

> 417.2. **TV Guide Index: 1978-1982 Cumulative Supplement: By Author and Subject: January 7, 1978-December 25, 1982**. Radnor, PA: Triangle Publications, 1982. 176p. LC 83-51316.

> 417.3. **TV Guide Index: 1983-1987 Cumulative Supplement: By Author and Subject: January 1, 1983-December 26, 1987**. Radnor, PA: Triangle Publications, 1988. 299p. ISBN 0-9603684-8-5.

> 417.4. **TV Guide Index**. Radnor, PA: Triangle Publications, 1983- . Annual. LC 87-656546.

418. **Western Journal of Speech Communication**. Los Angeles, CA: Western Speech Communication Association, 1937- . Quarterly. ISSN 0193-6700.

Western Journal of Speech Communication is among the major general scholarly journals in the field. It has published numerous features of significance that have influenced current communication research. The journal features articles that cover all aspects of communication—"rhetorical and communication theory, interpersonal communication, public address, philosophy of communication, language behavior, intercultural communication, argumentation, organizational communication, oral interpretation, group communication, free speech, and applied communication"—as well as "all possible theoretical orientations." The result is rather eclectic and refreshing—a diverse mixture of qualitative and quantitative treatments of subjects and issues from both humanistic and social scientific perspectives. Both MLA and APA styles of documentation are respected; issues typically include five articles; no reviews are included. Topics in interpersonal communication have included disengagement of relationships, the role of personal attractiveness, impression formation in sex-role socialization, and coping with loss. Historical and rhetorical assessments of John Milton, Ronald Reagan, Jesse Jackson, John C. Calhoun, and Mikhail Gorbachev have appeared. Other studies have addressed the media's coverage of specific political events and broader subjects, such as international terrorism, as well as Japanese-American/Caucasian relations in Hawaii. A recent special issue is titled "Microcomputers in Communication Research and Teaching." Touching upon every area of communication, the journal offers basic readings that support both teaching and research. *Western Journal of Speech Communication* is indexed in *CA* (entry 163), *CIJE* (entry 165), and *LLBA* (entry 175).

419. **Women's Studies in Communication**. Norman, OK: Organization for Research on Women and Communication, 1977- . 2/year. ISSN 0749-1409.

Most significant for research on topics in intercultural communication, this journal features four to six articles per issue that treat the relationship of gender and communication. Articles are relevant to interpersonal, organizational, and small group communication; the mass media; and language and rhetoric. A significant number of studies have compared male and female communicative strategies and practices—the expressions of love used by men and women, leadership behavior of men and women, and male and female nonverbal behavior. Other articles have focused on women's media use, the presentation of female characters in children's picture books, and sexist language. Special issues devoted to specific themes, like "Feminist Scholarship in Communication," are also published occasionally. A selection of one to three reviews of new books appears in each issue. *Women's Studies in Communication* is unindexed at this time.

420. **Written Communication: A Quarterly Journal of Research, Theory, and Application.** Newbury Park, CA: Sage, 1984- . Quarterly. ISSN 0741-0883.

Written Communication publishes articles that present theoretical, historical, and empirical research on writing. Main topics on interest include "assessment and evaluation of writing, impact of technology on writing; social consequences of literacy; cognition and composing; structure of written text; and connections among writing, reading, speaking, and listening." "Linguistic Politeness in Professional Prose: A Discourse Analysis of Auditor's Suggestion Letters, with Implications for Business Communication Pedagogy" and "Effectiveness in the Environmental Impact Statement: A Study of Public Rhetoric" are typical features. Other topics recently discussed include children's narratives, orality and literacy, text comprehensibility, use of computers in teaching composition, news writing, jargon, writing summaries, and second language writing proficiency. Announcements of conferences and calls for papers usually conclude each issue. No reviews of new books are published. *Written Communication* is indexed in *CA* (entry 163) and *LLBA* (entry 175).

421. **Youth & Society.** Newbury Park, CA: Sage, 1969- . Quarterly. ISSN 0044-118x.

Most significant for research on current intercultural communication, *Youth & Society* focuses on parental, peer, and social influences on child and adolescent behavior as well as analysis of behavior. Particular attention has centered on the influence of mass media on behavior. Articles have examined the effects of video watching, rock lyrics, and science fiction films. A special issue, 18.4 (June 1987), was titled "Adolescents and Rock 'N' Roll" and included features on the influence of MTV and the revival of the Grateful Dead as a popular cultural phenomenon. Other articles have examined the family as a social and educational support network. No reviews are included. *Youth & Society* is indexed in *A&HCI* (entry 155), *CA* (entry 163), *CC* (entry 164), *CIJE* (entry 165), *LLBA* (entry 175), and *SSCI* (entry 185).

Of several other journals that are significant sources of research on youth and communication, *Adolescence* (San Diego, CA: Libra Publishers, 1966-), quarterly, examines topics related to parent-child communication as well as the influences of individuals, groups, environment, and culture on adolescent behavior. Similarly *Journal of Youth and Adolescence* (New York: Plenum, 1972-), bimonthly, examines such topics as the influence of parental criticism on adolescent behavior, the family as social and educational support network, gender differences and communication and interaction, and the effects of divorce, drug abuse, and alcohol abuse on adolescent behavior.

9
Research Centers
and Archives

422. Advertising Research Foundation. 3 East 54th Street, New York, NY 10002. (212) 751-5656.

This independent, nonprofit foundation undertakes original research on significant advertising industry issues, in addition to acting as a consultant in other research studies and conducting workshops and seminars. The foundation's library holds over 2,500 volumes on advertising and marketing research. The foundation publishes the *Journal of Advertising Research* (entry 368).

423. American Film Institute. Louis B. Mayer Library, P.O. Box 27999, 2021 North Western Avenue, Los Angeles, CA 90027. (213) 856-7655.

The American Film Institute's large archive and library is open to graduate students, historians, writers, and scholars interested in the development of American film and television. The archive includes unpublished television and film scripts, newspaper clippings, stills, and several special collections. Its holdings are described in detail in Mehr's *Motion Pictures, Television, and Radio: A Union Catalogue of Manuscript and Special Collections in the Western United States* (entry 215).

424. Annenberg Television Script Archive. Annenberg School of Communication, University of Pennsylvania, 3620 Walnut Street, Philadelphia, PA 19104. (215) 898-2024.

Operated as a unit of the University of Pennsylvania's School of Communication, the Television Script Archive makes available to students, writers, and scholars over 28,000 American television scripts. Researchers should write in advance for permission to use the collection. Duplication of scripts is prohibited without advance written permission of copyright owners. The archive's online catalog, TSAR, provides subject access to the collection. In addition, the Annenberg School of Communication has recently published the *Index to the Annenberg Television Script Archive* (entry 219).

425. British Film Institute. Library Services, 127 Charing Cross Road, London WC2H OEA, England. (01) 2551444.

The British Film Institute (BFI) maintains one of the world's most significant collections on film and television. Its large library of films, books, journals, and reports includes a particularly strong television collection, which is described in *TV Documentation: A Guide to the BFI Library Services Resources* (London: [BFI] Library Services, 1985). Other excellent descriptions of the institute's collections include the *Catalogue of the Book Library of the British Film Institute* (Boston, MA: G. K. Hall, 1975) and the *British National Film & Video Catalogue* (entry 210). BFI publishes the quarterly *Sight and Sound* (London: BFI, 1982-), and the *Monthly Film Bulletin* (London: BFI, 1934-). Extended use of the BFI's facilities and resources typically requires membership.

426. **Broadcast Pioneers Library.** 1771 N Street, N.W., Washington DC 20036. (202) 223-0088.

The oldest active archive devoted to broadcast history and supported since 1966 by the Broadcast Pioneers Educational Fund, the Broadcast Pioneers Library is based on a collection of materials begun in 1942 by H. V. Kaltenborn. The collections include special materials related to the history of radio and television broadcasting in the United States as well as substantial materials on the history of telegraphy. Holdings include more than 4,500 photographs and 1,200 audiotapes of speeches and interviews (with over 300 oral history interviews) of early or otherwise notable television and radio broadcasters. The collection was opened to the public in 1971. Fees are charged for use, however, and scholars are advised to write for appointments in advance.

427. **Center for Advanced Study in Telecommunication (CAST).** Ohio State University, 210 Baker Systems, 1971 Neil Avenue, Columbus, OH, 43210-1271. (614) 292-8444.

Founded in 1988, this new center sponsors symposia and programs on a full range of topics in telecommunication and publishes the *Working Files* series on research in progress. Interested scholars are invited to contact the center for the *CAST Calendar* of local, national, and international programs and conferences in telecommunication. In addition, CAST has recently assumed the publication of *Communication Booknotes* (entry 344).

428. **Center for Advanced Technology in Telecommunication.** Polytechnic University, 333 Jay Street, Brooklyn, NY 11201. (718) 260-3050.

This center is one of nine cooperative research centers affiliated with the Centers for Applied Technology Project of the New York State Science and Technology Programs located at the Polytechnic University. Established in 1983, the Center for Advanced Technology in Telecommunications supports research on telecommunications systems, materials, devices, and networks; publishes findings in journals and reports; sponsors lectures and meetings; and offers postgraduate programs in telecommunications management and information systems engineering.

429. **Center for Applied Linguistics.** 1118 22nd Street, N.W., Washington, DC 20037. (202) 429-9292.

Crosscultural communication, adult language education, English as a second language, the teaching of languages that are not widely taught, literacy, and language variation are among the major focuses of research at the center. Founded in 1959, the center operates the ERIC Clearinghouse on Languages and Literatures and publishes books, reports, and audiocassettes aimed at new non-English-speaking immigrants to America and their teachers. The collections of the center's library are described in the somewhat dated *Dictionary Catalog of the Library of the Center for Applied Linguistics* (entry 211).

430. **Center for Study of Popular Culture.** Bowling Green State University, Popular Culture Center, Bowling Green, OH 43202. (419) 372-2981.

Researchers in popular culture and folklore as these are reflected and promoted in radio, television, newspapers, film, and other media should know of this active research center. The center publishes major periodicals in the field of popular culture, including *Journal of Popular Culture* (entry 385), the quarterly *Journal of American Culture* (Bowling Green, OH: Bowling Green State University, 1978-), and the semiannual *Journal of Cultural Geography* (Bowling Green, OH: Bowling Green State University, 1980-), in addition to numerous scholarly books.

431. **Communications Library**. University of Illinois at Urbana-Champaign, 122 Gregory Hall, 1810 South Wright Street, Urbana, IL 61801. (217) 333-2216.

One of the world's largest and most comprehensive collections of communications materials, the University of Illinois's Communication Library collects books, serials, and other documents in mass communication, public relations, radio and television broadcasting, telecommunications, communication theory, advertising, newspaper and magazine publishing, and related areas. The *Catalog of the Communications Library* (entry 220) and its quarterly acquisitions list record the library's holdings. Advertising historians will be particularly interested in the library's D'Arcy Collection, which features files of magazines and newspaper clippings (alphabetically arranged by subjects and brand names) from the late 1800s through 1960. Researchers are advised to write in advance to use the D'Arcy Collection.

432. **East-West Center**. Institute of Culture and Communication, 1777 East-West Road, Honolulu, HI 96848. (808) 944-7666.

Founded in 1970 and supported by the governments of the United States and several Asian and Pacific countries, the East-West Center is devoted to research on the effects of communication processes on culture and economics and on the roles of business markets, competition, and modernization in economic development. The center sponsors an international film festival and a performing arts series and offers seminars, workshops, and other development programs related to crosscultural and mass media professions. It maintains a large library of books, journals, and documents on communications and culture in Asia, the Pacific, and the United States. Among the center's numerous publications are Middleton and Jussawalla's *The Economics of Communication* (entry 63); Daniel Lerner and Lyle M. Nelson's *Communication Research: A Half-Century Appraisal* (Honolulu, HI: University of Hawaii Press, 1977); Godwin Chu's *Communication and Development in China* (Honolulu, HI: East-West Center, 1976); and Hayato Yamanaka's *Japanese Communication Studies of the 1970s* (Honolulu, HI: University of Hawaii Press, 1986).

433. **Gannett Center for Media Studies**. Columbia University, 2950 Broadway, New York, NY 10027. (212) 280-8392.

The research interests of the Gannett Center include mass communication and mass communication technology, media freedom and media accountability, the impact of new communication technology on the communication industry, sports and the media, libel, and politics and the media. Its publications include the quarterly *Gannett Center Journal* (New York: Gannett Center for Media Studies, 1987-), books, and working and occasional papers. The center annually conducts a summer Leadership Institute for Journalism and Mass Communication Education, which is open to professional journalists and students; sponsors conferences, workshops, and seminars; and maintains a library.

434. **International Mass Media Research Center**. 173, Ave. de la Dhuys, 93170 Bagnolet, France. (43) 60 56 90.

Interested in the development of critical left-wing studies and the bibliography of communication and ideology, the center publishes *Marxism and the Mass Media* (entry 61), an irregular bibliographic series that serves as the catalog of its library.

435. **Library of Congress. Motion Picture, Broadcasting, and Recorded Sound Division**. James Madison Memorial Building, Room 338, First Street and Independence Avenue, S.E., Washington, DC 20540. (202) 287-5840.

This division of the Library of Congress contains a very important and extensive collection of television and radio programs on videotapes, audiotapes, films, and sound recordings, the majority of which have been placed in the library in compliance with copyright laws. Gifts and purchases have also supplemented the collection. Noted collections include the National Broadcasting Company Radio Collection and the Armed Forces Radio and Television Series. *Radio Broadcasts in the Library of Congress, 1924-1941* (entry 212) and *3 Decades of Television: A Catalog of Television Programs Acquired by the Library of Congress, 1949-1979* (entry 213), among other catalogs, record parts of the full collection.

436. **Media Action Research Center**. 475 Riverside Drive, Suite 1370, New York, NY 10115. (212) 865-6690.

Founded in 1974, the Media Action Research Center is devoted to the study of television's influences on women, minorities, children, and other audiences and, more generally, the media's influences on social and cultural values. The center publishes *Media and Values: A Quarterly Resource for Media Awareness* (Los Angeles, CA: Media Action Research Center, 1977-), as well as books and reports.

437. **The Media Institute**. 3017 M Street, N.W., Washington, DC 20007. (202) 298-7512.

The Media Institute provides and supports research and critical evaluation of media performance, focusing on print and broadcast media news coverage as well as new communication technologies, communication policy, First Amendment rights, and Hispanic media. The institute operates the Hispanic Media Center and the First Amendment Center for the Mass Media and sponsors the "Washington, DC, Luncheon Series" featuring speakers from media and communication industries. Publications of the institute have analyzed the media's news coverage of issues related to energy, toxic chemicals, media abuses, and international information and include Ana Veciana-Suarez's *Hispanic Media USA: A Narrative Guide to Print and Electronic Hispanic News Media in the United States* (Washington, DC: Media Institute, 1987).

438. **The Museum of Broadcasting**. 1 East 53rd Street, New York, NY 10002. (212) 752-4690.

The museum's collection primarily consists of thousands of videotapes and audiotapes of radio and television programs from the 1920s through the present, including political broadcasts, early radio series, news events, and musical and dramatic programs. Catalogs of the museum's collection include *Subject Guide to the Radio and Television Collection of the Museum of Broadcasting* (New York: Arno Press, 1979) and *Catalog of the Museum of Broadcasting* (New York: Arno Press, 1980). In April 1989, the Television Information office (TIO) merged with the museum as part of efforts to fulfill the museum's research functions.

439. **Pacific Pioneer Broadcasters**. 1500 North Vine, Hollywood, CA. Mailing Address: P.O. Box 4866, North Hollywood, CA 91607. (213) 462-9606; 461-2121.

Open to researchers by advance appointment only, the center features special collections on the history of radio and television broadcasting from the early 1920s to the 1950s, including radio program music scores, oral histories by early radio personalities, recordings of radio broadcasts, and television and radio scripts.

440. **Public Affairs Video Archives**. Purdue University, Stewart Center, G-39, West Lafayette, IN 47907. (317) 494-9630.

Established in 1987, the Public Affairs Video Archives records all C-SPAN broadcasts. The archive is authorized to distribute copies of broadcasts solely for educational and research purposes. Although the archive is open to the public, researchers should arrange to use the collection in advance. *Public Affairs Video Archives Catalog* (entry 217) provides a detailed description of the collection.

441.   **Public Broadcasting Service**. Program Data and Analysis, 475 L'Enfant Plaza West, S.W., Washington, DC 20024. (202) 488-5227.

The Public Broadcasting Service maintains a collection of nearly 35,000 items dating from 1935 to the present related to public television programming, including both film and video recordings of news programs, congressional hearings, science documentaries, personality interviews and profiles, and musical and dramatic performances. The service also houses and maintains the records concerning the distribution and content of these programs as well as related slides and photographs.

442.   **Roper Center for Public Opinion Research**. University of Connecticut, P.O. Box 440, Storrs, CT 06268. (203) 486-4440.

Devoted to research on public social and political attitudes and behavior as well as on media and media policy, the Roper Center maintains a collection of over 10,000 computer tapes of polling surveys taken from 1936 to the present both in the United States and abroad. The center gathers data from a broad variety of nonproprietary polls, such as the Roper, Gallup, and Harris organizations; NBC News; *Los Angeles Times*; and the like. Fee-based online access to these survey data is available in the center's Public Opinion Location Library (POLL) database. Researchers should contact the center for the fee schedule. The center intends to make the database available on DIALOG in 1990. In addition, the Roper Center publishes the bimonthly *Public Perspectives* (Storrs, CT: Roper Center for Public Opinion Research, 1989-).

443.   **Silha Center for the Study of Media Law and Ethics**. University of Minnesota, School of Journalism and Mass Communication, 111 Murphy Hall, 206 Church Street, S.E., Minneapolis, MN 55455-0418. (612) 625-3421.

Established in 1954, the Silha Center sponsors symposia and conferences on issues concerning mass media law and ethics and also maintains the archives of the now defunct National News Council. The center's publications include Christians and Jensen's *Two Bibliographies on Ethics* (entry 25).

444.   **UCLA Television Archives**. Academy of Arts and Sciences, University of California, Los Angeles, Department of Theatre Arts, 504 Hilgard Avenue, Los Angeles, CA 90024. (213) 206-8031.

The Academy of Television Arts and Sciences (entry 448) provides restricted access to the holdings of its Television Archives, including more than 15,000 books, 350 periodical titles, and other archival materials, such as scrapbooks, photographs, slides, scripts, and the like. Researchers are advised to call or write in advance to use the collection. *ATAS/UCLA Television Archives Catalog* (entry 209) records the archive's holdings.

445.   **Vanderbilt Television News Archive**. Vanderbilt University, Jean and Alexander Heard Library, Nashville, TN 37240-0007. (615) 322-2927.

This archive contains videotapes of all network television evening news programs and selected special news programs from 5 August 1968 through the present. Researchers can arrange to use the collection's resources either in the archive or by videotape rental. The archive's monthly *Television News Index and Abstracts* (entry 218) includes complete details about rental and viewing and serves as a description and index of the collection.

446. **Wisconsin Center for Film and Theater Research**. University of Wisconsin, 6039 Vilas Communication Hall, Madison, WI 53706. (608) 262-9706.

Jointly administered by the State Historical Society of Wisconsin and the University of Wisconsin, the *Wisconsin Center for Film and Theater Research* contains over 150 collections on the history and development of radio, television, theater, and motion pictures in the United States and abroad. The center's *Sources for Mass Communications, Film, and Theater Research* (entry 214) serves as a guide to the full collection.

447. **Women's Institute for Freedom of the Press**. 3306 Ross Place, N.W., Washington, DC 20008. (202) 966-7783.

Focusing on the contributions and activities of female media professionals and media directed at women, the institute supports research on all forms of mass media, conducts programs, and maintains a library. It publishes the *Directory of Women's Media* (entry 229).

10
Societies and Associations

448. **Academy of Television Arts and Sciences (ATAS).** Founded 1948. 3500 West Olive Avenue, Suite 700, Burbank, CA 91505. (818) 953-7575.

Members of this association include television and film industry professionals. Formerly the Hollywood chapter of the National Academy of Television Arts and Sciences (entry 475), ATAS sponsors the Television Hall of Fame, presents the Prime Time Emmys, and maintains the Television Academy Archives. ATAS publishes the *Emmy Directory* (Burbank, CA: Academy of Television Arts and Sciences, 1976-) and *Emmy Magazine* (Burbank, CA: Academy of Television Arts and Sciences, 1979-).

449. **Accrediting Council on Education in Journalism and Mass Communication (ACEJMC).** Founded 1929. School of Journalism, University of Kansas, Lawrence, KS 66045. (913) 864-3973.

ACEJMC accredits programs in schools and departments of journalism and mass communication. Its 25 members include journalism education associations and related professional groups. ACEJMC establishes accreditation standards and publishes a list of accredited programs.

450. **Advertising Council (AC).** Founded 1942. 825 Third Avenue, New York, NY 10022. (212) 758-0400.

Funded by members of the American business, media, and advertising communities and by the American Association of Advertising Agencies (entry 455), the Ad Council coordinates public service advertising campaigns in support of major nonpartisan national causes, such as the prevention of child abuse, alcoholism, and forest fires. It publishes Public Service Advertising Bulletin (New York: Advertising Council, 1947-).

451. **Advertising Research Foundation (ARF).** Founded 1936. 3 East 54th Street, New York, NY 10022. (212) 751-5656.

ARF publishes the *Journal of Advertising Research* (entry 368). Members include advertising agencies, research organizations, associations, media, and advertisers. Colleges and universities are eligible to join as associate members. ARF maintains an information center.

452. **American Academy of Advertising (AAA).** Founded 1958. c/o Dr. Robert L. King, Department of Business Administration, The Citadel, Charleston, SC 29409. (803) 792-7089.

AAA publishes the *Journal of Advertising* (entry 367). Membership is limited to college and university teachers of advertising. AAA annually presents awards for outstanding contributions to advertising education and conducts research in the field.

453. **American Advertising Federation (AAF).** Founded 1967. 1400 K Street, N.W., Suite 1000, Washington, DC 20005. (202) 898-0089.

This important organization, also known as the Ad Fed, boasts a membership of nearly 50,000, including advertisers, clubs, agencies, trade associations, students, and other interested individuals. AAF sponsors the Addy Awards, given to advertisers, agencies, individual writers, and others for "the very best advertising campaigns" at the national and local levels; promotes student competitions; and publishes *AAF Communicator* (Washington, DC: AAF, 1976-), *American Advertising* (Washington, DC: AAF, 1984-), and other newsletters.

454. American Association for Applied Linguistics (AAAL). Founded 1977. 1325 18th Street, N.W., Suite 211, Washington, DC 20036. (202) 835-1714.

AAAL is affiliated with the International Association for Applied Linguistics. Members are interested in the application of linguistics. In cooperation with the British Association for Applied Linguistics, AAAL publishes *Applied Linguistics* (London: Oxford University Press, 1980-).

455. American Association of Advertising Agencies (AAAA). Founded 1917. 666 Third Avenue, 13th Floor, New York, NY 10017. (212) 682-2500.

An association for advertising agencies, with approximately 800 members organized in 28 committees, AAAA is dedicated to the advancement of the profession. AAAA represents advertising agencies in the Advertising Council (entry 450) and sponsors the AAAA Educational Foundation, which offers grants and scholarships. More important, AAAA actively regulates advertising and monitors advertising practices. AAAA publishes *AAAA Bulletin* (New York: AAAA, 1978-) and several membership newsletters.

456. American Speech-Language-Hearing Association (ASHA). Founded 1925. 10801 Rockville Pike, Rockville, MD 20852. (301) 897-5700.

With over 60,000 members, including speech-language pathologists and audiologists, ASHA serves as the accrediting agency for postsecondary educational institutions, hospitals, and clinics and as the certifying body for professionals who provide speech, language, or hearing services to the public. Formerly known as the American Speech and Hearing Association, ASHA is affiliated with the American Association for the Advancement of Science and with the International Association of Logopedia and Phoniatrics. ASHA publishes *Journal of Speech and Hearing Disorders* (Rockville, MD: ASHA, 1936-) and *Journal of Speech and Hearing Research* (Rockville, MD: ASHA, 1958-).

457. American Women in Radio and Television (AWRT). Founded 1951. 1101 Connecticut Avenue, N.W., Suite 700, Washington, DC 20036. (202) 429-5102.

With approximately 3,000 members, including radio, television, cable, and network professionals organized in five regional and over 50 local groups, AWRT holds conferences on media ownership, maintains the AWRT Foundation, and sponsors competitions. AWRT publishes the bimonthly *News and Views* (Washington, DC: American Women in Radio and Television, 1983-).

458. Association for Business Communication (ABC). 100 English Building, 608 South Wright Street, University of Illinois, Urbana, IL 61801. (217) 333-1007.

With a membership of over 2,500 college teachers of business communication, public relations writers, and others interested in writing for business, ABC publishes *Journal of Business Communication* (entry 372) and *Bulletin of the Association for Business Communication* (Urbana, IL: ABC, 1935-). It also sponsors research and competitions.

459. **Association for Communication Administration (ACA).** Founded 1971. 311 Wilson Hall, Murray State University, Murray, KY 42071. (502) 762-3411.

Members of ACA include chairpersons of schools, divisions, and departments of communication in colleges and universities. With a primary focus on speech communication in higher education, ACA compiles statistics, conducts workshops and seminars, and maintains a library. Its publications include *ACA Bulletin* (Murray, KY: ACA, 1972-) and a biennial directory *Communication Media in Higher Education* (entry 232).

460. **Association for Education in Journalism and Mass Communication (AEJMC).** Founded 1912. College of Journalism, 1621 College Street, University of South Carolina, Columbia, SC 29208-0251. (803) 777-2005.

Consisting of over 2,000 college and university journalism teachers and other interested individuals, AEJMC publishes several major journals, including *Journalism Quarterly* (entry 390), *Journalism Educator* (Columbia, SC: AEJMC, 1958-), and *Journalism Monographs* (entry 389), as well as *Journalism Abstracts* (entry 174) and *Journalism and Mass Communication Directory* (entry 202). AEJMC compiles statistics on journalism education enrollment, sponsors research, and maintains a list of job openings. Its numerous divisions focus on all aspects of journalism and mass communication and sponsor workshops and newsletters.

461. **European Institute for the Media (EIM). Institut Europeen de la Communication (IEC).** Founded 1983. Manchester University, Manchester, M13 9PL, England. (61) 2736055.

Devoted to the use of the media to enhance international communication and understanding, EIM supports research and provides fellowships to Third-World residents, maintains a large library, and compiles statistics. EIM publishes *Media Bulletin* (Manchester, England: EIM, 1983-) in English and French, the latter being the official language of the organization. It also published *Mass Communication in Western Europe* (entry 87).

462. **Federal Communications Bar Association (FCBA).** Founded 1935. P.O. Box 34434, Bethesda, MD 20817. (202) 331-0606.

Approximately 1,700 attorneys who practice before the Federal Communications Commission make up the membership of this organization. FCBA sponsors meetings in conjunction with the Practising Law Institute and the American Bar Association and publishes the important *Federal Communications Law Journal* (entry 355).

463. **IEEE Communications Society (IEEE CS).** c/o Institute of Electrical and Electronic Engineers, 345 East 47th Street, New York, NY 10017. (212) 705-7867.

A subgroup of the Institute for Electrical and Electronic Engineers, IEEE CS focuses on the collection and dissemination of information on developments in the field of communications. With a membership of over 23,000 divided into 56 local groups, IEEE CS publishes *IEEE Communications Magazine* (entry 360), *IEEE Journal on Selected Areas in Communications* (New York: IEEE, 1953-), and *IEEE Network Magazine* (New York: IEEE, 1987-), among other publications.

464. **Institute for Public Relations Research and Education (IPRRE).** Founded 1956. 310 Madison Avenue, Suite 1710, New York, NY 10017. (212) 370-9353.

Publisher of *Public Relations Review* (entry 406), IPRRE conducts public relations research, offers scholarships for public relations education, and sponsors competitions.

465. **International Advertising Association (IAA).** Founded 1938. 342 Madison Avenue, 20th Floor, Suite 2000, New York, NY 10017. (212) 557-1133.

IAA membership consists of individuals from 71 countries who are primarily associated with advertising or marketing products or services. The publisher of a number of reports and monographs, including the annual *World Advertising Expenditures* (New York: IAA, 1953-) and a membership directory, IAA conducts advertising research, sponsors educational programs, and maintains a library.

466. **International Association for Mass Communication Research (IAMCR).** Founded 1957. Center for Mass Communication Research, University of Leicester, 104 Regent Road, Leicester, LE1 7LT, England. (533) 523864.

Consisting of approximately 1,000 individuals, institutes, research groups, organizations, and universities that specialize in mass communication, this international organization publishes monographs and symposium reports. Its official language is French.

467. **International Association of Business Communicators (IABC).** Founded 1970. 870 Market Street, Suite 940, San Francisco, CA 94102. (415) 433-3400.

An organization of public relations professionals and communication managers, IABC conducts research in communication, provides job listings, and maintains a library. IABC publishes *Communication World* (San Francisco, CA: IABC, 1970-), which includes the *World Book of IABC Communicators* directory (described in entry 206).

468. **International Communication Association (ICA).** Founded 1950. P.O. Box 9589. Austin, TX 78766. (512) 454-8299.

With an international membership of over 23,000, including college and university teachers, business professionals, military personnel, government employees, public relations professionals, and others, ICA is devoted to the promotion of research on human communication. ICA sponsors *Communication Yearbook* (entry 95), *Human Communication Research* (entry 358), and *A Guide to Publishing in Scholarly Communication Journals* (entry 8), as well as the bimonthly newsletter *International Communication Association—Communique* (Dallas, TX: ICA, 1953-), which features association and industry news.

469. **International Public Relations Association (IPRA).** Founded 1955. Case Postale 126, CH-1211, Geneva 20, Switzerland. (22) 910550.

With about 800 members, IPRA sponsors awards and competitions, supports the International Foundation for Public Relations Research and Education, and publishes *IPRA Review* (London: Whiting & Birch, 1976-) and a membership newsletter. Professionals who have held senior-level appointments in public relations organizations for five or more years are eligible for membership. Its U.S. chapter, founded in 1950, is located at 21 East Tenth Street, Apt. 10A, New York, NY 10003, (212) 254-7953.

470. **International Society for the History of Rhetoric (ISHR).** Founded 1975. c/o Michael Leff, Department of Communication Arts, University of Wisconsin, Madison, Madison, WI 53706. (608) 262-2543.

Membership includes about 800 scholars and others interested in the history and theory of rhetoric. ISHR publishes *Rhetorica* (entry 409) as well as *Rhetoric Newsletter* (Madison, WI: ISHR, 1978-).

471. **International Telecommunication Union (ITU).** Founded 1865. Palais des Nations, CH-1211, Geneva 10, Switzerland. (22) 7995111.

Formerly called the International Telegraph Union, ITU is particularly interested in the development of international cooperation in telecommunication and the promotion and operation of technical facilities. ITU allocates and regulates radio frequencies; provides technical assistance in space technologies for developing countries; establishes rates; sponsors worldwide meetings and conferences; and publishes a wide variety of tables, statistics, regulations, and bibliographies of telecommunications literature in Chinese, English, French, Russian, and Spanish. ITU also publishes English-, French-, and Spanish-language editions of the important *Telecommunication Journal* (entry 412). ITU also maintains an extensive library on telecommunication electrical engineering, and electronics.

472. International Telecommunications Satellite Organization (Intelsat). Founded 1964. 3400 International Drive, N.W., Washington, DC 20008. (202) 944-6800.

This is an intergovernmental organization representing nations that abide by two international telecommunication agreements. Each national telecommunication authority designs, develops, constructs, establishes, maintains, and operates part of the global communication satellite system. Intelsat publishes an annual report.

473. Linguistics Society of America (LSA). Founded 1924. 1325 18th Avenue, N.W., Suite 211, Washington, DC 20006. (202) 835-1714.

LSA's members include educators and linguists interested in scholarly analysis, research, and publication in the fields of language and literature. Its publications include *LSA Bulletin* (Washington, DC: LSA, 1970-) and *Language* (Washington, DC: LSA, 1925-). LSA is a member of the American Council of Learned Societies.

474. Modern Language Association of America (MLA). Founded 1883. Ten Astor Place, 5th Floor, New York, NY 10003. (212) 475-9500.

With over 26,000 members in 75 divisions, MLA includes college and university teachers of English and other modern languages and literatures. MLA sponsors research, competitions, and awards and maintains an extensive publication program. Its major publications include *MLA International Bibliography* (entry 178) and *PMLA* (New York: MLA, 1884-). The fourth issue of PMLA is a membership directory. MLA is a member of the American Council of Learned Societies.

475. National Academy of Television Arts & Sciences (NATAS). Founded 1946. 111 West 57th Street, Suite 1020, New York, NY 10019. (212) 586-8424.

With a membership of more than 14,000 professionals in television performing, directing, writing, cinematography, and other related fields, NATAS sponsors the Emmy Awards and publishes *Television Quarterly* (New York: NATAS, 1962-).

476. National Association of Broadcasters (NAB). Founded 1922. 1771 N Street, N.W., Washington, DC 20036. (202) 429-5300.

Members of NAB include representatives of radio and television stations and television networks. In addition to operating the Broadcasting Hall of Fame and maintaining a library, NAB publishes *Radio Week* (Washington, DC: NAB, 1988-) and *TV Today* (Washington, DC: NAB, 1988-).

477. National Association of Public Television Stations (NAPTS). Founded 1980. 1350 Connecticut Avenue, N.W., Suite 200, Washington, DC 20036. (202) 887-1700.

The organization is composed of public television licensees actually involved in planning, researching, and presenting issues and concerns of public television before the government. NAPTS collects, analyzes, and disseminates current information on public television systems.

478. **North American Telecommunications Association (NATA).** Founded 1970. 2000 M Street, N.W., Suite 550, Washington, DC 20036. (202) 296-9800.

More than 700 companies that manufacture, supply, sell, maintain, lease, or use telecommunication systems comprise this group. NATA maintains a library, compiles statistics, presents awards, and publishes *Directory of Telecommunications and Education Programs* (Washington, DC: NATA, 1987-) and a newsletter.

479. **Public Relations Society of America (PRSA).** Founded 1948. 845 Third Avenue, New York, NY 10022. (212) 826-1750.

With over 11,000 members, PRSA is open to professional public relations practitioners in business and industry, government, education, health and welfare organizations, and trade and professional groups. In addition to sponsoring a speakers bureau, accreditation programs, competitions, and awards, the society publishes *Public Relations Journal* (entry 405) and *Public Relations Register* (entry 206), important journals in the field.

480. **Public Relations Student Society of America (PRSSA).** Founded 1968. 33 Irving Place, New York, NY 10003. (212) 995-2230.

PRSSA is devoted to strengthening relationships of students in public relations programs with professionals working in the public relations field. Membership consists of more than 5,000 students organized in over 150 local chapters. PRSSA publishes a membership newsletter.

481. **Southern States Communication Association (SSCA).** Founded 1930. Department of Communication Arts, Appalachian State University, Boone, NC 28603. (704) 262-2403.

An affiliate of the Speech Communication Association (entry 482), SSCA consists of individuals, departments, and other institutions (organized in 12 state groups and several divisions) that are interested in promoting communication. SSCA publishes *Southern Communication Journal* (entry 411).

482. **Speech Communication Association (SCA).** Founded 1914. 5105 East Blacklick Road, No. E, Annandale, VA 22003. (703) 750-0533.

A venerable association, SCA consists of speech teachers, speech clinicians, media specialists, communication consultants, theater directors, students, and other individuals interested in public communication. SCA's primary function is to support study and research in communication, particularly speech communication. The organization and its numerous commissions, committees, and sections present awards, sponsor international debate tours, and publish a number of important journals, such as *Communication Education* (entry 345), *Communication Monographs* (entry 346), and *Quarterly Journal of Speech* (entry 407). SCA also published the three editions of Matlon's *Index to Journals in Communication Studies* (entry 177), among other publications.

483. **World Communication Association (WCA).** Founded 1968. c/o Ronald L. Applbaum, Pan American University, Edinburg, TX 78539. (512) 381-2111.

Members include students, scholars, and educators interested in promoting communication studies in colleges and universities. Regional groups focus on radio, television, film, electronics, and written communication. WCA sponsors symposia and competitions, presents awards, and publishes *World Communication* (Edinburg, TX: WCA, 1985-) and *Communication Research Reports* (Morgantown, WV: WCA, 1984-).

Appendix
Database Service Suppliers and Vendors

A. C. Nielsen Company
1290 Avenue of the Americas
New York, NY 10104
(212) 708-6908

American Library Association
50 East Huron Street
Chicago, IL 60611
(312) 944-6780

Baseline, Inc.
838 Broadway
Fourth Floor
New York, NY 10003
(212) 254-8235
(800) 242-7546

Billboard Information Network
1515 Broadway
New York, NY 10036
(212) 764-7424

BRS
BRS Information Technologies
1200 Route 7
Latham, NY 12100
(517) 783-1161
(800) 345-4277

CompuServe Information Services
5000 Arlington Centre Boulevard
Columbus, OH 43220
(614) 457-8600
(800) 848-8990

DataTimes Corporation
14000 Quail Springs Parkway
Suite 450
Oklahoma City, OK 73134
(405) 751-6400
(800) 642-2525

Dialcom, Inc.
6120 Executive Boulevard
Rockville, MD 20852
(301) 881-9020
(800) 435-7342

Dialog Information Services, Inc.
3460 Hillview Avenue
Palo Alto, CA 94304
(415) 858-3785
(800) 334-2564

Dow Jones and Company, Inc.
P.O. Box 300
Princeton, NJ 08543-0300
(609) 520-4000

Executive Telecom System, Inc.
The Human Resource Information Network
9585 Valparaiso Court
Indianapolis, IN 46268
(317) 872-2045
(800) 421-8884

General Electric Information Services
401 North Washington Street
Rockville, MD 20850
(301) 294-5405

Interactive Market Systems
55 Fifth Avenue
New York, NY 10003
(212) 924-0200
(800) 223-7942

Knowledge Index
(see Dialog Information Services, Inc.)

Management Science Associates, Inc.
6565 Penn Avenue at Fifth
Pittsburgh, PA 15206-4490
(412) 362-2000

Market Science Associates
1560 Broadway
Third Floor
New York, NY 10036
(212) 398-9100

Mead Data Central
P.O. Box 933
Dayton, OH 45401
(513) 859-1611
(800) 227-4908

Networking and World Information, Inc.
333 East River Drive
East Hartford, CT 06108
(203) 282-3700

NewsNet, Inc.
945 Haverford Road
Bryn Mawr, PA 19010
(215) 527-8030
(800) 345-1301

Orbit Search Service
Pergamon Orbit InfoLine, Inc.
8000 Westpark Drive
Suite 400
McLean, VA 22102
(703) 442-0900
(800) 456-7248

Profile Information
Sunbury House
79 Staines Road West
Sunbury-on-Thames
Middlesex TW16 7AH
England
44 (932) 761444

Tech Data
Information Handling Services
Department 406
15 Inverness Way East
P.O. Box 1154
Englewood, CO 80150
(303) 790-0600
(800) 241-7824

Telmar Group, Inc.
902 Broadway
New York, NY 10010
(212) 460-9000

VU/TEXT Information Services, Inc.
325 Chestnut Street
Suite 1300
Philadelphia, PA 19106
(215) 574-4400
(800) 323-2940

West Publishing Company
50 West Kellogg Boulevard
P.O. Box 64526
St. Paul, MN 55164-0526
(612) 228-2500
(800) 328-0109
(800) 328-9833

Western Union Telegraph Company
1 Lake Street
Upper Saddle River, NJ 07458
(201) 825-5000
(800) 527-5184

Wilsonline
H. W. Wilson Company
950 University Avenue
Bronx, NY 10452
(212) 588-8400
(800) 367-6770
(800) 462-6060 (in New York)

Author/Title Index

This index lists titles of works given full annotations, authors, editors, translators, compilers, series, and corporate bodies associated with the publication of the works included. Numbers cited in the index are entry numbers.

Subject Index

This index covers entries for all reference works, periodicals, organizations, and authors named in the annotations in the guide. Numbers cited in the index are entry numbers.